SEEPERSAD AND SONS:

NAIPAULIAN SYNERGIES

FRIENDS OF MR BISWAS

The Naipaul House
26, Nepaul Street   St James, Trinidad and Tobago

Friends of Mr Biswas Executive Committee Members:
Professor Kenneth Ramchand (Chair)
Professor Brinsley Samaroo, Professor Rajendra Ramlogan, Dr David Rampersad, Dr J Vijay Maharaj, Dr Natalie Persadie, Ms Lenore Dorset, Ms Valerie Taylor, Ms Anu Lakhan.

Friends of Mr Biswas Publications:
General Editor: Kenneth Ramchand
Editorial Committee for the first publication: Prof. Ken Ramchand, Dr J. Vijay Maharaj, Dr David Rampersad, Ms Anu Lakhan.

Conference planning committee:
Prof. Ken Ramchand, Prof. Brinsley Samaroo, Prof. Paula Morgan, Dr Karen Eccles, Dr Radica Mahase, Dr J Vijay Maharaj, Ms Natalie Persadie, Ms Lenore Dorset, Dr Primnath Gooptar.

SEEPERSAD AND SONS:

NAIPAULIAN SYNERGIES

EDITED J. VIJAY MAHARAJ

PEEPAL TREE

First published in Great Britain in 2019
Peepal Tree Press Ltd
17 King's Avenue
Leeds LS6 1QS
England

© 2019 J.Vijay Maharaj, authors
and Friends of Mr Biswas

ISBN13: 97818452324386

All rights reserved
No part of this publication may be
reproduced or transmitted in any form
without permission

CONTENTS

Acknowledgements   7

J. Vijay Maharaj
Introduction: Synergies Everywhere   9

Kenneth Ramchand
1: Being and Becoming a Writer: Family Ambitions   17

Bhoendradatt Tewarie
2: Family Love Tested by Artistic Ambition   27

Nicholas Laughlin
3: Naipaul's Letters Between a Father and Son
(and Mother and Sister)   35

Aaron Eastley
4: Biswas before *Biswas*:
Plotlines and Perspectives from the Chaguanas Correspondent   50

Brinsley Samaroo
5: "In but not of the society": the crusading and critical eye
of Seepersad Naipaul (1906-1953)   60

Arnold Rampersad
6: In Seepersad's *Guardian* Circle: J.E. Rampersad
and the Making of "McGee"   70

Robert Clarke
7: Our St James   91

Andre Bagoo
8: Strangers in the House: Cinema, Sexuality
and Politics in V. S. Naipaul's "Tell Me Who to Kill"   103

J. Vijay Maharaj
9: Shastri Maharaj: A Grain of Mustard   112

Sharon Millar
10: *Guerrillas* and "Buying Horses"   120

Keith Jardim
11: Beauty Surrounds the Darkness:
Novels that Taught Me How to See   131

Raymond Ramcharitar
12: Prelude to a Reading of an Excerpt from *Here*   141

Kevin Frank
13: Muddling the Middle: Cynical Representations
of Ethnic Relations in V.S. and Shiva Naipaul   153

Jim Hannan
14: "My Sense of Distance and Time Was Shaken":
Globalisation before its Time in the Work of V.S. Naipaul   164

Hywel Dix
15: From Tonka Beans to Magic Seeds:
V.S. Naipaul's Late Career Fiction of Self-Retrospect   175

Elizabeth Jackson
16: Constructions of Masculinity in Vidia Naipaul's
A House for Mr Biswas and Shiva Naipaul's *Fireflies*   187

Paula Morgan
17: Naipaulian Mothers and Motherlands   199

Fariza Mohammed
18: Karma and the Naipaul Brothers   206

Meghan Cleghorn
19: Sadomasochism, Incest and Power Relations   217

Varistha Persad
20: Finding Safe Spaces   230

Nivedita Misra
21: From Tramp to Traveller:
Mirrors of Immigrant Experiences in *In a Free State*   240

Contributors' Biographies   251

Index   256

ACKNOWLEDGEMENTS

Without the vision and the solid financial assistance of the National Gas Company of Trinidad and Tobago Limited and the then Ministry of National Diversity and Social Integration, the conference that attracted the articles on which this book is based would never have taken place. Friends of Mr Biswas also benefited from the good names, and from the creative and practical inputs of our official collaborators – the National Archives, GORTT; The Chaguanas Borough Corporation, and the Department of Literary, Cultural and Communication Studies, University of the West Indies, which was continuously involved in the project.

The following institutions and departments were indispensable: Republic Bank; the Office of the Principal, Marketing and Communications, The Alma Jordan Library and the Open Campus, all of the UWI; and The National Library and Information Services. We also thank the Trinidad daily newspapers – the *Express*, *Guardian* and *Newsday* – for their kind coverage of the conference.

Victor Edwards and his Iere Theatre group, warm Friends of Mr Biswas, opened the conference with a brilliant performance of work by Seepersad Naipaul.

The names of the following persons are registered in this book for their influence and their particular services: Dr Rodger Samuel, Ms Bettie Mc Comie, Ms. Vaneisa Baksh, Ms Jacinta Mitchell, Ms Roma Wong Sang, Chaguanas Mayor Gopaul Boodhan, Professor Paula Morgan, Mr Chan Chadeesingh,

Finally we thank the Executive Committee of Friends of Mr Biswas, the Conference Planning Committee and the Editorial Committee, especially the Editor, Dr Vijay Maharaj.

The next Conference to be held in 2020 is to address The Literature of Trinidad and Tobago since 1970, and we look forward to a continuation of support and participation.

INTRODUCTION

SYNERGIES EVERYWHERE

J. VIJAY MAHARAJ

Ever since the desire for federation was sown in the West Indies and deep disappointment followed its ignominious collapse, we have lamented its loss and our apparent incapacity for unity. Threaded through our grief (and sometimes seemingly hapless floundering with other unification projects), there has been, however, an awareness that before any association is possible, individual self-knowledge is critical. However, intensive exploration of the latter has often been forestalled in academia by the widespread pursuit of pan-global concepts such as the postcolonial and pan-Caribbean ones that seek to transcend parochial national borders and language differences.[1]

As Gordon Rohlehr puts it: the "revolution of self-perception… grows increasingly more complex and multi-faceted… It challenges conventional notions of history and is part of a vast world-wide movement to relocate the submerged cultures of the devastated in the kingdom of human and humane achievement."[2] However, while this emplotment on global and regional terrains is necessary – because those who have experienced colonialism certainly do have much in common, and there are certainly deep cultural similarities across the Caribbean – there is also much that is unique to individual nations, ethnicities, cultures and individuals, which is worthy of study.

In Caribbean human sciences such microcosmic examination has offset the general trend towards broad overviews and this has been nowhere more apparent than in literary studies, where it has occurred on par with what has happened in Australia, Africa or, as V.S. Naipaul delightedly reported in *A Million Mutinies Now,* in India. A conference was held in Trinidad and Tobago at the end of 2015 called Seepersad and Sons: Naipaulian Creative Synergies. It aimed to examine the localness of the Naipaul legends and trouble the common-sense perceptions of this subject. The outcome, it was hoped, would be the renewal of our sense of the importance of every artistic contribution to our self-knowledge and our understanding of how our societies generate the arts and people that they do. This seemed particularly urgent as Caribbean literature has become a staple offering at most Euro-American universities, as well as those across the postcolonial world, and thus more a career field than a tool of national and regional self-understanding.

We anticipated that this would by no means produce a coherent, unified perspective and so it happened. Sometimes this was very obvious as in the presentation reproduced here as Chapter 13, in which Kevin Frank claims that "we have clear insight into V.S. Naipaul's view, which, through the evidence over his career, could be summed up as follows: 'A writer is doing his work well when people dislike, perhaps even despise him'".[3] Frank denounces this position and contrasts it with Seepersad Naipaul's dictum: "Write sympathetically".[4] He argues that the Naipaul brothers have invited dislike because of their lack of objectivity regarding race – that all important marker of life in the Caribbean. As Shalini Puri argues, in Trinidad and Tobago's "public discourse... racial stereotypes are unusually prominent [because] racialisation of politics in post-colonial Trinidad [involves] the persistence and active redeployment of colonial stereotypes."[5] Puri further contends: "What these stereotypes produce for contemporary dominant nationalist discourse is the fiction of a seamless and monolithic racial community with common interests, pitted against another seamless and monolithic racial community with common interests".[6] Frank certainly seems to be of a similar view.

Frank's position is, however, different from that in most other chapters, for example, in Chapter 15: "From Tonka Beans to Magic Seeds: V.S. Naipaul's Late Career Fiction of Self-Retrospect". In this chapter, Hywel Dix reads V.S. Naipaul qua V.S. Naipaul in making internal comparisons of his work and the responses to it. He states: "Over the course of half a century, V.S. Naipaul has been absorbed retrospectively into a literary canon from which he was an outsider during the late stages of colonial history. This retrospective recognition of his early work has had the effect that his more recent work has remained eclipsed by it".[7] Frank, on the other hand, positing the necessity for ontological transfiguration in order to ensure cultural citizenship in the nation and the region, argues that "the nature of creolisation as an essence of Trinidadian and Tobagonian and, more broadly, Caribbean culture, despite the legacy of both open and more subtle resistance to that process, makes it a fertile patch of ground for evaluating the Naipauls' – Seepersad and his sons – contributions to the Caribbean literary tradition, our cultural formation, and our ongoing pursuit of ontological transfiguration".[8]

It is therefore perhaps worth mentioning that placing no hope in essences or transfigurations, V.S. Naipaul and the other two Naipaul men have said in various ways that:

> I don't think there is any magic in any racial inheritance... the problems of the Indians are no different from the problems of everybody else here. I don't think it is possible for any one here, of any community, to seek the camouflage of some larger cultural entity, because that again is only a form of 'dropping out'. Wasn't the retreat into Negritude a form of 'flight'? One can always create hope but how lasting has been the redemption?[9]

And as Jim Hannan points out in Chapter 14, "My Sense of Distance and Time Was Shaken": Globalisation before its Time in the Work of V.S. Naipaul: "Naipaul is capable of deploying, and dismissing, the local colour prized in Commonwealth Literature, but also of moving from anecdotal observation to the kind of sweeping, universalising statements disavowed by postcolonial theory".[10]

Such connections and divergencies evident among Hannan, Dix and Frank characterise all twenty-one chapters that comprise this book and reveal a set of distinctive synergies. Writing appositely in a style that is more ghazal than the formal academic essay, in the way it segues by association from idea to idea, in his opening address reproduced here as Chapter 1, Kenneth Ramchand presciently foretells much of what would be the focus of the presentations that came before and after his talk on the first night of the conference. He states that "I meant to call this address "Coming Home to Ourselves and to the Place or Places that Make and Sustain Us", since that is one of the dramas we see played out in the writings of the three Naipauls. Given the condition of our society, that is a journey all of us need to make".[11] In this, he could easily have been identifying a main theme of all the essays and the major point made by the six arrayed below Chapter 1, which ends with the photographic essay by Robert Clarke, appropriately called "Our St James". In this essay, Clarke's photographs tell a story of how the multi-ethnicities of Trinidad and Tobago form its singular ethnic identity in a dynamic process of synergistic interactions.

Those social synergies seem to be reproduced not only in the lives of the Naipaul family but also in the individual papers, despite the absence of any prior interactions among the authors. Such synergies are apparent in other linkages between the opening address and later chapters. For example, Ramchand asks: "Is it too wild to notice that the older brother in "Tell Me Who to Kill" is like a mother to his younger brother and to think that this is an unconscious reflection of the kind of mothering in the family as well as an ironic comment on the negligible role of males in the caring of children?".[12] No essay is actually able to do much more than notice this fact, but the conference certainly revealed an interest in this story, which is one of V.S. Naipaul's most provocative, written as it is in a dense stream-of-consciousness mode. In Andre Bagoo's contribution, Chapter 8 – Strangers in the House: Cinema, Sexuality and Politics in V.S. Naipaul's 'Tell Me Who to Kill'", he looks both at the role that film played in the creation and meaning of the story and at the ambivalence of gender roles in the relationship of the two brothers. The idea of mothering is taken up further via this story and others in Paula Morgan's contribution in Chapter 17, "Naipaulian Mothers and Motherlands", which wonders about V.S. Naipaul's apparently ambivalent perceptions of the maternal roles of Indo-Caribbean women. Morgan's chapter is in turn complemented by Elizabeth Jackson's "Constructions of Masculinity in Vidia Naipaul's *A House for Mr Biswas* and Shiva Naipaul's *Fireflies*" in Chapter 16, which examines apparently paradoxical aspects of male privilege within the families portrayed in those novels.

Another focus was the role of journalism as the common factor in the works of the father and the sons. Aaron Eastley expresses it in Chapter 4, "Biswas before *Biswas*: Plotlines and Perspectives from the Chaguanas Correspondent", in this way:

> I think it is fair to say that the quality of the fiction produced by all three Naipauls owes a great deal to the discipline and creativity they learned through their work as reporters – writers making stories out of materials at hand. This all started, of course, with Seepersad's work for the *East Indian Weekly* and the *Trinidad Guardian* as a largely self-educated man in his early twenties. As a newspaperman Seepersad Naipaul pioneered for his sons a path similar to that taken by other brilliant prose stylists of the Western world. One recalls, almost exactly a century before Seepersad, the young Charles Dickens, who entered his craft as a court reporter and traveling correspondent before branching out into fiction with his early collection of literary vignettes, *Sketches by Boz*. Similarly, roughly a half-century before Seepersad, Mark Twain got his start with the Virginia City *Territorial Enterprise* en route to his early short story collection *Roughing It*. Then there is a contemporary of Seepersad, Ernest Hemingway, whose few months of work for the *Kansas City Star* prior to WWI led to a lifetime of intermixed work as a foreign correspondent, war correspondent, and novelist.[13]

Arnold Rampersad, in Chapter 6, "In Seepersad's Circle: J. E. Rampersad and the Making of 'McGee'", charts the local context and similar inspiration of his father, Jerome Ewart Rampersad, who was also a journalist and "brilliant prose stylist".[14] He thereby performs the invaluable task of validating the significance of Seepersad Naipaul's journalistic work. Rampersad's essay both points to the importance of journalism in Trinidad's national discourse and confirms it as a space where high quality writing was appreciated. This recalls the contention of Barbara Lalla and Valerie Youssef that "part of the validation of a novelist's perspective... lies in the precise and accurate depiction of the historical circumstance within which it is contextualised".[15]

Brinsley Samaroo, Bhoendradatt Tewarie and Nicholas Laughlin all offer their own contributions to such a contextualisation project, in their case to the context of the Naipaul family as both a support for the writing careers of the sons, and a site of conflict. Indeed Tewarie's and Laughlin's essays in Chapters 2 and 3 comprise a trenchant critique of the ways in which individual ambition can undermine family desires and ambitions. In combination with Samaroo's essay they work to show how important Seepersad Naipaul's efforts were despite, as Tewarie shows, their belated appearance long after his death. To use Samaroo's words:

> In spite of the demands made upon him by the necessity to earn money for the family, he accomplished much in his stress-shortened life. Seepersad was an insider who was able to stand outside of his society and write about it. In his first brilliant period of journalism (1929-1934), he brought the techniques of the fiction writer, a wicked sense of fun, a little malice, and a focus on character and situation to his work; in his second period (1938-1946) when he did not have so much of a byline, he had more time to work on his short stories at home and make an acolyte of Vidia. All of this led to the publication of *Gurudeva and Other Indian Tales* in 1943. In his third period (1950-1953) he continued writing non-fiction articles on a wide variety of subjects (abuse of Indian women, education for girls, non-Hindu persons and cultural expressions, local government, and national politics) while doing all he could to get out a book of his collected stories and begin a novel or an autobiography.[16]

Historical context was not of course the only area that was greatly clarified by the conference, so were present legacies as the brief accounts of other chapters have shown. In addition, the way the Naipauls' work has breached the boundaries of fiction and journalism is further explored in Nivedita Misra's "From Tramp to Traveller" where she examines the relationship of the apparently journalistic travelogues of the the Prologue and Epilogue within the two stories and novella that comprise *In a Free State*.

In keeping with Kenneth Ramchand's plea for the recognition of literary creation to the well-being of the nation-state, the conference also explored the legacies of the Naipauls' example by including creative writers and artists among the presenters. The rationale was simple. As Mervyn Morris said of his inaugural professorial lecture on "Making West Indian Literature" (2007), "[it] deals in part with where I'm coming from and what I do as a West Indian poet." He argued that he did this because: "Critics can be important to a literature. But the literature must be produced before it can be sifted for analysis. It may be that, even in the academy, we should pay more attention to nurturing production and trying to understand its processes."[17] This has increasingly become standard practice in the Caribbean academy and it was with the aim of understanding the processes of literary relationship that the conference included several practitioners. Although slightly financially better off than Seepersad Naipaul, they are walking his walk because they are located, like him, in Trinidad and Tobago, and write and paint despite enormous obstacles, including the lack of facilities or appreciation for their efforts. Chapters 9 to 12 reproduce their presentations.

Chapter 9, "A Grain of Mustard", comprises commentary on and twenty paintings by the artist Shastri Maharaj, who like the Naipaul brothers has gained an international reputation through his representation of similar themes. Unlike them, however, and like their father, Maharaj often paints "sympathetically" rather than satirically, and in this chapter J Vijay Maharaj looks at his work. Chapter 10, "*Guerrillas* and 'Buying Horses'" by Sharon Millar, is also concerned with sympathetic representation, as is Chapter 11, "Beauty Surrounds the Darkness: Novels that Taught Me How to See", by Keith Jardim. Millar reflects briefly on the process that led her to writing the story "Buying Horses". In this story we see that like V.S. Naipaul, as well as the many filmmakers and calypsonians who have all been intensely interested in the role of white women in the Black Power movement, as represented, for example, in *The Bank Job* (2008) directed by Roger Donaldson, Millar foregrounds a character she calls simply "the English girl". Millar's story revisits the real-life narratives on which V.S. Naipaul's novel *Guerrillas* draws and re-imagines them and in the process writes back to that novel. In this extract from his forthcoming novel, Jardim also expresses concern over the kind of world that V.S. Naipaul observes fearfully in *Guerrillas* – here escalated into a terrain of guns and drugs, a local world manipulated by global strings. Jardim tries both to imagine both how local entanglements occur and create the kind of prose fiction that in its care with artistic expression lives up to the example of the Naipauls.

Raymond Ramcharitar has also shown a great deal of interest in the manifestations of a society seemingly out of control, and he, like the Naipaul brothers, has no qualms about not being sympathetic, as is evident, for example, in his collection, *The Island Quintet: Five Stories*. Chapter 12, "A Prelude to a Reading of *Here*", is, however, an introduction to and an extract from his exquisitely beautiful autobiographical poem, *Here*. As he has pointed out on a number of occasions *Here* was written under the anxiety of influence created by the prior existence of the work of Derek Walcott. Although, unlike Walcott's work, in which the gods are Mediterranean and Judaeo-Christian, for Ramcharitar they begin with Brahma and the nine planets, include the ever-ubiquitous goddess Kali and end with the incarnation of the gods as the intellectual giants in whose footsteps Ramcharitar walks, including the Naipauls, Lloyd Best and of course Walcott himself. This is perhaps not surprising if we recall Dipesh Chakrabarty's point that:

> For most "Hindus", ["Hindu" in quotes to indicate its socially constructed and contingent nature] if not for most Indians, gods, spirits, and the so-called supernatural have a certain 'reality'… [T]o talk about the violent jolt that the imagination has to suffer in order to be transported from a temporality co-habited by gods and living beings to one from which the gods are banished is not to express an incurable nostalgia for a long-lost world. Even for the members of the Indian upper classes, this experience of travelling across temporalities can in no way be described as merely historical".[18]

This is certainly evident in the works of the Naipauls and in Maharaj's paintings. Ramcharitar's response is to re-historicise the gods and to make them contemporaneous even though he may object to being categorised as "Hindu" – socially and historically contingent or not.

The final group of essays is by four postgraduate students of the University of the West Indies, St Augustine, whose work can therefore be seen as aspects of the ongoing interest in the work of the Naipauls in their homeland Trinidad and Tobago. One of them, Fariza Mohammed, has taken a break after completing her masters on which the essay in Chapter 18 of this book is based. The essay is entitled "Karma and the Naipaul Brothers", which is self-explanatory but deceptively simple in relation to Mohammed's exploration of the topic. Chapter 19, "Sadomasochism, Incest and Power Relations", by Meghan Cleghorn, examines changing concepts of sexuality and gender, and discusses their relevance to the reading of the Naipauls' works. Chapter 20, "Finding Safe Spaces" by PhD candidate, Varistha Persad, like Jim Hannan in Chapter 14, reads V.S. Naipaul's consideration of the tenets of globalization in his novel *A Way in the World*, in his case through the lens of postmodernist critical theory. The last chapter, "Tramp and Traveller", engages with that most troublesome of V.S. Naipaul's books, *In a Free State*, and provides a final reminder that like biblical Jacob, we will be besieged by the Naipauls' work for a very long time to come in our own individual and collective versions of "wrestling with angels".

This book, *Seepersad and Sons: Naipaulian Synergies*, as well as the conference of the same name from which the chapters are drawn, distinguishes itself by making an intervention into the prevalent academic focus on just one member of the Naipaul family – V.S. Naipaul – and into readings of his work from avowedly generic postcolonial perspectives. By contrast, the conference and the book return the first three male writers of this family of writers to their local contexts. This approach underwrites the work of the organisation called the Friends of Mr Biswas which was responsible for making the conference happen and attempting to ensure that its proceedings are published.

Like the couplets of a ghazal, each chapter can be read on its own, but the synergies each forms in relation to others can be experienced by reading the book – *Seepersad and Sons: Naipaulian Synergies* – as a whole. The book title drops the "Creative" in the conference title in deference to the multiplicities of synergies uncovered in the presentations. The publication of these proceedings will bring closure to the first conference effort of the Friends of Mr Biswas and provide an opening for planning the next.

Endnotes

1. Interestingly the bulk of study takes this approach even as every single one declaims the lack thereof. See for example Véronique Maisier, *Violence in Caribbean Literature: Stories of Stones and Blood*. (Lanham MD: Lexington Books, 2014) which uses what the writer calls a "comparative transnational approach" (xvi); Yolanda Martínez-San Miguel, *Coloniality of Diasporas: Rethinking Intra-Colonial Migrations in a Pan-Caribbean Context*. (Basingstoke: Palgrave Macmillan, 2014) or Kristian Van Haesendonck & Theo D'haen (eds.) *Caribbeing: Comparing Caribbean Literatures and Cultures*. (New York: Rodopi, 2014).
2. Gordon Rohlehr, "Articulating a Caribbean Aesthetic: The Revolution in Self-Perception", in *My Strangled City and Other Essays* (Port of Spain: Longman, 1992), 1-16, quoted in Jennifer Rahim, "Issues and Developments in Caribbean Literary Theory and Criticism", *Research Methods in Caribbean Literary and Discourse Culture*, ed. Barbara Lalla, Nicole Roberts, Elizabeth Walcott-Hackshaw and Valerie Youssef, 15-40, p. 15.
3. Frank, xxx. (8)
4. V.S. Naipaul, foreword to *The Adventures of Gurudeva and Other Stories* (London: Andre Deutsch, 1976), 14.
5. Shalini Puri, "Race, Rape, and Representation: Indo-Caribbean Women and Cultural Nationalism", in *Matikor: The Politics of Identity for Indo-Caribbean Women*, ed. Rosanne Kanhai (University of the West Indies, St Augustine, 1999), 238-282, p. 240.
6. Puri, 240.
7. Dix, 173-184
8. Frank, 151-161
9. Paper delivered to the first conference on East Indians in the Caribbean in 1976, reproduced in *East Indians in the Caribbean: Colonialism and the Struggle for Identity*, eds. Bridget Brereton and Winston Dookeran (New York: Kraus International Publications, 1982).
10. Hannan, 162-172
11. Ramchand, 15-24
12. Ramchand, 18
13. Eastley, 48-57
14. Rampersad, 68-88
15. Barbara Lalla and Valerie Youssef, "Introduction: Caribbean Research and Scholarship in Literature, Discourse and Culture", in *Research Methods in Caribbean Literary and Discourse Culture*, ed. Barbara Lalla, Nicole Roberts, Elizabeth Walcott-Hackshaw and Valerie Youssef (Mona: University of the West Indies Press, 2013), 1-13, p. 2-3.
16. Samaroo, 58-67
17. Mervyn Morris, "Making West Indian Literature", *Anthurium: A Caribbean Studies Journal* 10, no. 2 (2013): 1-16, p. 1.
18. Dipesh Chakrabarty, "Marx After Marxism: A Subaltern Historian's Perspective" *Economic and Political Weekly* 28, no. 22 (29 May 1993): page numbers do not match between in-text citation (see end of p. 12 and page range in Works Cited on p. 14).

1: KEYNOTE ADDRESS

BEING AND BECOMING A WRITER: FAMILY AMBITIONS

KENNETH RAMCHAND

In the name of Friends of Mr Biswas, I welcome you and thank you for attending the Opening Ceremony of the Conference called Seepersad and Sons: Naipaulian Creative Synergies. I begin with a restrained statement about the state of our society and the necessity of the arts and sciences.

I meant to call this address "Coming Home to Ourselves and to the Place or Places that Make and Sustain Us", since that is one of the dramas we see played out in the writings of the three Naipauls. Given the condition of our society, that is a journey all of us need to make. The talk would have been a defence of the arts and humanities in these materialistic times when all value is economic value, when the aim of education is to push children to come first in examinations, and when universities all over the world have been driven to the treason of selling out to the marketplace.

The arts and the humanities have a major role to play in the humanising of society, and in stimulating persons to feel the immensity and beauty of the universe of which they are a part, to believe in life's possibilities, and to see happiness as the prime goal of life. An education that gives scope to the self-expression and self-discovery facilitated by the arts and humanities may be our best hope to arrest our society's unfeeling drift into ever-increasing levels of crime and violence, and the unholy self-slaughter of crimes against the person.

To summarise, our society desperately needs to rediscover the promise of the arts of the imagination. This conference is therefore timely.

Two key motifs
Over the next two days we will be exploring themes and issues that are important to how we relate to ourselves, to one another, and to the world. These themes include: ethnic relations, sex and sexuality, gender issues; family relations, religion, race and politics, immigration,

and globalisation. Arising out of these themes are two key motifs. The first is the three writers' lifelong struggles through their writing to come home to themselves: to come to some kind of understanding of who they were; to acknowledge their different selves; and to explore how their different selves might relate to their social identities and to their being.

The second motif running through my overview is a sense of a continuous striving against self-inflicted dislocation and placelessness. Seepersad's sons can be seen in their works to be in the throes of rejecting any "home" that is connected with the political agendas of a specific nation. At the same time, they are redefining "home" as a commodity that you can hold in your head regardless of geography or political nation, and sometimes against your will. The question this raises is important: what and where is home and can one belong to more than one country? More extremely, can home be any country but the country of your birth and growing up?

A third point
My third movement lists four major observations that need to be made early about this conference.

i. The conference brings together three writers from Trinidad and Tobago, each of whom has made a contribution to the literature of the island and the wider region. Let us take note: these are Trinidadian writers.

ii. The three writers originate from an ethnic group that found itself placed among other ethnic groups and among the ghosts and relics of the first peoples in the landscape. But I want to make it clear: their works help us to understand the development of Trinidad and Tobago as a fusion society, where the mixing of multiple heritages has caused much stress but has released incredible energy and creativity. Like most of our other artists, the Naipaul writers offer insights into the seepages between the cultures of the different ethnic groups in the island that helped to make the fusion society.

Seepersad knew all of this but did not know he knew it. He was not afraid of contamination by the Western works of philosophy and literature that formed part of a colonial education; he saw no mimicry in taking an interest in fiction and seeking to learn from accounts of the lives of leading men and women from India; he looked around him at the community out of which he came and saw institutions dying, and people changing, and wrote what he saw. They were all part of him. His short stories are not the idyllic evocation of "the Indian community" that V.S. tends to suggest. These stories are of a piece with the social and cultural criticism of his journalism.

Seepersad's journalism was multi-cultural, that is to say Trinidadian. It covered pan-making and pan-tuning, the calypso, survivors of slavery, time-expired indentureds, rice-growing, remarkable persons, local politics and political intrigue, cultural and religious commonalities and differences – Ramlila and Sonny Ramadhin. His accounts of politics in the Indian community are the stuff that could have made an earlier version of V.S.'s *The Suffrage of Elvira* (1958). He had an instinctive way of seeing the society and its cultures and he encouraged Vidia to cultivate it.

V.S. did it his own way. In his self-presentations he describes his growth as a writer as a process running parallel with his discovery, through selective travel to India, Africa, Europe and America, of the sources of a complex heritage that was present but dark in the islands of his childhood. To the child, all that lay outside his grandmother's house was in darkness. As a writer he made it his mission to light up these areas for the sake of constructing his true self:

> When I became a writer, those areas of darkness around me as a child became my subjects. The land; the aborigines; the New World; the colony; the history; India: the Muslim world, to which I felt myself related; Africa; and then England where I was doing my writing.[1]

His island and region were ancient and global though he did not know it at first. He came to discover through research and his travel missions the antiquity of his civilisation and the submarine globalism of the region of his birth.

iii. The works of these three writers express dramatically the complex and sometimes confused evolution of descendants of Indians in Trinidad from the early 1900s up to the early years of the twenty-first century. We see diasporic figures clinging to and losing touch with the realities of their original culture: bruised souls responding to and being bewildered by the changes taking place in the island and in the larger world over the same period. Once again it was the patriarch who first stumbled upon the theme of the enigma of arrival. In his journalism he wrote about the plight of Indian castaways in the city after the first journey, the hopes of many to board the ship for the return, and their puzzled arrival at a place grown unfamiliar. They wanted to get on the ship and come back to Trinidad. In *Gurudeva and Other Indian Tales* (1943) the Presbyterianised headmaster Sohun is used by the constructive Seepersad to spell out the crisis of the descendants of Indians who cannot be entirely Occidental nor entirely Oriental and who, Sohun confidently affirms, will arrive at being distinctly West Indian.

iv. Much of the impetus of the conference comes from a phenomenon: the three writers, Seepersad, Vidia and Shiva belong to a single family, the Naipaul family. The general effect of the family relationships on the Naipaul writings bears deep exploration. Family relationships are a felt presence in A *House for Mr Biswas* (1961). In *The World Is What It Is* (2008), Patrick French observes that while V.S. was writing *A House for Mr Biswas,* he tapped deliberately into family memories and family sensibility: "Vidia kept in close touch with his family, their letters feeding the book and Vidia's own attitudes feeding the letters his siblings sent him".[2] Is it too wild to notice that the older brother in "Tell Me Who to Kill" (*In a Free State*, 1971) is like a mother to his younger brother and to think that this is an unconscious reflection of the kind of mothering in the family as well as an ironic comment on the negligible role of males in the caring of children?

Be that as it may, the close relationship between Seepersad and Vidia in the Port of Spain years between 1938 and 1943 – the year when Seepersad self-published *Gurudeva and other Indian Tales* – was crucial in pointing Vidia to his vocation as writer. In the letters between Seepersad and Vidia, father and son praise, encourage and stimulate each other. It should be noticed for future exploration, however, that for all the exchanges between father and son on writing and about getting published, it was over twenty years after his father's death that Vidia felt ready to push for publication of *Gurudeva and Other Stories*.

On 22 October, 1953, the day of Seepersad's cremation, Kamla reminded Vidia that the thing his father most wanted but never saw was to have his book published;[3] nearly nine months earlier (February 2, 1953) she had pleaded with Vidia: "According to Ma and Sati, Pa's greatest worry is that he cannot get his stories published. Sati wrote saying that he sent you one but you have done nothing about it so far. Now something immediate regarding the publishing of his stories means life or death for him and consequently life or death for us..."[4] Although Henry Swanzy, editor of *Caribbean Voices* and a British person, had praised Seepersad's writing highly,[5] Vidia seemed to hold that Seepersad's stories would not go over well with British readers. It may well be that Vidia's fixation on getting his first book published and establishing his own literary career did not leave much room for helping anybody.

To Shiva, the thirteen-year age gap between himself and Vidia (b. 1932) almost made them different generations. The tensions this brought to their personal relationship is explored in Shiva's essay "My Brother and I".[6] Vidia's love for Shiva was never in doubt, but he behaved towards him like an exasperated father. As an author, Shiva sought encouragement and writing advice from Vidia, and did get some editing help with at least one manuscript. But Vidia was not his brother's mentor. Between the brothers there was the anxiety of influence, with Shiva striving to move out of the shadow of "the Absolute"[7] whose role as example and exemplar he nevertheless readily acknowledged. And then there was the anxiety of influencing. Nearly twenty years after Shiva's death Vidia expressed the anxiety of influencing:

> I was really hoping when my brother came along – before I was told of his alcoholic idleness – that he would, as it were, show me a new way. But he was just using me as a template. He was patterning himself on me.[8]

Shiva did not have the kind of dialogue with Seepersad that Vidia had, but one day, at the age of fifteen, he discovered the riches of his father's bookshelves, and in the sun-drenched sitting-room of number 26 Nepaul Street he entered imaginary worlds larger and more stimulating than the immediate environment which he considered "poor in possibility", and so "tawdry and confining".[9] This was a turning point in the life of the previously unmotivated QRC student. Seepersad's reading and writing, which gave Vidia the ambition to be a writer, had returned to arouse the second son.

There have been notable literary and artistic colonies in the island, but none of them lasted long, and none of them was a nurturing literary community. As I have hinted, the literary community that was the Naipaul family was a source of creative tension even as it provided recognition and the support that our society still seems to be unable or willing to offer to artists. It was the nearest we have come to having a literary community. Naipaulian studies will need to look more closely in future at the visible and invisible, conscious and unconscious influences of family on the works of the three Naipauls.

In passing, it should be noted that V.S. Naipaul's time with West Indian writers at the BBC *Caribbean Voices*, where he also served as presenter/editor, was a period when he was part of a literary community. V.S. has tended to play this down. It could be argued that the immediate cause of his rediscovery of his life at Luis Street and his first experience of Port of Spain as the raw material with which his fiction could begin was his fraternising with these writers, and his reading of so many scripts by would-be West Indian writers hoping to get broadcast on *Caribbean Voices*. In 1955, he was sitting at a typewriter in the freelances' room when the now famous sentence came to him:[10] "Every morning when he got up, Hat would sit on the bannister of his back verandah and shout across, 'What happening there, Bogart?'"[11] When he finished the story, his colleagues in the freelances' room were enthusiastic and encouraging. Other stories came fast. This was the making of *Miguel Street*.

I would like now to look at the writers themselves, and some of the issues that arise in their writings. To Seepersad Naipaul (1906-1953), the founding father of the literary line, his first son V.S. Naipaul wrote in July 1951: "You are the best writer in the West Indies, but one can only judge writers by their work".[12] Vidia was saying that Seepersad had all the strokes but he was not playing a test match innings. When was he going to make a book? This was a hard thing to tell a man who had such an impressive portfolio as a journalist and had published a collection of stories in 1943. But Seepersad took it to heart because he was as obsessed as his son was with the idea of producing a book. Seepersad tried to fulfil his writerly ambitions in more dispiriting circumstances than his sons, though to hear Vidia bemoaning what he went through you would not think so.

In spite of Vidia's encouragement, Seepersad never had the time to get around to writing the novel or autobiography he desperately wanted to deliver: "This is the time I should be writing the things I so long to write. *This is the time for me to be myself.* When shall I get the chance? I don't know. I come home from work, dead tired. The *Guardian* is taking all out of me..." [my italics].[13] On May 2, 1952 he complained to Vidia again about how working for the *Guardian* made it hard for him to do any sustained writing: "In this I must struggle for existence and feel just hemmed in by hard, unescapable facts and forces."[14] It wasn't only the *Guardian*. He was a selfless provider for his family and tended to put their needs and dreams above his own. He was full of anxiety. About the book. About being himself. About being trapped. His sons were the same. All three writers suffered from depression and anxiety and all three had nervous breakdowns.[15] It was like a trademark.

My next two points are that it was Seepersad who first built the bridge between journalism and fiction; and that Trinidad never left the consciousness of Seepersad's sons.

In spite of the demands made upon him by the necessity to earn money for the family, Seepersad accomplished much in his stress-shortened life. He was an insider who was able to stand outside of his society and write about it. In his first brilliant period of journalism (1929-1934), he brought the techniques of the fiction writer, a wicked sense of fun, a little malice, and a focus on character and situation to his work; in his second period (1938-1946) when he did not have so much of a byline, he had more time to work on his short stories at home and make an acolyte of Vidia. All of this led to the publication of *Gurudeva and Other Indian Tales* in 1943. In his third period (1950-1953) he continued writing nonfiction articles on a wide variety of subjects (abuse of Indian women, education for girls, non-Hindu persons and cultural expressions, local government, and national politics) while doing all he could to get out a book of his collected stories and begin a novel or an autobiography. The crossovers between fiction and journalism that became marked in the work of Vidia and Shiva began intuitively and naturally with Seepersad. He did not have to talk the kind of nonsense his older son did about journalism being a better form than the novel for capturing our fast-moving times. Who ever said that the purpose of the novel was to catch the world as it jumped about from day to day? But Vidia did make a fine self-promoting art of fusing fiction, journalism, autobiography and biography, emphatically so in later works like *The Enigma of Arrival* (1987) and *A Way in the World* (1994) which he subtitled as "A Sequence".

Seepersad was an early outstanding man of letters in Trinidad and Tobago, the first person of Indian origin to achieve that status. He was a writer all his life but he did not have the required ruthlessness or irresponsibility. He did not allow himself to be a failure, but he was not enough of a vivisector. I wonder how he would have felt about the callous opening sentence of *A Bend in the River* (1979): "The world is what it is; men who are nothing, who allow themselves to become nothing, have no place in it."[16]

In Shiva's third novel, *A Hot Country* (1983), there is an extreme statement of the issues and anxieties that wasted Shiva and that underlie the work of all three writers. Dina, with the very English surname Mallingham, is a passive, depressed, educated light-skinned woman (part Portuguese, part Indian) for whom the country is sinking to a bottom that has no bottom, and to whom life itself has no meaning or purpose. Her grandfather Mahalingam (Shiva is being a little naughty here) had surrendered his name, religion and anything he could have called his own when he became a Presbyterian. In the next generation, Dina's father learned to live with the sense that he had been misguided and he progressed even further on the weary road to false identity. Dina suffers as a child from the void in which her father lived with his Portuguese wife, and she finally puts words to the condition that has sapped her of vitality: "I grew up, you know, without allegiance to anything. I'm nothing but a mongrelised ghost of a human being living in a mongrelised ghost of a country. There's nothing holding me together. Every day I have to re-invent myself".[17] Shiva was the bleakest of them all.

I turn now to Trinidad in their consciousness. Seepersad never left Trinidad, but Vidia and Shiva shook the dust. Among the pieces in Shiva's posthumous collection *An Unfinished Journey* (1986) there is a long item that suggests he was doing a travel book about Sri Lanka. The last paragraph Shiva wrote is the last paragraph in the Sri Lanka fragment.

In this paragraph, his new friend Tissa is talking about his admirable mother-in-law: "All the men in her family have made nothing of their lives. Not her father, not her husband, not her brothers, not her sons-in-law. The women have been the strong ones. It is often like that in Lanka." Shiva narrates: 'Tissa lopes along beside me. Holding up the blade of grass, he lets a gust of wind sweep it away from his fingertips. He buries his hands in his pockets. "Is it like that in your island as well?"[18] This is the last sentence Shiva wrote.

Like Vidia he insisted that he would not return to little folks' Trinidad. But however far they wandered Trinidad never left them alone. "Is it like that in your island as well?" I think that question literally killed Shiva. Trinidad nagged the brothers. On the occasion of his accepting the Trinity Cross, Vidia was asked questions aimed at finding out if he still considered the region a backward place. He did not answer directly. "These are immense questions", he said. "My life's work is about that."[19] The island that exasperated the man was in the writer's blood. In 1956, the writer in him spoke: "From the writing point of view, this land is pure gold. I know it so well, you see. Pure, pure gold..."[20]

Each of these writers is worth reading in his own right. But, obviously, they were not passing ships. They were all three heading in the same direction: being a writer. At first they carried the same freight and baggage – the social and cultural context out of which they came. Then Seepersad got stranded. In August 1951, in the middle of describing to Vidia how he was trying to cope and how hard it was to really go to work at writing after a day at work, he couldn't hold back: "The fact is, I feel trapped."[21] Some of the pain this stoic man kept swallowing back may be seen in something he wrote to Vidia: "Perception is rare and intelligence is by no means widespread. Those who have it to any unusual degree often suffer terribly: they are the most lonesome creatures in the world... Yet, more often than not it is from such people that the world derives its true greatness... Sometimes in our very loneliness you will produce that which will be something new and which you otherwise could not produce... AND DO NOT SAY YOU RESIGN YOURSELF TO OBSCURITY. Or if you do, say that in obscurity you will do your work."[22]

Ostensibly, he is trying to bolster Vidia. But this is so autobiographical. Seepersad never used the word "shipwreck" but he conjured the image. The shipwreck that was the aftermath of the voyages into indenture was his unconscious and motivating theme. Build then the new ships, Brathwaite wrote.[23]

The sons were able to escape. On the new ships they travelled beyond the bounding main, taking on board new material and new understandings as they strove to fulfil the vocation as writer that had chosen them. They wanted to believe they were full-blooded global creations (as if anything global has any blood); they were haunted nevertheless by the undeniable fact that memory can eject neither the island and the native shores, nor the first immigrant experience, the ancestral journey that brought them from that other place that became an area of darkness.

I have said that the writings of all three Naipauls are driven by anxiety. In the writings of all three there is also yearning and nostalgia coming from they know not where. In all, there is the fear of extinction. To the three of them, to write was to live. On reading Shiva's second novel, *The Chip Chip Gatherers* (1973), Diana Athill, an editor at Vidia's first publisher, Andre Deutsch, felt that there had to be "some very rare and awe-inspiring gene roaming about among the Naipauls".[24] If there is something genetic in the case, I hope we hear about it in some form during the conference.

This conference attempts to give the kind of lead that could only come from our perspective as inhabitants of the country and region that formed and tested these three writers, and gave them their themes and obsessions. For too long we have evaded our responsibility to think of our writers, first of all in terms of what they mean to us in whose language they write. There are certain noises writers make that can only be heard by those whose language they write in. If there are to be new directions in West Indian literary studies, it is with this realisation that we must begin.

It is the unique purpose of this conference not just to point to the obvious connections and differences, but more daringly to probe the mysteries of place and person and heritage, the nebulous conjunctions and influences among the three writers, between them and their family and between them and this their native land. I have referred to the ghostly influence of Seepersad when Shiva came upon his father's eclectic and purposeful collection of books, to the uncanny interpenetrations between Vidia and Seepersad seen and felt in the overpowering *Letters Between a Father and Son* and in Vidia's sometimes invisible absorption of so much of Seepersad's sketches and hints. It is our hope that this first inquiry will offer unique insights into the work of three important Trinidadian writers and make an inspiring contribution to Naipaulian and West Indian literary studies.

Endnotes

1. V.S. Naipaul, "Two Worlds" (Nobel Lecture), in *Literary Occasions* (New York: Knopf, 2003), 190.
2. Patrick French, *The World Is What It Is: The Authorised Biography of V.S. Naipaul* (London: Picador, 2008), 202.
3. Kamla Naipaul, quoted in V.S. Naipaul, *Letters Between a Father and Son* [1999], ed. Gillon Aitken (London: Abacus, 2000), 304.
4. Kamla Naipaul, quoted in V.S. Naipaul, *Letters* [1999], 237.
5. French, 85.
6. Shiva Naipaul, *An Unfinished Journey* (London: Hamish Hamilton, 1986), 23-29.
7. Shiva Naipaul, *An Unfinished Journey*, 25.

8. V.S. Naipaul, interview by Patrick French, 22 January 2004, in French, *The World Is What It Is*, 425.
9. "Poor in possibility"; "tawdry and confining." (19)[SOURCE?]
10. See French, 157, and "Prologue to an Autobiography" in V.S. Naipaul, *Finding the Centre* (London: Andre Deutsch, 1984), 32.
11. V.S. Naipaul, *Miguel Street* [1959], (New York: Vanguard Press, 1960), 9.
12. V.S. Naipaul, *Letters* [1999], 116.
13. Seepersad Naipaul, quoted in V.S. Naipaul, *Letters* [1999], 25.
14. V.S. Naipaul, *Letters* [1999], 95.
15. French, 17, 95, 271.
16. V.S. Naipaul, *A Bend in the River* (London: Andre Deutsch, 1979), 9.
17. Shiva Naipaul, *A Hot Country* (London: Hamish Hamilton, 1983), 160.
18. Shiva Naipaul, *An Unfinished Journey*, 136.
19. French, 456.
20. French, 176.
21. Seepersad Naipaul, quoted in V.S. Naipaul, *Letters* [1999], 120.
22. Seepersad Naipaul, quoted in V.S. Naipaul, *Letters* [1999], 69.
23. Kamau Brathwaite, "New Ships", *The Arrivants* (Oxford: OUP, 1973), 124-129
24. Diana Athill, quoted in French, *The World Is What It Is*, 423.

2: FAMILY LOVE TESTED BY ARTISTIC AMBITION

BHOENDRADATT TEWARIE

Gillon Aitken was Naipaul's literary agent for many years. He accompanied V.S. to Trinidad when, as principal of the St Augustine campus of the University of the West Indies, I hosted V.S. Naipaul for a week in 2006. Aitken introduced the letters between Seepersad Naipaul and V.S. Naipaul in the book *Letters Between a Father and Son* (1999). He wrote:

> The task of introducing this extraordinary and moving correspondence is a delicate one. In these letters between a father and son, the older man worn down by the cares of a large family and the distress of unfulfilled ambitions, the younger on the threshold of a broad and brilliant literary career, lies some of the raw material of one of the finest and most enduring work of the twentieth century: V.S. Naipaul's *A House for Mr. Biswas*.[1]

The contrast that Gillon draws between "the distress of unfulfilled ambitions" in Seepersad Naipaul, with V.S. being on the "threshold of a broad and brilliant literary career" is what I want to explore in the first part of this presentation.

The exchanges between Seepersad and Vidia came to an end with Seepersad's death in 1953. Seepersad's last letter to his son (September 24th 1953) contains all the worry and care of a father and family man. He is concerned about his inability to earn, the sequence of earners who will support the family materially, and the ambitions of the younger siblings. He asks his older son to consider returning home to help support the family,[2] knowing full well that his real opportunities lay outside, not in Trinidad and Tobago. He is hopeful that V.S. Naipaul will, at least, come home to visit. By October 3, 1953, however, succumbing to three heart attacks, Seepersad Naipaul passed on.[3]

This is how Sati (one of V.S. Naipaul's sisters) writes to her brother about her father: "Materially he must have left us just a bit above the average, but mentally he has left us millionaires."[4] There is no denying Seepersad Naipaul's role as a philosophical anchor and intellectual leader of the Naipaul home and household. But the central concern of Kamla, V.S. Naipaul's eldest sister and Sati (second sister and third in line after V.S.) after their father dies, is the book that their father Seepersad wrote and what would happen to it. In her letter to Mr Bayley, V.S. Naipaul's tutor, asking him to break the news of his father's death, Kamla, oldest in the family, writes at the end (October 5, 1953): "The publishing of his stories and book must be done. He gave his life to that."[5]

Sati wrote again to her brother (October 7, 1953): "As Pa's elder son you have one more duty to perform. That is the publishing of his book. That Vido was Pa's life. That's what he slaved over and gave his life to, and though he wouldn't be here to see this great love of his materialise, we would all be here to take our 'hats off to him'".[6]

Letters Between a Father and Son is, at its core, a book about a father's legacy, after years of infuriating struggle to be a writer; his gift to his son was the ambition to become one; and the debt of the son was to help his father to make real his dream. The book's context is the groundbreaking triumph of the talented son, a literary genius who built on the foundations of his father's own originality in presenting the world in which he lived, from the perspective of those who inhabited that world, and the different ways they related to it. Within the story the letters present a fierce tug of war between family love and obligations on the one hand and artistic ambition on the other.

Seepersad Naipaul's book, *The Adventures of Gurudeva and Other Stories*, was not published until 1976 – twenty-three years after he died. V.S. Naipaul tells us honestly why it had not happened before in his foreword to the collection: "…I did not think the stories publishable outside Trinidad, and I did nothing about them."[7] This was despite the fact that he had once written to his father saying that he, Seepersad, was the best West Indian writer of the time,[8] and despite assuring him that he was actively engaged in trying to get it published, whereas, in fact, on his own admission, he had done nothing about it. In Patrick French's words in *The World Is What It Is* (2008): he "opted for inertia and silence" and said in a later interview "The manuscript was in a bad state. I didn't think the work was ready for publishing. I didn't want to wound him by making it explicit."[9]

Yet the letters between father and son reveal V.S. Naipaul's support for his father's work, including editing, submitting, and reading his short stories on the BBC's *Caribbean Voices* programme. Seepersad himself could not understand why his son appeared to be making no serious effort to look for a publisher for his book, and enclosed a list of authors' agents since his son seemed to be failing at the task.[10] When, twenty-three years after Seepersad's death, V.S. Naipaul honoured his obligation and edited and wrote an introduction to his father's stories, it was regarded by the world more as the son's gift to his father, as an act of generosity or charity on his part. Too much time had passed for Seepersad Naipaul's talent to matter other than historically, for his legacy to matter to contemporary critics and the literary world. *The Adventures of Gurudeva and Other Tales* became a V.S.

Naipaul phenomenon. By this time V.S. Naipaul had already established an unassailable reputation as a writer. It was his reputation, perhaps, that may have helped to sell more copies of *Gurudeva* than Seepersad could have ever have envisaged, but it was mostly read and reviewed in the context of appreciating the contemporary author's antecedents rather than Seepersad's talents. In the end, *The Adventures of Gurudeva and Other Tales* is a book sponsored by V.S. Naipaul, which helps to give his context, to anchor his achievement. It is not about Seepersad. The publication of the book as a period piece scarcely realises the "unfulfilled ambitions" of Seepersad Naipaul as a writer.

In "Prologue to an Autobiography" in *Finding the Centre* (1984) – the title of the book makes reference to a phrase used two or three times in letters by Seepersad to Vidia in their exchanges on the art of writing – V.S. Naipaul acknowledges that "The ambition to be a writer was given to me by my father".[11] In the period between 1984 and 2000, except for *Beyond Belief* (dealing with the Muslim world), Naipaul seems to have focused a good deal on his own personal journey – the antecedents, the contexts, the sources of material for writing, his way of seeing as a writer (articles collected in books such as *The Writer and The World* (2000) and *A Writer's People* (2007). It was in that context that *Letters Between a Father and Son* is published in 1999, a collection that makes clear just what the son owed the father.

Seepersad Naipaul was not the only member of his family that V.S. Naipaul tapped for source material. He wrote to his sister Mira, who was at the time in Edinburgh, to ask for material – things she might remember about the family. In making his request he explained to her, "now you mustn't think that this is a form of cheating. Gogol wrote to his mother for stories when he was writing those stories of Russian rural life."[12] In a letter to his younger brother, Shiva, who seems at some point to have indicated his lack of interest in writing fiction, V.S. asks him to think of "odd incidents for him" and he indicates that this would be no loss to Shiva, since he, Shiva would not be writing fiction anyway.[13]

V.S. evidently had no qualms about drawing material from his father, mother and siblings and other family members. To borrow from his father's work was, from V.S. Naipaul's point of view, the prerogative of the artist. Publication of his father's work could not be a priority in the larger scheme of his own artistic ambitions. This has been the pattern of V.S. Naipaul's life. Nothing or no one stands in the way of artistic ambition. This is true of other immediate family members. True in the case of his first wife, Pat. True in the case of his Argentinian lover, Margaret. In the relationship with Seepersad over the publication of *Gurudeva* we see the beginnings of this emergent tendency, this ruthlessness of personality, so deftly explored and presented by Patrick French in his authorised biography. The story that Patrick French really tells is the triumph of will of the gifted artist over the human being, with all his deficiencies and failings.

So what of V.S. Naipaul's relationship with his younger brother, Shiva? This is the issue I wish to explore in the second half of this article. In a letter of 1952 from his sister Mira, Shiva writes, "Dear Vido, I send you a kiss."[14] It is a touching gesture from a boy of seven to an elder brother whom he adores and who, by that time, might have become something of a mythical figure in his consciousness. When V.S. Naipaul left Trinidad for Oxford, Shiva was hardly four years old.

In 1956, when Vidia Naipaul visited Trinidad for the first time since leaving Oxford – a visit which yielded the novel *The Suffrage of Elvira* – would you believe that he slapped-up eleven-year-old Shiva? This is how V.S. writes to sister Kamla in a 1957 letter about it: "I struck Shiva once or twice. I cannot say how bitterly I regret that now; at times I almost wish the hand that struck would drop off".[15]

When Shiva, suddenly, at the young age of forty, died from a heart attack, V.S. Naipaul was devastated, broken, distraught. This is how Patrick French records his grief from one of his letters to his friend, Lady Antonia Fraser. "It's a great grief; and it has brought, suddenly, a new feeling of loneliness (though we seldom met)... since my father's death in 1953, I have never really known grief as sharp as this."[16]

So, within the framework of the actions and feelings outlined in the preceding three paragraphs, one gets the flavour of the relationship between V.S. and his younger brother – love and affection, intolerance and anger, remorse for things done, and regret for things not done and for opportunities missed. V.S. Naipaul's body erupted in eczema when Shiva died[17] – so affected was he by the death of his brother.

The tension between family love and its obligations and the will to artistic achievement, identified in the relationship between Seepersad and Vidia, replays itself in the relationship between Vidia and Shiva. Seepersad's angst over not being published would have reinforced V.S. Naipaul's feelings that a writer is not really a writer unless a book is published. He experienced his own frustrations in trying to get his first work of fiction published. The desire of father and son, to have a first publication out in bookstores, collided. In 1953, when his father died V.S. Naipaul had already given himself to the vocation of writing, but he had not yet published a book.

Shiva became a writer without Vidia's overt help, though he, no doubt, would have benefited from the relationship. By the time Shiva submitted his work to Andre Deutsch, he had the benefit of V.S. Naipaul's reputation, who by that time (1970) had published seven works of fiction (including the critically acclaimed *A House for Mr. Biswas*) and three of nonfiction. And V.S. Naipaul, struggling for material at the time, after cannibalising his father's work and mining the stories, incidents, events and characters, from his memory and from exchanges of letters with his loved ones, would have begun the next phase of his career by exploring new landscapes, characters very different in dimension from those in his early works and contexts not limited to insular environments – anything that could be described as books of local colour. This is the period in which books such as *The Mimic Men*, set in London and the imagined Isabella, and *In a Free State* (Washington, London, an imagined African country) begin to manifest.

Shiva Naipaul had won a scholarship and followed in V.S. Naipaul's footsteps to Oxford. He, too, wanted to be a writer but with Vidia's reputation there were challenges. This is how French describes Shiva's challenge to being a writer. "Standing above him was the banyan tree, in whose shade nothing could grow: Vido. From his earliest days, Shiva had been made aware that he had to match his elder brother's achievements, and wrote later, 'no one ever quite lives up to the demands of an Absolute'".[18] From the beginning, the relationship between the two brothers in England was not very good. They were very different personalities, perhaps, with very different approaches to life. "Vidia adored Shiva", wrote French, quoting Francis Wyndham, "but was very heavy-handed with him."[19] There are so many psychological possibilities to explore here that could possibly explain why, but I will not venture there in this article.

The tone of the relationship continued until Shiva died. V.S. remained the banyan tree, but Shiva's talent was real and he began to receive critical acclaim, became a darling of the *Spectator* crowd, which helped to boost him up, and created a kind of Naipaulian complexity and confusion. (French even suggests that *Gurudeva*, *House for Mr. Biswas* and *Fireflies* could be regarded as something of a trilogy.[20] Two Naipaul novelists drawing on similar material competing in the literary market place and operating in overlapping circles in London. It was very difficult for both, no doubt. The complexity of the relationship of two writing brothers, in a world in which opportunities were circumscribed, is caught quite well in these lines from French: "Vidia sat down to read the manuscript of Shiva's new book *North of South,* and made 'correction after correction' big and small... In the evening Vidia told me how much he loved Sewan [Shiva], always had, but Sewan rejected him when he first came to England."[21] His brother remained on his mind. Vidia telephoned him to give instructions on the craft of the writer: "it is not the writer's business to complain but to explore".[22] Shiva, on the other hand, often complained that Vidia never raised a hand to help him and he had to do it all on his own.[23]

So what is the point?

Well here again, between these two brothers, very different in personality and disposition, who really did not engage with each other much in spite of being together in England at the same time, we witness the tensions between family love and obligations on the one hand and artistic ambition on the other. Vidia's inconsolable grief and the extreme physical reaction after Shiva's death can perhaps be explained best in these terms, though, in the case of both father and brother, he seems driven more by artistic ambition than by love or the need to meet obligations. V.S. Naipaul had a mentor in Seepersad. V.S. Naipaul never became a mentor to Shiva and sometimes made light of his work. From V.S. Naipaul's viewpoint, Shiva, as a writer, seemed to be a weak imitation and unnecessary competitor with an unhealthy lifestyle. V.S. Naipaul can be judgmental and harsh in his relationship with those close to him and with Shiva Naipaul, he definitely was. Again, there is much to explore here but this is not the time.

The act of creation is a complex phenomenon and the artist is often a complex being. The artist lives for those moments when creation becomes possible. He/she jealously guards creative space, creative time, and opportunity for personal creative accomplishments to be experienced and acknowledged by others. The artist is not about good works, he/she is about good work; he/she is not about love per se, but passion for the act of creation. Even when there is love, what is more important is the stimulus of love and romance to the passion to create. For the true artist there is no integrity higher than artistic integrity and there is no love greater than love for the creation of art and the validation of the artistic self, by increasing acceptance of the art one creates. Family love comforts and secures a human being, but it does not seem to satisfy the driven artist, whose deep hunger drives him/her to create above all else. Relationships and engagement are sources of information in the universe, stimuli to creativity, food for reflection and imaginative conversion and transformation. Relationships might have deep value in their own right but they do have a definite, perhaps definitive value in providing material for artistic creation.

There is just one more dimension on which I wish to close and that has to do with the summoning of the human will in the service or support of artistic ambition.

In *A Bend in the River*, V.S. Naipaul's 1979 novel about individual survival in the face of a collapsing, disintegrating society and economy, the protagonist and narrator in the novel begins with the following sentence: "The world is as it is; those who are nothing, who allow themselves to become nothing, have no place in it."[24] In my 2006 interview with V.S. Naipaul, published in *Journal of West Indian Literature* and recorded on film, I asked the author whether those words quoted above reflected his own thinking.[25] He reflected and admitted that it probably did. This issue, therefore, of the assertion of individual will and its link to the will to triumph and to artistic ambition is very important in the Naipaul context. Put another way, in the case of V.S. Naipaul's own psychological make up, ambition and drive and the assertion of human will to succeed is important for human beings to triumph over the world as it is, and no less so for the artist, perhaps even more for the creative writer.

This perception of the crucial role of determined will in human affairs becomes for Naipaul, over time, a philosophical perspective and deeply held belief. Obviously, even before the articulation of such a belief, it was already in construction during his formative years as a writer, and reinforced later as personal ideology by his triumph in the literary world in the face of formidable difficulties.

Endnotes

1. Gillon Aitken, introduction to *Letters Between a Father and Son* [1999], ed. Gillon Aitken (Abacus, 2000), ix.
2. Seepersad Naipaul in Naipaul, *Letters* [1999], 295-7.
3. Patrick French, *The World Is What It Is: The Authorised Biography of V.S. Naipaul* (London: Picador, 2008), 125.
4. Sati Naipaul to Peter Bayley and VSN, (October 5, 1953), *Letters Between a Father and Son*, ed. Nicholas Laughlin and Gillon Aitken (London: Picador, 2009), pp. 371-372.
5. Kamla Naipaul, quoted in V.S. Naipaul, *Letters Between a Father and Son*, ed. Nicholas Laughlin and Gillon Aitken (London: Picador, 2009), 370.
6. Sati Naipaul, quoted in V.S. Naipaul, *Letters* (2009), 372.
7. V.S. Naipaul, foreword to *The Adventures of Gurudeva and Other Stories* (London: Andre Deutsch, 1976), 19.
8. V.S. Naipaul, *Letters* [1999], 116.
9. Patrick French, *The World Is What It Is: The Authorised Biography of V.S. Naipaul*, 114.
10. French, op. cit., 119.
11. *Finding the Centre* (London: Deutch, 1984), 33.
12. *Letters*, V.S. to Mira, quoted in Patrick French, op. cit., 228.
13. Quoted in French, 228
14. In a letter from Mira to V.S., 1952, quoted in French, 89
15. *Letters Between a Father and Son*, ed. Nicholas Laughlin and Gillon Aitken (London: Picador, 2009), 444
16. French, 425.
17. Savi Naipaul Akal, *The Naipauls of Nepaul Street* (Leeds: Peepal Tree Press, 2018), 195
18. French, 251.
19. Francis Wyndham, interview by Patrick French, 27 August 2003, quoted in French, 252.
20. French, 293.
21. French, 384.
22. French, 384.
23. French, 424-425
24. V.S. Naipaul, *A Bend in the River* (London: Andre Deutsch, 1979), 9.

25. V.S. Naipaul, interview by Bhoendradatt Tewarie, "Interview with V.S. Naipaul: Writer and Critical Thinker," *Journal of West Indian Literature* 16, no. 2 (2008): 62-74, http://www.jstor.org/stable/23019881.

3: NAIPAUL'S LETTERS BETWEEN A FATHER AND SON (AND MOTHER AND SISTER)

NICHOLAS LAUGHLIN

[Author's note: this substantially expanded version of my presentation at the *Seepersad and Sons* conference is the result of an invitation from Prof. Alison Donnell to turn my notes into a formal essay for publication in a special issue of *Caribbean Quarterly* on Caribbean Literary Archives. My thanks to Prof. Donnell and her anonymous readers for their comments and suggestions.]

In October 1953, when the twenty-one-year-old Vidia Naipaul heard his father had died, he sent a telegram to his family in Trinidad saying "everything I owe to him."[1] That is the exaggeration of grief, but only a slight exaggeration. And although Vidia soon outgrew the intellectual influence of Seepersad, the example of his father's devotion to writing, of his almost desperate anxiety about being a writer, has motivated and also haunted the prodigious son throughout his long career.

Naipaul's relationship with his father has its supreme literary monument in his novel *A House for Mr. Biswas*. But its chief biographical record is the sequence of family correspondence collected in *Letters Between a Father and Son*, a book with a complicated and revealing history, involving two editions (published a decade apart in 1999 and 2009, the latter ultimately withdrawn), two editors, two rival literary agents, a biographer, the tangled relations of a large and far-flung family, and the even more tangled negotiations of publishing-world politics. The intricacies of this history are unknown to – one may even say concealed from – most readers of the published correspondence. But it may perhaps serve as a telling case study in the opportunities and dangers, the politics and personalities involved, in making a literary archive public by turning it into a book.

Letters exist because of geography: because of the distances between people. In the case of the Naipaul family correspondence, they exist because in August 1950 the elder son Vidia left Trinidad to take up a scholarship at University College, Oxford – but also because, as fewer people know, Vidia's sister Kamla, the eldest of the Naipaul siblings, preceded him by a year. She left Trinidad in 1949, also on scholarship, to study in India, at Benares Hindu University. So the earliest letters "between a father and son" are actually between a sister and brother: Kamla writing to Vidia from almost the other side of the world, and Vidia replying with bits of family gossip, suggested reading lists, and criticisms of her handwriting, or confessing an adolescent crush. Once Vidia himself was safely off the island, the correspondence became a three-way affair, between Oxford, Benares, and Nepaul Street in St. James, the west Port of Spain neighbourhood that was home to the Naipauls. The core of the book, as its title implies, is the series of letters between Seepersad and Vidia, but it's crucial to remember that, in both the published selection and the complete sequence preserved in the archive, this is a broader family correspondence, continuing after Seepersad's death and through the decade of the 1950s, with many letters written by and addressed to Seepersad's wife (and Vidia's mother) Droapatie, Kamla, the other Naipaul sisters, in particular Sati, and even the occasional scribble from Vidia's brother Shiva, still a young boy at this time.

The original letters – which now repose in the Naipaul Archive at the University of Tulsa's McFarlin Library – survive because they were kept separate from V.S. Naipaul's other literary papers, a substantial number of which were destroyed in the kind of accident archivists have nightmares about. In his authorised biography *The World Is What It Is*, Patrick French describes how Naipaul "spent a lifetime meticulously recording himself." "Always conscious of his own projected destiny," French writes, Naipaul "had preserved everything":[2] manuscripts; notebooks; correspondence; BBC scripts; newspaper clippings; and much else. A large portion of these papers, covering Naipaul's early career in the 1950s and 60s, had been entrusted to Ely's, a storage company in Wimbledon, for supposed safekeeping. But in 1992, thinking to have his archive valued for sale, Naipaul discovered instead and to his horror that, thanks to a clerical error, Ely's had mistakenly incinerated the box of files that had contained a third of his papers.[3]

French notes succinctly the significance to a biographer of the loss of Naipaul's Oxford diaries, the manuscript of his unpublished first novel *The Shadow'd Livery*, and the journals recording his travels in the Caribbean (the subject of *The Middle Passage*) and India.[4] To Naipaul, the loss was also financial. As long as two decades earlier, in 1972, he'd attempted to interest a library or university in purchasing his papers, suggesting a price of £40,000.[5] Having discovered the destruction of a sizeable portion of this asset, Naipaul tasked his literary agent with finding a buyer for what survived. "Using impeccable logic," French writes, "Gillon Aitken argued to various interested American institutions that the loss of the boxes at Ely's made the remaining material especially valuable." The University of Tulsa in Oklahoma – already the home of the Jean Rhys papers and the archive of André Deutsch, Naipaul's first publisher – made the winning bid:

"$470,000, covering material to the end of 2002, with an additional $150,000 to become available for papers generated during the five years after that date, making a total of $620,000."[6]

So in 1994, along with the other papers not stored at and incinerated by Ely's, Naipaul's family letters made a further and final journey to Tulsa. His side of the correspondence – the letters he wrote to "home" – had previously been kept in a bank vault in Trinidad. A note in Naipaul's handwriting filed with the correspondence in the Tulsa archive says he retrieved the letters from Trinidad intending to use them as the basis for a book about his Oxford days, never written. But now they were to see the light of publication, as part of another deal negotiated by Aitken, who offered various British publishers the travel book that was to become *Beyond Belief* – Naipaul's revisiting of the Islamic countries he'd written about in *Among the Believers* – with an edition of Vidia and Seepersad's "Oxford" letters thrown in to sweeten the deal. "The letters were a questionable commercial project," Aitken later admitted to French, and the publishers Little, Brown offered a mere £225,000 for the two books. "I had to write Vidia a careful letter; he wasn't pleased."[7] Aitken himself took on the task of editing the letters – or at least was officially credited for this – introducing them with a note remarking on Naipaul's "understandably disengaged approval of the project,"[8] and the book duly appeared in bookshops in the autumn season of 1999. A US edition soon followed, published by Alfred A. Knopf, and a selection from the sequence of letters also appeared in *The New Yorker's* issue of 13 December 1999, helping drum up public interest in this commercially "questionable" book.

As published in this original edition, *Letters Between a Father and Son* tells a poignant family story, offering intimate insights into the relationship between Vidia and Seepersad Naipaul – a relationship the son had contemplated in his writing oftentimes over the decades, most extensively in the essay "Prologue to an Autobiography". The letters are also revealing of the influences and concerns of V.S. Naipaul as a young writer, of the precocious confidence of his ambitions but also of his anxieties, and shows how some of the important themes and lines of inquiry of his later books took root early on – such as the movement of peoples between and within countries and cultures, the making and remaking of the self in response to these dislocations, and their accompanying tensions and illusions. The letters enrich readers' understanding of *A House for Mr Biswas,* a canonical work of twentieth-century literature, which reimagines Seepersad and Vidia Naipaul as Mohun Biswas and his son Anand, Nepaul Street as Sikkim Street, the Naipauls' Capildeo cousins as the overbearing Tulsis. And the letters give us glimpses into the social life of an urban, semi-creolised Indo-Trinidadian family at a key period in Trinidad's history, the decade before independence in 1962.

These aspects were all noted by the early reviewers of *Letters Between a Father and Son*, a few of whom also considered the question of where this book fits in the Naipaul canon, and whether we should think of it as a literary work, or as something else. Reading the correspondence, from time to time you get the sense that Seepersad certainly, and Vidia perhaps, felt conscious of the possibility that the letters could someday have a public audience. It's most overt in Seepersad's letter dated 22 October 1950, in which he gives the book its eventual title: "Your letters are charming in their spontaneity," he writes to his son, suggesting that if Vidia would write regular letters describing "things and people" at Oxford, Seepersad could compile them in a volume to be called "LETTERS BETWEEN FATHER AND SON, or MY OXFORD LETTERS".[9]

Reviewing the volume in the *London Review of Books*, the English critic James Wood made an astute observation about the way the letters seem to document Vidia's growing sense of Seepersad as someone a novel could be written about. "Vidia's letters contain both warm respect for his father," Wood wrote, "and the beginning of a necessary objectification of Pa, a novelist's weaning, in which the young man begins to see his father as others might – as a character. He writes home: 'If I didn't know the man, I would have said: what a delightful father to have.'"[10]

So the value of these letters as a document of the development of an important writer – certainly the major prose writer of the Anglophone Caribbean tradition, and a major writer of world literature in the twentieth century – seems indisputable. But very few readers of the 1999 edition of *Letters Between a Father and Son* could have known that on editorial grounds it was a defective text. It was riddled with errors of transcription which may not have affected the book's immediate readability, but certainly damaged its accuracy as a document – in some cases, changing the meaning of what Naipaul and his correspondents wrote, and elsewhere interfering with the nuances of the epistolary conversation in these pages.

Some of these errors are almost comically hapless, as in the letter written by Vidia to Kamla in September 1950, in which he describes his departure from Trinidad, beginning his journey to Britain. In the 1999 edition, it reads:

> "I learned that the plane was delayed. I was mad. I refused to believe it. But it was so. So I kicked my heels in anguish at Woodbrook until 11, then took my luggage into dear old PA 1192 and we got to Diane at about 12. The waiting room was swarming with people"[11]

– and on it goes. Some Trinidadian readers must have felt a slight confusion on first reading this passage. Woodbrook is the Port of Spain neighbourhood where Vidia's Capildeo cousins lived; "dear old PA 1192" was Seepersad's car, a Ford Prefect. But who was Diane? This mysterious woman is not mentioned anywhere else in the letters before or after, there is no explanatory note, and there appears to be no Naipaul or Capildeo relative named Diane. But according to the published letter, this was the last person Vidia was taken to see before he left Trinidad. The mystery was solved – anticlimactically – when I finally read the original letter in Naipaul's handwriting. Piling his luggage into the family Ford, Vidia was driven not to "Diane" but merely and logically to Piarco, Trinidad's airport, about an hour east of Port of Spain. (The confusions are not limited to Trinidadian place names: later in the same letter, the 1999 edition gives the capital of Puerto Rico, where Vidia's plane refuelled, as "San Fran", rather than San Juan.)[12]

Another example, in which a transcription error completely misrepresents what Naipaul actually wrote, comes from a letter dated 21 September 1949, written by Vidia to Kamla, giving her his impressions of India – a country he would not visit for more than a decade yet – and specifically his opinions of Prime Minister Jawaharlal Nehru. The 1999 edition reads: "From Nehru's autobiography, I think the Premier of India is a first-class showman using his saintliness as a weapon of rule."[13] It is an odd assessment of a politician who was seen as a national and anticolonial hero by many, but surely not as a saint. In fact, the transcription accidentally skips two lines of the original typewritten text, and conflates separate comments on Nehru and Mohandas Gandhi. What Naipaul actually wrote (with italics added here to indicate the missing text) was:

> "From Nehru's autobiography, I think the Premier of India is a first-class showman *with a host of third-rate supporters. I don't know whether I could agree with Nichols' condemnation of Gandhi as a shrewd politician,* using his saintliness as a weapon of rule."[14]

Thus were readers of the letters deprived of young Vidia's considered opinion of the late Mahatma.

The 1999 edition of the letters contains numerous examples of similar misreadings and misinterpretations – often the kind likely to be made by an editor with limited knowledge of Trinidad's geography and social history. But it also contains errors resulting from other kinds of contextual confusion. For instance, the letters were arranged by their first editor into "chapters" named according to the three terms of the university academic year. In the 1999 edition, they are Michaelmas, Lent, and Summer; but at Oxford, the terms are rather named Michaelmas, Hilary, and Trinity. (You could call this a kind of terminological inexactitude.)

It seems no one had an inkling of these problems until Patrick French examined the original documents in the Tulsa archive during his research for *The World Is What It Is*. "These letters... were not transcribed accurately," French writes tersely, explaining his decision to make his own fresh transcriptions. He went on to promise that "a corrected and expanded edition is being prepared."[15] For French had persuaded Naipaul's new publisher, Picador – who had acquired the rights to all of Naipaul's backlist, alongside the new biography – that they should issue a corrected version of *Letters Between a Father and Son*. Furthermore, and given the kinds of errors riddling the 1999 edition, he convinced them to hire a new editor – one from Trinidad, grounded in the place of Naipaul's origins, and so presumably unlikely to confuse "Piarco" with "Diane".

Here, this essay becomes a personal narrative. In July 2006, following an introduction by French and a cordial exchange of correspondence, I met Gillon Aitken at his office in London to talk about my tackling a fresh edition of the letters. We agreed on three objectives: to correct transcription errors in the 1999 edition, to beef up the book with relevant additional letters which might have turned up in the process of cataloguing the archive, and to expand the endnotes. Aitken made it clear that Naipaul would not be involved in the process, and not available to answer questions about tricky references requiring annotation. Naipaul would never read the text, Aitken explained, repeating what he'd already claimed in his introduction to the 1999 edition. The letters summoned too many painful memories for the writer; Naipaul understood the value of having the letters published (and, it did not need saying, appreciated the book royalties), but would remain "detached". At the time, none of this seemed odd. But perhaps I should have paid closer attention when Aitken, in a subsequent email, said he would not even discuss the new edition of the letters with Naipaul, once more citing the writer's detachment from the book and Aitken's knowledge of his client's preferences.[16]

Thus in January 2007 I paid a visit to Tulsa – fortuitously enjoying a mild winter – and spent several days in the McFarlin Library leafing through Naipaul's original papers. Then followed several months at my desk at home in Trinidad, reading and rereading a thick stack of photocopies, transcribing, proofreading, and re-proofreading what became a significantly different version of *Letters Between a Father and Son*. For I exceeded the brief instigated by French and agreed by Aitken – to correct, expand, re-annotate; because, as I read my way into the material of the correspondence, I realised the task wasn't so simple.

First of all, there was a basic editorial principle to decide: how to reproduce the text of the original letters, which were sometimes handwritten and sometimes typewritten, composed sometimes carefully and sometimes in haste, with their various authors' idiosyncrasies of style and spelling. Though Aitken wrote that, as editor, he had "adopted a policy of non-intrusion,"[17] the 1999 edition in fact approached the letters from an editorial stance of intervening to standardise and smoothen: changing the punctuation and sometimes the grammar of the texts, correcting slips of the pen or the typewriter (while, however, introducing new slips of the word processor), quietly removing postscripts and marginalia. I decided instead to offer the reader a text as close as possible, within the bounds of conventional typography, to the experience of reading the original documents – which meant retaining their idiosyncrasies and inconsistencies, and indeed sometimes their infelicities, as long as these did not hinder comprehension.[18]

For example, Vidia tended to use ampersands when he was writing by hand, but spelled out his *ands* when he was typing; he dropped the apostrophes in his *don'ts* and *won'ts* when typing, but not when writing with his pen. These differences may seem trivial, but they influence the flow and rhythm of the sentences as you read them, and I thought it valuable for readers of the book to experience these just as the original recipients of the letters did. I even persuaded myself I had Naipaul's approval for this approach, in a sort of a way, as he'd once declared in a 1984 interview that "a writer's writing should not be interfered with. I like people to punctuate their own way... I never forgive people who change my things."[19] It also occasionally happens in the letters that one of the correspondents uses a word or grammatical construction common in Trinidadian English but usually erroneous in standard British usage, as when Vidia writes of "fulling out", not filling in, his Oxford application forms.[20] To keep the phrase as he wrote it is to preserve a tinge of his accent.

There were other little particularities I thought worth preserving in the published text. In a couple of letters written to her parents by Kamla from Benares, she includes marginal notes in stilted Hindi,[21] which she obviously expects them to understand, telling us something perhaps not irrelevant about the linguistic situation at Nepaul Street. Or there is the letter Seepersad writes to Vidia in August 1953 after Kamla's return home, in which he uses an air-letter form Kamla had begun writing on but abandoned,[22] hinting at the necessary thrift in a household struggling to make ends meet. Or the letter from Vidia to his mother Droapatie in January 1957, announcing that he has received the proofs of *The Mystic Masseur*, and complaining about the publisher's illustration for the dust jacket, with two small sketches to demonstrate how badly André Deutsch's artist had depicted an Indo-Trinidadian turban. I scanned Vidia's doodles and had them reproduced in the new text.[23]

The 1999 edition also lacked much of the contextual apparatus which might help a broad range of readers to more fully understand the letters: information about Trinidad in the 1940s and 50s, about Indo-Trinidadian family structure, about the Naipaul and Capildeo families, about Oxford in the 1950s, about the authors Vidia and his father read closely and discussed, and much else. The book offered only a few cursory pages of endnotes inadequate to the task. So I extensively re-annotated the letters, trying to anticipate readers' curiosity about people and places, and I gave the book a brief "epilogue" which describes the later years of the main characters, the members of the Naipaul family.

But the most significant and substantial change in my revised edition were the seventy-nine previously unpublished letters I added to the 170 of the original, increasing the size of the book by almost half. Most important, these included thirty-one new letters by Vidia and twenty-three by Seepersad – so that the revised edition contains all the letters between father and son discoverable in the Tulsa archive, some of which were apparently overlooked before the papers were fully catalogued. The 2009 edition also includes seventeen new letters by Kamla, seven by Droapatie, and one by Sati – a narrow selection from the dozens of additional family letters from this period in the archive. The most affecting of these new letters may be the pair written by Kamla and Sati in the days immediately after Seepersad's death, addressed to Vidia's tutor Peter Bayley and intended to break the tragic news gently.[24] In the event, before the letters arrived in Oxford, Vidia was summoned to London by his cousin Bas Mootoo, and learned of Seepersad's fatal heart attack from her.

Almost half of these new letters come at the end of the sequence, in the years from 1954 to 1957. The 1999 *Letters Between a Father and Son* trails off after the death of Seepersad: there are merely six letters and one telegram from Vidia to his mother and sisters, which cover his transition from graduation to publication, a period of three and a half years. I decided this gave a misleadingly abbreviated version of what you could call the final "chapter" of the story told in the book, climaxing in the publication of *The Mystic Masseur,* Vidia's debut novel and the tangible achievement of his and Seepersad's dream. I decided to flesh out that final chapter, and make it clear that after Seepersad's death there continued to be a regular and often equally intense correspondence between mother and sisters and son.

The "revised and expanded edition" of *Letters Between a Father and Son* was finally published in early April 2009, "edited by / Nicholas Laughlin / and / Gillon Aitken", as the title page read.[25] It went almost unnoticed in the press, as it was perhaps not obvious at a glance that this was almost a new book, in all but name; and furthermore Picador had decided against sending out review copies, as they considered the book merely a revision of a backlist title.[26] Then, almost a year later, I received a mildly apologetic email from the head of Picador, saying that "Sir Vidia Naipaul... has decided that he would prefer the letters to stand alone without... any commentary and has therefore asked that we print the book in future without the editorial notes."[27] What did I think of that? I thought it was a bad idea, and replied as much, but I acknowledged that Sir Vidia was the copyright holder, and this was his decision to make. A few months later, I got a further email: "I am sorry to have to tell you that Vidia decided that he wanted to revert to the original edition of the Letters for our next reprint."[28] In other words, Picador were discarding my text and reverting to the error-filled 1999 version. There was no further explanation.[29]

I was bothered by this turn of events, but quickly decided to – as it were – take it on the chin and move on. Naturally, I also tried to figure out what could have prompted this withdrawal of my edition of the letters, after it had gone through the appropriate processes of editorial approval. There were various factors in play. *The World Is What It Is* had been published, and French's meticulously researched and unvarnished biography had provoked strong reactions: praise for its deeply intelligent scrutiny of Naipaul's life, work, and perplexing personality, but anger from some Naipaul confidantes who felt the great writer had been betrayed by his biographer.[30] Also, Naipaul had recently fired Gillon Aitken, his agent for decades past, in favour of a former protégé of Aitken's (and now his eager rival). Perhaps the proximity of the letters project to these other events had something to do with it.[31]

But I came to suspect that a major element in Naipaul's decision was that I'd substantially changed the nature and scope of the *Letters*, and probably in ways that did not suit the author's sense of his own life story. The Naipaul origin myth – "the ambition to be a writer was given me by my father"[32] – perhaps requires that the relationship between Seepersad and Vidia, between father and son, not be diluted by the adjacency of mother and sister. And that is effectively what I had done – deliberately – by allowing more prominence to Droapatie and Kamla, especially in the concluding section of the revised *Letters*. In fact, I'd chosen to end the book with a letter from Droapatie – to give her the last word, in a sense.

It is a delightful and revealing letter, written a few weeks after *The Mystic Masseur's* publication date. Droapatie begins by saying how nice it is to get a letter from Vido every week. Then she explains in detail why she must ask him to continue contributing financially to the Nepaul Street household. The grocery bill is $150. The light bill is $6. The phone bill is $10. His sister Meera needs new glasses. But among all these expenses, Droapatie managed to save $5 to do a puja for the success of the book. "At the end of two weeks" she thereupon points out, "2 hundreds copies were sold. I definitely think it is a success, and I thank God for it."[33] As an aside: while there's a great deal in the family correspondence about books and writing, there's also an obvious pragmatic interest in money. There are bills to pay, typewriters to repair; the correspondents go to considerable trouble sending each other transatlantic postal orders for what sound like fairly small sums. The family was often, as Kamla put it, very hard up. We should recognise that Naipaul's anxiety about getting a book written and published was primarily but only partly about a young writer's literary ambitions: he also simply needed to earn money, to support himself and his family in Trinidad.

So I entirely understand why Naipaul (or his representative) might think I had turned *Letters Between a Father and Son* into a rather different book to the one he wished it to be, by trying to recover the voices of the mother and sister who were vitally important in Vidia's personal life in the 1940s and 50s, but who have not enjoyed an equivalently central role in the subsequent Naipaul mythology. This was, nonetheless, an intention I was led to by the evidence in the very archive the writer himself took such pains to assemble and preserve.

In 2004, reflecting on the partial incineration of his papers more than a decade before, Naipaul told French: "I am a great believer in the record, that the truth is wonderful and that any doctored truth is awful... I think the completeness of a record is what matters."[34] These are sentiments to encourage any biographer, and indeed French has made it clear that Naipaul never requested a single revision to his authorised but often unflattering portrait in *The World Is What It Is*. However, there is a crucial distinction between "doctoring" the record, as Naipaul puts it, and shaping a narrative from the raw materials of the archive. Sequestered in the climate-controlled stacks at the University of Tulsa, accessible only to researchers approved by Naipaul or his agents, the family correspondence is available to most readers at present only in the form determined by an authorised editor.[35] The edition of the letters currently in print – the 1999 version, complete with mysterious Diane and saintly Nehru – embodies the narrative of filial affection and literary fulfilment which Seepersad imagined when he gave a name to the correspondence still in progress. But a consideration of the full archive of letters may suggest a less obvious narrative of family ties and literary ambition within the Nepaul Street household, rooted in a relationship ignored by the title *Letters Between a Father and Son*.

Here, I follow a faint line of thought triggered by a mischievous hint in *The World Is What It Is*. Describing Naipaul's composition of *The Middle Passage*, French scrutinises the book's infamous opening passage: Naipaul's encounter with the "immigrant-type" West Indian passengers on the boat-train from Waterloo Station in London to Southampton. French suggests this episode may have been inspired by a letter written by Kamla Naipaul to her brother – which French quotes – describing her own journey on the boat-train at the end of a visit to Britain.[36] It is indeed barely the merest trace of a suggestion, but French leaves his reader wondering if Naipaul borrowed his sister's story for his own book. This reminds me of the letter dated 24 November 1949, written by Vidia, still in Trinidad, to Kamla in Benares. "I want you to promise that you will write a book in diary form about your stay in India," Vidia says. "Study conditions; analyse the character. Don't be too bitter. Try to be humorous. Send your manuscript in instalments to me. I will work on them... Your book will be a great success from the financial point of view. I can see it even now – My Passage to India – A Record of Six Unhappy Months – by Kamla Naipaul."[37]

Vidia is at least half joking in this letter, but it nonetheless may prompt the reader to ask if Kamla did ever seriously contemplate writing about her time in India, or writing any other kind of book; and *when* she might have managed to do this, inasmuch as when she returned to Trinidad from university in India she was expected to take up a teaching job to support the family. Seepersad's expectation of Vidia, on the other hand, was that he should stay in Britain as long as necessary to complete a book, and advance the cause of Seepersad's own writing, an increasing worry in his last months.

In one of the more celebrated passages of *A Room of One's Own*, Virginia Woolf invents a character named Judith Shakespeare, sister to the better-known William.[38] Shakespeare's sister is a kind of thought experiment, through whom Woolf considers what might have befallen a woman in Shakespeare's place and time, with similar intelligence, literary talent, and curiosity about the world, but barred by social convention from fulfilling these. (It's no spoiler to say she doesn't end well.) The example tempts me into my own thought experiment: given the opportunity and encouragement, and assuming she had the desire, what kind of book could Naipaul's sister have written? "The record" should show that Kamla did write a book: of some sort, never published, and which I briefly held in my hands. I met Kamla Naipaul Tewarie only once, near the end of her life, when a mutual friend took me to visit. I regret that I don't recall many details of our conversation. But I do remember she offhandedly mentioned she'd once tried to write about her parents, and she sent someone to fetch the typescript from somewhere in the house. It was spiral-bound, and there was a family photo at the front, with the title *Seepersad and Droapatie*. I had it in my hands for just a minute and didn't manage to do more than glance at the first pages. Kamla said she'd once tried showing it to her brother's agent, with no result. And the book, such as it was, disappeared again. (French certainly saw it also, as he quotes a few sentences of Kamla's text in his biography.[39])

If Kamla's typescript still exists, it surely forms part of the "complete record" of the major author V.S. Naipaul and the minor author Seepersad Naipaul, both of them duly recognised in the Tulsa archive (as brother and son Shiva Naipaul is recognised in the archive of his own papers, recently acquired by the British Library). But just as surely, the correspondence collected in *Letters Between a Father and Son* – including Kamla Naipaul's letters, unacknowledged in the book's title – forms part of her record as sister, daughter, teacher, unpublished writer, and member of one of the most extraordinary families the Caribbean has yet produced.[40] Comparing the 1999 and 2009 editions of the *Letters* may stimulate fruitful discussion of editorial methods, literary politics, the vicissitudes of publishing, the crafting of biographical narratives, and the nature and value of the objects that do (or don't) get preserved in archives. It should also remind us that, as material collections assembled by men and women with intentions and ideologies, archives by necessity exclude, and choose to ignore or forget.

Readers of the published *Letters* might also productively reflect on the conventions and motives that shape our ideas of authorship. Nothing could be plainer about the book than that V.S. Naipaul is credited – on cover, spine, and title page – as its sole author. He holds the copyright and receives the royalties. This seems unremarkable, even obvious, until you remember that, in both the 1999 edition and the expanded 2009 edition, approximately half the letters in the book, and thus half the published text, were written by others: Seepersad, Kamla, and the other family members who joined the correspondence.[41] Even Seepersad, the father who precedes the son in the book's published title, is not formally recognised as co-author. You might attribute this omission – if omission is the fitting word – to the practicalities of commercial publication. Perhaps it also reveals something about the ways in which an archive may be used in shaping an author's public persona. The letters themselves tell a story about an author inventing his literary identity, his notion of his relationship to literature, and how this might be perceived by others; and the circumstances of the letters' publication, half a century later, tell a later chapter of that ongoing story. The *Letters* are the author's authorised version of his archive, shaped by his sense of literary destiny. After all, "everything of value about me is in my books," Naipaul has written. "I am the sum of my books."[42]

Meanwhile, though my edition of *Letters Between a Father and Son* is officially out of print, there are copies secreted – archived – in libraries and individual readers' bookshelves. And in its pages you can find the words of a mother and sister which complicate the story – the record – of a father and his famous son.

Afterword

"What kind of book could Naipaul's sister have written?" When I asked this question at the *Seepersad and Sons* conference in October 2015, I had no idea that a tangible reply was already taking form: a memoir at that very time was being completed by Savi Naipaul Akal, the fourth daughter and fifth child of Droapatie and Seepersad (after Kamla, Vidia, Sati, and Mira). Published in May 2018 by Peepal Tree Press, *The Naipauls of Nepaul Street: A Memoir of Life in Trinidad and Beyond* combines Naipaul Akal's detailed recollections of family history over seven decades with a measured but frank assessment of the brother who left 26 Nepaul Street to become one of the most celebrated and controversial writers of his time. In her note of acknowledgements, Naipaul Akal explains why she felt compelled to write her book:

I had begun a biography of my mother in 2006. For various reasons I had to set it aside, unsure of when or if ever I would get back to it. My mother has remained a woman largely hidden in the shadows cast by the lives of my father and my two brothers, who were the published writers in the family. I believed strongly that she deserved some public recognition for her intelligence, pragmatism, stoicism, and strength. She had stood by my father through difficult and dark days. She had nursed Vidia through his bouts of asthma as a child. She had also believed in and encouraged Shiva, who lost his father while still very young. Certainly, she was always confident about the worth and the promise of her five daughters – from Kamla, the oldest, to Nella, who was a baby when Pa died. I believed that they, too, deserve a greater measure of illumination than they have received.

Endnotes

1. V.S. Naipaul, *Letters Between a Father and Son*, ed. Nicholas Laughlin and Gillon Aitken (London: Picador, 2009), 377 (letter 201). Unless otherwise indicated, quotations from the Naipaul correspondence are from this revised and expanded 2009 edition, in which the letters are numbered chronologically for ease of reference.
2. Patrick French, *The World Is What It Is: The Authorised Biography of V.S. Naipaul* (London: Picador, 2008), 462.
3. French also records that on the same day Naipaul was informed of the loss of the papers at Ely's – 8 October 1992 – he received a second piece of bad news: "the Swedish Academy made an announcement of the winner of that year's Nobel Prize in Literature: Derek Walcott." French, *The World Is What It Is*, 462.
4. French, notes to *The World Is What It Is*, 531.
5. This information comes from a letter from Naipaul to his then protégé Paul Theroux: "The only asset I have," Naipaul writes, "is my manuscripts > (drafts etc.)< & my other papers (correspondence etc). A pretty complete documentation of my writing life from 18 to 40." French, *The World Is What It Is*, 323.
6. French, *The World Is What It Is*, 468-469
7. French, *The World Is What It Is*, 474
8. Gillon Aitken, introduction to *Letters Between a Father and Son* (1999), xiii.
9. *Letters Between a Father and Son* (2009), 47 (letter 20).
10. James Wood, "Tell Me What You Talked", review of *Letters between a Father and Son*, by V.S. Naipaul, *London Review of Books*, 11 November 1999, http://www.lrb.co.uk/v21/n22/james-wood/tell-me-what-you-talked
11. V.S. Naipaul, *Letters Between a Father and Son*, ed. Gillon Aitken (London: Little, Brown, 1999), 12.
12. The correctly transcribed letter (letter 13) appears in the 2009 edition on pages 26–29.
13. *Letters Between a Father and Son* (1999), 5.

14. *Letters Between a Father and Son* (2009), 11 (letter 4). "Nichols" is the British writer Beverley Nichols, author of *Verdict on India*.
15. French, notes to *The World Is What It Is*, 508-509.
16. Personal correspondence from Gillon Aitken, 9 August 2006.
17. Gillon Aitken, introduction to *Letters between a Father and Son* (1999), xiii.
18. For a more comprehensive summary of the editorial principles I adopted in preparing the revised text, see my editor's note in *Letters Between a Father and Son* (2009), xv-xx.
19. V.S. Naipaul, interviewed by Mel Gussow, "It Is Out of This Violence I've Always Written," *New York Times*, 16 September 1984, http://www.nytimes.com/books/98/06/07/specials/naipaul-violence.html
20. *Letters Between a Father and Son* (2009), 9 (letter 4).
21. *Letters Between a Father and Son* (2009), 304-05 (letters 159 and 160).
22. *Letters Between a Father and Son* (2009), 357 (letter 190).
23. *Letters Between a Father and Son* (2009), 438 (letter 241).
24. *Letters Between a Father and Son* (2009), 369-73 (letters 199 and 200).
25. My contract with Macmillan Publishers, owners of the Picador imprint, stipulated "a credit to the Editor" but did not rule out a co-credit to the editor of the 1999 edition, even though Aitken had made no active editorial contribution to the 2009 edition, other than approving the revised text as Naipaul's agent.
26. I'd tried but failed to persuade Picador to publish the expanded edition of the letters under a new title, to make it clearer to readers, reviewers, and booksellers that it was substantially different to its predecessor. At a meeting with a Picador editor on 23 September 2008, I learned that the publisher was planning no special publicity for the new edition. Soon after the new edition appeared, the *Evening Standard* ran a brief notice on 21 April 2009, calling it a "significantly enhanced version (of an already desperately touching book)". As far as I know, this is the closest thing to a review of the revised *Letters* ever published.
27. Personal correspondence from Paul Baggaley, 22 February 2010.
28. Personal correspondence from Paul Baggaley, 5 July 2010.
29. I can hardly blame Picador for following the binding wishes of the eminent copyright-holder in discarding the revised edition of the letters, even if the effective result is a distortion of the texts. More frustrating was the muddle in the last stage of the book's production in which I was not given the opportunity to check my final corrections to the text. As a result, more than one minor typo made it into print – particularly annoying since the original reason for a revised edition was precisely to eliminate errors.
30. Indeed, the second Lady Naipaul – her husband's staunchest defender – later recounted her visit to a "witch doctor" in Uganda, and her temptation to have an appropriate curse placed on "the wretched two-timing biographers." The revelation came in an article she wrote for the British society magazine *Tatler*, and was picked up by the press on several continents, reported as literary news. See, for instance, "Naipaul, Theroux and the

witch-doctor", *The Week*, 1 December 2008, http://www.theweek.co.uk/people/40343/naipaul-theroux-and-witch-doctor

31. Given that all of Naipaul's professional correspondence will eventually be deposited in the Tulsa archive, and his habit of discarding almost none of his papers, it is likely that the archive itself may, in time to come, elucidate the reasons for the reversion to the 1999 edition of the *Letters*.
32. V.S. Naipaul, "Prologue to an Autobiography", in *Literary Occasions*, ed. Pankaj Mishra (New York City: Knopf, 2003), 67. The phrase is repeated almost exactly from Naipaul's 1983 foreword to *A House for Mr. Biswas*, also collected in *Literary Occasions*, 129.
33. *Letters Between a Father and Son* (2009), 449 (letter 249).
34. French, *The World Is What It Is*, 462.
35. According to the McFarlin Library's Department of Special Collections and University Archives, "Mr. Naipaul has made all of his pre-publication notes, drafts, manuscripts, and typescripts... open to scholars under the University's usual policies for access to unpublished materials... Mr. Naipaul has asked, however, that access to family and professional correspondence files... be restricted for the time being to scholars who have obtained his prior approval." "V.S. Naipaul Archive", McFarlin Library website, http://www.lib.utulsa.edu/speccoll/collections/naipaulvs/index.htm
36. French, *The World Is What It Is*, 207.
37. *Letters Between a Father and Son* (2009), 14-15 (letter 6).
38. Virginia Woolf, *A Room of One's Own* (London: Penguin, 1945), 48-50.
39. French, *The World Is What It Is*, 17.
40. In his introduction to the 1999 edition, Aitken does recognise that "Kamla occupies a special position in this book," and thanks her for allowing her letters to be reproduced, though the volume's copyright notice states V.S. Naipaul is the sole copyright-holder. Gillon Aitken, introduction to *Letters Between a Father and Son* (1999), xii-xiii.
41. To be precise, 92 of the 170 letters in the 1999 edition (54 per cent) and 123 of the 249 letters in the 2009 edition (49 per cent) were written by Vidia.
42. V.S. Naipaul, "Two Worlds", in *Literary Occasions*, 181, 182-183.

First published in *Caribbean Quarterly: A Journal of Caribbean Culture,* vol. 62, nos. 3 and 4, September–December 2016 (special issue on Caribbean Literary Archives, ed. Alison Donnell), pp 110–125.

4: BISWAS BEFORE *BISWAS*: PLOTLINES AND PERSPECTIVES FROM THE CHAGUANAS CORRESPONDENT

AARON EASTLEY

Few literary families can rival the achievements of the Naipauls. Though V.S.'s fame obviously outstrips that of his father and brother, the three taken together would be hard to match in any other country or time period. Certainly the historical importance of Seepersad as the first major East Indian writer in the West Indies cannot be dismissed, and the work of Shiva deserves much more attention than it has received to date.

What each of the three Naipauls has achieved in the realms of both fiction writing and travel writing/journalism is extraordinary. More importantly, the combination of those genres has proved vital. I think it is fair to say that the quality of the fiction produced by all three Naipauls owes a great deal to the discipline and creativity they learned through their work as reporters – writers making stories out of materials at hand. This all started, of course, with Seepersad's work for the *East Indian Weekly* and the *Trinidad Guardian* in the 1930s as a largely self-educated man in his early twenties. As a newspaperman Seepersad Naipaul pioneered for his sons a path similar to that taken by other brilliant prose stylists of the Western world. One recalls, almost exactly a century before Seepersad, the young Charles Dickens, who entered his craft as a court reporter and travelling correspondent before branching out into fiction with his early collection of literary vignettes, *Sketches by Boz*. Similarly, roughly a half-century before Seepersad, Mark Twain got his start with the Virginia City *Territorial Enterprise*, en route to his early short story collection *Roughing It*. Then there is a contemporary of Seepersad, Ernest Hemingway, whose few months of work for the *Kansas City Star* prior to WWI led to a lifetime of intermixed work as a foreign correspondent, war correspondent, and novelist. Dozens of others could be mentioned, all forming a league of journalist-creative writers among whom the three Naipauls now take a prominent place.

Although Seepersad Naipaul only seriously began writing short stories around 1939, he had his start much much earlier in the form of several highly creative sketches he produced as the Chaguanas Correspondent for the *Trinidad Guardian* in 1932 and 1933. Many of his best articles read like short stories, and when he began writing actual short stories he drew upon this material. But the influence did not stop there. His sons, particularly V.S., or "Vidia" (as family and friends knew him), were also greatly influenced by these early works.

In "Prologue to an Autobiography", V.S. Naipaul fondly recalls the pride he felt as a teenager in the early 1940s knowing that his father was a public figure, a well-known reporter in Port of Spain. He pinpoints the genesis of his own writerly ambition back to the work his father "had done for the *Guardian long before*" [my emphasis].[1] He recalls that among Seepersad's prized possessions "there was a big ledger in which my father had pasted his early writings for the Guardian".[2] "This ledger", V.S. explains, "became one of the books of my childhood. It was there... that I got to love the idea of newspapers and the idea of print".[3] I would argue that it was there, too, that he may well have gotten inspiration for several of his own early narratives, including some of the *Miguel Street* stories and the novels *The Mystic Masseur* and *The Suffrage of Elvira*. This brings me to the particular topic of this article: the intriguing connections between Seepersad Naipaul's early journalism and V.S. Naipaul's early stories and novels. This is why I am calling the article "Biswas before *Biswas*": looking at the influence of the work of Seepersad (later immortalised through the character of Mohun Biswas), as seen in V.S.'s early fiction leading up to *A House for Mr Biswas*.

In looking at the connections between Seepersad's early journalism and V.S.'s early fiction, two trends jump out at once. First, both father and son did their first high quality, successful work as writers by fashioning lighthearted but poignant vignettes of colorful local characters. Second, each made much of the local drama surrounding religion and politics. Seepersad really came into his own as a reporter and a writer when he was assigned to cover his hometown of Chaguanas in early 1932. He had been writing for the *East Indian Weekly* and the *Trinidad Guardian* for roughly four years, and had written some very creditable articles, most notably a couple of dozen opinion pieces on Trinidadian East Indian issues printed under the pseudonym "The Pundit", as well as a running column entitled "East A Calling". But beginning in March 1932, the first of a series of more specific local pieces appeared. These are what might be termed "found" pieces. Seepersad did not just wait for something newsworthy to happen; he made news by digging up interesting stories and transforming them into something newsworthy through the quality of his telling. Similarly, a little more than two decades later, V.S. Naipaul found his voice and subsequent success at the BBC by manufacturing short stories from his memories of "characters" based on the inhabitants of the street he had known as a boy in Port of Spain.

These early efforts paved the way in the work of both father and son for more significant, serious-humorous writings centering on the issues of religion and politics. Seepersad wrote several excellent articles looking at various aspects of Hinduism in Trinidad. Other articles dealt with politics and governance: everything from elections to Road Board meetings. These articles foreshadow the central motifs of V.S.'s early novels – *The Mystic Masseur*, in which fictional Hindu faith healer, Ganesh Ramsumair, runs for office in the 1946 Trinidad General Election, and *The Suffrage of Elvira*, which caricatures the religious-political ploys of an election not unlike the Trinidad General Election of 1950.

I chart some of the similarities and then compare and contrast the work of father and son by focusing specifically on the issue of tone. At their best, both Seepersad and V.S. communicate genuine appreciation for the humanity and the genius, even, of the Trinidadian "characters" they write about. These characters may have been chosen for their eccentricity, but this does not automatically make them absurd. On the contrary, I would argue that there is little or no condescension in the representation of the denizens of Chaguanas in Seepersad's early journalism, and more irony than mockery in the representation of the denizens of Miguel Street in V.S.'s stories. The same, unfortunately, cannot be said of many of the characters in V.S.'s early novels, *The Mystic Masseur* and *The Suffrage of Elvira*. Only in *A House for Mr Biswas* is there a return to compassion, a renewed perception of redeeming qualities.

I fully recognise the slippage involved in comparing satirical fiction with objective journalism. It is not surprising that Seepersad's journalism gives greater credibility to Trinidad than V.S.'s fiction; Seepersad's own fiction operates in a much more satirical vein than his newspaper writing. Yet the fact remains that Seepersad's journalistic depictions of Trinidadian life are both much less acerbic and much more warmly comical than V.S.'s. This, I think, relates back to fundamental differences in character, in mentality, in personality. Despite enduring extreme hardships of his own, Seepersad seems to have been possessed of a confidence and human sympathy that V. S., plagued by a vicious and largely self-inflicted double-consciousness, apparently lacked – at least initially. The confidence, human sympathy, and at least outward optimism of Seepersad, I would suggest, are among the factors that make him a writer who was truly ahead of his time.

The literary ingenuity that makes V.S. Naipaul's characters in *Miguel Street* enduring originates in their audacity, adaptability and mimic pretensions. There is Bogart the bogus tailor, Popo the playacting carpenter, Elias the stupid student, Titus Hoyt his inept instructor, Man-Man the make-believe Messiah, B. Wordsworth the would-be poet, and Big Foot the boxer who gets beaten. Some of these "characters" are mere pretenders, others more earnest failures. A few have actual occupations, but even these are undermined in various ways. All are flawed. Consider Bogart, who affects the speech of an American movie star and has a sign made advertising himself as a tailor: "Tailor and Cutter: Suits made to Order, Popular and Competitive Prices".[4] He might seem legitimate, but the narrator lets us know: "I never could imagine him competing with anyone; and I cannot remember him making a suit".[5] Similarly, Bogart's neighbor Popo "like[s] standing in front of the sign" which says: "Builder and Contractor, Carpenter, And Cabinet-maker", but "he had quite a little panic when people who didn't know about him came to inquire. 'The carpenter fellow?' Popo would say. 'He don't live here again'".[6] A more dramatic pretender is Man-man, a madman (by local reputation) who divines that there is fame and possibly fortune to be had in religion. For some time, he follows this vocation, preaching regularly and actually amassing quite a following.[7] But when the momentum of his early successes excites him to stage his own martyrdom, his experiment takes a frighteningly absurdist turn as people respond to his cry: "Stone, stone, STONE me, brethren! I forgive you", by throwing some "really big stones". Man-man, "look[ing] hurt and surprised," indignantly curses the crowd.[8]

There are other more earnest failures. Titus Hoyt, another man with a sign, claims to be a teacher, but fails to help his earnest student, Elias, pass a single major exam. Elias ultimately gets a job, but only as a local "sanitary inspector".[9] B. Wordsworth, while an actual calypsonian, cares only about being the sort of poet who would win respect in England: a poet like Wordsworth. His is a rather bitter failure, as it is mostly a failure of self-belief. Finally, even the redoubtable Hat, a voice of pragmatic wisdom in many of the stories and a man of adaptability and pluck, is brought low by the authorities in the end, having been caught thinning his milk.[10]

These characters are, of course, very deliberately created for comic effect. And *Miguel Street,* taken as a whole, is a brilliant, nuanced collection that contains a handful of true literary gems. Yet the persistence of failure, and ludicrous failure at that, hangs heavily in the air. This strikes me all the more potently when I compare these character sketches to those produced years earlier by Seepersad – the news stories that V.S. grew up reading. Among Seepersad's local characters are Trinidad's Robinson Crusoe; an ancient woman who remembers the time of slavery; and a convict he dubs Trinidad's "Worst Man". None of these people have much in the way of wealth or education or status. Yet each is described with dignity and deference in a way that serves to bring out their human charm.

In a series of articles about Trinidad's "Robinson Crusoe", Seepersad introduces Daniel Martin, a 90-year-old hermit who lives in a handmade hut on the Caroni Coast. This story shows how Seepersad both searched for content and dramatised his own adventures as an investigative journalist. "Come let me show you the Robinson Crusoe of Trinidad",[11] his first article begins. "Well, of all things – !" he gives his thought at this. Then goes on: "But I followed by boat and tramped through half a mile of a marshy track that stopped abruptly before a small hut in a lone coconut plantation near the Felicity Bay." The article goes on to describe Martin: a man in rags – "And what rags!" – who also wears "four hats set one on top the other". Seepersad humorously observes that the combined hats "did the work of a hat as well as served the purpose of an umbrella." But this is not the essence of the article. Seepersad observes that "Daniel Martin is happy in those rags, and happier still to tell people of the cause that made him go to them. It is this, more than the fact that he is the Robinson Crusoe of Trinidad that makes Daniel interesting." What follows is the story of Martin's apparent coming down in the world, but also his finding a truer sense of himself. Once a prosperous planter, he was reduced to poverty by "Women, wine and spree." Yet he is philosophical about his life path. "'Some people call me a madman,' he told me as an afterthought, 'because I laugh while others in my position only cry. Why should I cry? I am glad I spent a happy youth. And I am as happy today in my loneliness as Robinson Crusoe was in his.'" Comedy and pathos, blended together, typify Seepersad's three articles about Martin.

Much the same can be seen in his sketches based on the conversations he has with Granny Constance, and Birbal Wilson – alias "Cut-throat" – designated Trinidad's worst man. The headlines, perhaps owing to the dash of editor Galt McGowan, prepare readers for the sensational, but the stories themselves are full of vibrant humanity. "I talked to Trinidad's grandest old lady yesterday," his article about Granny Constance begins, "Mrs. Constance Gravett of Xeres Road, who passed her eighty-eighth birthday last Sunday." The tone is lighthearted, as he recalls their opening exchange:

"Hard times, Nansense!"
　The dark shining eyes of Granny Constance, as she is more popularly known flashed brighter.
　"Ah hate to hear dem tush," she said.
　"Some people will grumble evin ef dey live in heaven."
　"One good work is better dan a tousand excuse, is wat I say."[12]

Similarly, he lets Wilson speak for himself, illuminating his residual humanity: "I am a human derelict. I have made a mess of life. And the least I can do is to lead a straight life from now."[13] This article ends with Seepersad's own empathetic feelings: "I shuddered as I left this man, with his thin finger over the hole in his throat, and with a heart so full of agonising memories."

Seepersad sees these people in no Orientalist shadow. His interest is human interest, and he never seems troubled by the thought that any of his "characters" might be perceived by others as somehow subhuman, or so much on the periphery of the "real" world that their lives do not matter. The common denominator in his stories is people making their way in the world with a lot of pluck, and suffering in real poignancy.

In view of what Seepersad achieves in these articles, I am left to wonder how it is that V.S. Naipaul came to present such a uniformly despairing vision in his sketches. Guessing at his motives is not, I think, an entirely fruitless exercise. Circumstantial evidence suggests that this vision of the characters in *Miguel Street* is likely a product of V.S.'s anxiety about perceived Trinidadian backwardness. A hint in this direction appears in the very first story. When the narrator says, "*I* never could imagine [Bogart] competing with anyone,"[14] V.S. does not seem far away from that *I*. There are strong overtones of the personal panic that V.S. speaks of near the end of his retrospective "Prologue to an Autobiography". He was, he admits, consumed in his early career by an abiding fear that he would not be able to make it as a writer in England. "It was that fear," he says, "a panic about failing to be what I should be, rather than simple ambition, that was with me when I came down from Oxford in 1954 and began trying to write in London".[15] As I have argued elsewhere, in his struggle to fill the role of a writer, Naipaul was, in effect, one of his own characters: a man playing a part, and trying to be real in a professional sense, but initially not able to produce anything that really counted.[16]

Like V.S., Seepersad also wrote for a largely alien audience – the predominantly white-elite readers of the 1930s-era *Trinidad Guardian* – but Seepersad did not seem to let that cloud his humanistic vision. Indeed, his article about "Trinidad's 'Worst Man'" may be seen as a precursor to V.S.'s breakout story, "Bogart". Like the character in the story, the real-life character eloped to Caroni, fell afoul of the law, and at one point lived as a fugitive in Venezuela. Yet this Bogart-type character was not the paltry pretender that V.S. would later envision. For while most readers would concur that V.S.'s Bogart never really goes to Venezuela or runs a brothel (he just pretends these things based on his mimicry of the Humphrey Bogart film star persona), Seepersad's "worst man" was, if anything, a much more formidable and tragic figure even than Humphrey Bogart's Rick Blaine in *Casablanca* – certainly he was a person whom Miguel Street's Hat could, without irony, have called "a man, among we men". And Seepersad describes him as such – with relish.

If anything, the tendency to undermine his characters is accentuated in V.S.'s first two novels. In *The Mystic Masseur* and *The Suffrage of Elvira*, V.S. moves from the casual comedy of the street into a much more drawn out – but no less ludicrous – farcical satire. Central to these satires are motifs of religion and politics. Ganesh Ramsumair, protagonist of *The Mystic Masseur*, is both a self-proclaimed faith healer and a budding politician. He both gains fame for his supposed religious power and wins a seat on the

Legislative Council in the General Election of 1946. Surujpat "Pat" Harbans, protagonist of *The Suffrage of Elvira*, is a businessman-turned-politician who seeks to beat his black political rival, Preacher, largely by courting the Hindu and Muslim voters of Elvira through community leaders Chittaranjan and Baksh. Those familiar with these books will readily recall the thousand inventive and genuinely comical ways that religion and politics are parodied in these novels. What is most interesting, however, in light of my current focus, is how V.S.'s representations once again echo the content but depart from the tone of newspaper articles written by Seepersad.

Certainly Seepersad Naipaul did not hesitate to draw attention to the religious and political problems of his day. In one early article, for instance, he writes of "Bogus Mediums Who Prey on Villages".[17] He relates how "so-called spiritualism, is conducted on strictly business lines", by quacks who "claim both the doctor's and spiritualist's prerogative", and come to their work armed with "fowls, rum, sweet oil and the all indispensable stock of candles". Here we see Ganesh Ramsumair in a nutshell – though certainly Ganesh is far more hilarious, harmless, and endearing. Yet he is a charlatan, absolutely. And this contrasts markedly with religious individuals depicted quite even-handedly in Seepersad's journalism. Consider, for example, Sadhu Dhooni Dass, of whom Seepersad records:

> Sadhu Dhooni Dass, the Hindu ascetic doing penance before a huge debris of fire on the bank of the Caparo river broke his stony silence for five minutes yesterday and spoke to me about himself.
>
> At first he would persist to speak only in Sanskrit, because he said, it was the language of his gods, but after repeated requests he consented to speak in Hindi.
>
> He said he is inflicting such corporal punishment on himself because he wants to become a faith-healer. If he succeeds he will go about healing sick people free.[18]

V.S. likely gleaned from his father's journalism, among untold other sources, something of his watchful eye for religious trickery. Yet he somehow missed the dignity that often graces religious fundamentalism.

Beyond this, events such as those depicted in V.S.'s *The Suffrage of Elvira* may well have been nuanced by Seepersad's coverage of events such as Chaguanas Road Board meetings, and the election of 1933. Like the contest described in *The Suffrage of Elvira*, the local Road Board meetings that Seepersad frequently covered in late 1932 and early 1933 could be very dramatic events. Consider just the titles of two articles out of more than a dozen: "Dramatic Scene at Road Board Meeting: Members Called 'Fools': Words Withdrawn After Debate";[19] "Appointment of Chaguanas Road Board Secretary Annulled: Dramatic Sequel to Stormy Meeting".[20]

More closely connected still are the articles describing Sarran Teelucksingh's race against E. A. Robinson in 1933 – a contest between an incumbent Indian and a black challenger, not unlike Harbans and Preacher in *Elvira*. Again, a few of the headlines suffice to show how colourful the contest was: "Political Parley in Caroni: Move to Heal a Party Split";[21] "Another Hindu Political Cleavage: Mr. E.A. Robinson's Supporters Split: Mr. Teelucksingh to Invade Enemy's Camp: Chaguanas Ablaze";[22] "Hindu War-God Invoked for 1933 Elections: Revolt against Mr. Teelucksingh: Support Pledged to Mr. E.A. Robinson: Pundit Leader".[23] What I would point out, however, is that while this was a highly contested race with plenty of drama, it was by no means as ludicrous and one-dimensional as the elections depicted in V.S. Naipaul's first two novels.

Returning, in conclusion, to the root issue of motive or philosophy, I would note that V.S. Naipaul's early caustic attitudes (articulated quite plainly in *The Middle Passage*, and reflected in the fictional representations of *The Mystic Masseur* and *The Suffrage of Elvira*) had mellowed somewhat by the mid-1990s when he published *A Way in the World*, wherein he explains that "the problem" with writing in the 1950s and 60s about "a place like Trinidad was that black people were simply not a subject".[24] Audience perceptions mattered a great deal to V.S. in the early 1950s, and he saw quite clearly that when it came to local West Indian life, outside of Trinidad, "no one was interested in the subtleties".[25] With this perception in mind, the achievement of *A House for Mr Biswas* stands out. In *Biswas*, V.S. Naipaul casts aside the crutches of religious and political farce and presents Mohun Biswas as a common man whose ambitions and emotions are as real and important and deserving of respect as anyone's. To cite just one textual example, the representation of Mr Biswas in the great storm in the "Green Vale" chapter of *Biswas* is parallel in literary potency to the climax of Shakespeare's *Lear*, and Mohun Biswas's final victories, though they may seem paltry to some, are actually magnificent. It is notable that V.S. produced this novel in the same environment, for the same biased reading publics, as his earlier novels.

I think V.S. himself recognised the progression of his own confidence, as in *A Way in the World* he writes of the comedic mode as one that, by the time he began *Biswas,* he "had begun to grow out of".[26] "The comedy that had become my writing tone," he relates, "... the jokeyness that was my double inheritance from my Trinidad background, ...was also a way of making peace with a hard world; was on the other side of hysteria".[27] *A House for Mr. Biswas*, he perceives, was a work "so different from the street book"[28] he had written earlier. He was a far more confident writer, and I am referring here especially to his confidence in presenting Trinidadian society. Even at that, as V.S. himself has admitted, "My father was a profounder man in every way."[29] Yet even the still somewhat farcical Biswas was apparently too legitimate a character for one prominent English critic to swallow: "You have passed a stool",[30] the critic told V.S. Naipaul after reading *Biswas*. Such attitudes explain a great deal about why V.S. may have written as he did, especially early on. Thankfully, by the time he set out to produce a version of his own father's life story, V.S. had matured. He felt "absolutely secure in this new book [*Biswas*]," he relates, "and for the first time, since [he] had begun truly to write, felt the need for no one's approval".³¹ I am not sure that Seepersad himself ever quite felt that way, but herein lies the tremendous importance of Gault MacGowan, editor of the *Guardian* in Seepersad's early years. It was MacGowan who encouraged Seepersad, and who specifically urged him to "write sympathetically",³² advice that Seepersad later passed along to V.S., who had determined midway through his first year at Oxford, "I think a man is doing his reporting well only when people start to hate him".³³ It would take V.S. several years to really heed that advice, and to discover that, as Seepersad summed up: "Write sympathetically, and this, I suppose, in no way prevents us from writing truthfully, even brightly".³⁴

Endnotes

1. V.S. Naipaul, *Finding the Centre* (London: Andre Deutsch, 1984), 36.
2. V.S. Naipaul, *Finding the Centre*, 37.
3. V.S. Naipaul, *Finding the Centre*, 37.
4. V.S. Naipaul, *Miguel Street* (New York: Vintage, 2002), 10.
5. V.S. Naipaul, *Miguel Street*, 10.
6. V.S. Naipaul, *Miguel Street*, 15-16.
7. V.S. Naipaul, *Miguel Street*, 42-3.
8. V.S. Naipaul, *Miguel Street*, 44.
9. V.S. Naipaul, *Miguel Street*, 32-7.
10. V.S. Naipaul, *Miguel Street*, 206.
11. Seepersad Naipaul, "Robinson Crusoe of Trinidad: Happy Poor Man on Lone Plantation: 'Wine, Women and Spree' – His Downfall: Ragged Clothes", *Trinidad Guardian*, 11 February 1932.
12. Seepersad Naipaul, "Old Woman of 88 Laughs at Hard Times: Homely Wisdom of Granny Constance: 'Ef You Work You Must Mek Out': Slavery Memories", *Trinidad Guardian*, 10 March 1933.
13. Seepersad Naipaul, "Amazing Interview with Trinidad's 'Worst Man'", *Trinidad Guardian*, 12 June 1932.
14. V.S. Naipaul, *Miguel Street*, 10.
15. V.S. Naipaul, "Prologue to an Autobiography" in *Finding the Centre* (London: Andre Deutsch, 1984), 84-5.
16. Aaron Eastley, "Area of Enigma: V.S. Naipaul and the East Indian Revival in Trinidad", *ARIEL* 41, no. 2 (2010): 23-45.
17. Seepersad Naipaul, "Bogus Mediums Who Prey on Villages: Spiritualism as a Paying Business: Law Cases 'Won' and Devils 'Driven Out': Poor Exploited", *Trinidad Guardian*, 11 May 1932.

18. Seepersad Naipaul, "Sadhu Plans to Be a Healer: Reason for His Penance", *Trinidad Guardian*, 25 March 1932.
19. Seepersad Naipaul, "Dramatic Scene at Road Board Meeting: Members Called 'Fools': Word Withdrawn After Debate", *Trinidad Guardian*, 24 September 1932.
20. Seepersad Naipaul, "Appointment of Chaguanas Road Board Secretary Annulled: Dramatic Sequel to Stormy Meeting", *Trinidad Guardian*, 12 October 1933.
21. Seepersad Naipaul, "Political Parley in Caroni: Move to Heal a Party Split", *Trinidad Guardian*, 20 July 1932.
22. Seepersad Naipaul, "Another Hindu Political Cleavage: Mr E.A. Robinson's Supporters Split: Mr Teelucksingh to Invade Enemy's Camp: Chaguanas Ablaze", *Trinidad Guardian*, 8 December 1932.
23. Seepersad Naipaul, "Hindu War-God Invoked for 1933 Elections: Revolt Against Mr. Teelucksingh: Support Pledged to Mr E.A. Robinson: Pundit Leader", *Trinidad Guardian*, 23 November 1932.
24. V.S. Naipaul, *A Way in the World* (New York: Knopf, 1994), 96.
25. V.S. Naipaul, *A Way in the World*, 96.
26. V.S. Naipaul, *A Way in the World*, 98.
27. V.S. Naipaul, *A Way in the World*, 98.
28. V.S. Naipaul, *A Way in the World*, 98.
29. Mel Gussow, "The Writer-to-Be and His Mentor", *The New York Times on the Web*, January 5, 2000.
30. V.S. Naipaul, *A Way in the World*, 96.
31. V.S. Naipaul, *A Way in the World*, 98.
32. V.S. Naipaul, *Letters Between a Father and Son*, eds. Gillon Aitken and Nicholas Laughlin (New York: Picador, 2009), 108.
33. V.S. Naipaul, *Letters Between a Father and Son*, eds. Gillon Aitken and Nicholas Laughlin (New York: Picador, 2009), 65.
34. V.S. Naipaul, *Letters Between a Father and Son*, eds. Gillon Aitken and Nicholas Laughlin (New York: Picador, 2009), 108.

5: "IN BUT NOT OF THE SOCIETY": THE CRUSADING AND CRITICAL EYE OF SEEPERSAD NAIPAUL (1906-1953)

BRINSLEY SAMAROO

World War One was a time of considerable challenges for the Caribbean. The hardships of the War were followed by the Great Depression of the late 1920s, which meant continuous hardships for the labouring class in the colonies. In Trinidad and Tobago, the problem was confounded by the great disparity in wealth and power between the sugar and oil barons on the one hand and the mass of workers on the other. Out of these adverse conditions there arose a body of literary activists who recorded the period for posterity. Equally, this group became agitators for change. There were others who took to political and trade union activism geared towards the same end. But this essay is interested in the first group and mainly in one figure in the group, Seepersad Naipaul.

Seepersad Naipaul belonged to the literary brigade writing about the society in general, but concentrating on that segment with which he was most familiar, namely the Indian population. He was one of the first to write about the rites de passage of the most recent arrivals to the region, namely the plantation Indians whose arrival dates back to 1838. Naipaul belonged to this segment of the society, but he was able to distance himself sufficiently so that he could look in, as if from the outside, criticising the society whilst actively agitating for positive change. This he did by contributing over many years to a host of periodical magazines as well as the daily *Trinidad Guardian* newspaper. Equally important was his fictional book *Gurudeva and Other Indian Tales*, published in Trinidad in 1943, at a time when to be published meant being published abroad. (The collection is today available to us because it was republished by his son as *The Adventures of Gurudeva and Other Stories* in 1976). Equally important were the synergies between his writing and those of his sons Vidia and Shiva. This paper seeks to highlight the major crusades waged by Seepersad Naipaul, the fate of these agitations and the ways in which he contributed to social change. The data thus uncovered reveals hints also of his literary influences on the writings of his sons with whom he forms the triumvirate of Seepersad and Sons.

> Mr Sohun saw the futility of the argument. He couldn't possibly put right all the wrong things in the world, but he could at least give a warning and wash his hands of the business.[1]

In these lines interjected in the action of the story, Seepersad Naipaul appears to be expressing his own view of his vision to effect change in the society. He could not, like Omar Khayyam, smash the whole thing and then remould it nearer to the heart's desire, but he could at least do his bit at effecting change. Mr Sohun was the Presbyterian schoolmaster in the village of Cacandee, West of Chaguanas. The village itself was symbolic of the Indian struggle for a place in the sun, since it was created out of alligator-infested swamplands by Cacandee, a Bengali bondsman who, after his indentureship, purchased what was considered by plantation owners to be useless lands. Out of this piece of nothing, the village of Cacandee grew, around which the well-known village called Felicity was created. Seepersad Naipaul was born in 1906, during the last years of indentureship and would have been fourteen when the system ended in 1920. His writings indicate a clear familiarity with former indentured workers, as well as Trinidad-born descendants. He therefore functioned within that environment, yet he was able to distance himself and, as an outsider, embark on a crusade of advocating change on a wide range of matters. Whilst he was proud of the Indian heritage, and that India should remain a source of inspiration, he believed that Indo-Caribbean people must regard their settlement here as a permanent one. Similarly, he believed that the descendants of African slaves should cherish their heritage, seeking out and preserving African cultural survivals.

The sources of Seepersad's writing are very varied, as were its outlets. He took to writing with a passion, seeking many local avenues for the expression of his ideas. During the brief life of the *East Indian Weekly* (1928 to 1932), for example, he was one of its major contributors, advocating one or other of his current campaigns, or engaging in debate with other young Indo-Trinidadians about the way forward. Later on, he wrote for *The Beacon*, which was a radical journal edited by Albert Gomes, featuring writers such as Alfred Mendes, Ralph de Boissiere, C.L.R. James and Clytus Thomasos. Additionally, he sought to prolong the life of other struggling periodicals such as *The East Indian Advocate*, *Spectator* and *Minerva Review* by regularly writing columns in these publications. A major source of Seepersad's writing was of course the *Trinidad Guardian*, for which he started writing in 1928, becoming its regular Chaguanas correspondent in 1932. He left the paper around 1934, but returned in 1938 as the city reporter and feature writer, leaving again in 1950 only to return finally in 1951, two years before his death.

What were the issues to which Seepersad was devoted? At the top of the list were the abuse of Indian women by their spouses and the denial of education to girls. In "The Adventures of Gurudeva" he writes movingly of Gurudeva's brutalising of his wife Ratni, of her acceptance of that fate and of her parents' acceptance of that condition:

> So, too, he beat Ratni; not from any overwhelming surge of anger, nor from any conscious wickedness, but because the privilege and prerogative of beating her was his, by virtue of his being her husband. He was not doing anything shameful. He was only beating his wife.[2]

The only sympathy which a battered Ratni receives is from her sisters-in-law Dhira and Mira, who console her by an attempt at rationalisation:

> It is all a very one-sided operation. They want us all to be like Sita – that is, to try as far as possible to be like her; but on the other hand, *they* are far from being like Rama... They do not even try. It is not fair. But wipe your tears, little sister. It is our karma.[3]

Ratni later decides to leave Gurudeva because he has found a new love in Daisy, daughter of the Presbyterian catechist, whom the villagers describe as a lady with "good looks but dotty tricks".[4] Ratni decides to take Gurudeva to the village panchayat, accusing him of bigamy. However, the wily Gurudeva is able to convince his peers that Raja Dasrath of Ramayana fame had three wives so that he, Gurudeva, was acting in keeping with that Hindu tradition. The panchayat frees him of any blame and Ratni now has to make her way in the world! Later on the panchayat accepts Gurudevas's marriage to Daisy, but orders that she must abandon her Western Presbyterian lifestyle and live like an Oriental, Hindu woman. Gurudeva now meets his comeuppance. When he conveys this directive, Daisy bursts into a tantrum, using her newly-found American lingo, recently acquired by her association with the Yankees who are encamped at the nearby Carlsenfield during the Second World War:

> You must be nuts too! You and the set of you! ... Me! Turn Hindu? Ha! Man don't make me laugh. Me wear ghangri and orhani and chappals and long hair? Me give up rouge and lipstick? You can all go to hell.[5]

Daisy then packs up and leaves for Port of Spain, where the American boys are. When they are gone after the war, she later returns to Chaguanas, accommodating those whom she had earlier avoided as rough and oily. Here is a parallel Indian version of the "Jean and Dinah" story made famous by the calypsonian Slinger Francisco, whose sobriquet is Mighty Sparrow. The primary differences in the two stories is not, however, only the locations to which the women return, it is also how masculinity is represented in relation to the new kind of financial freedom women found in the American presence. Sparrow begins the calypso as follows:

> Well the girls in town feeling bad
> No more Yankees in Trinidad
> They going to close down the base for good

> Them girls have to make out how they could
> Brother is now they park up in town
> In for a penny, and in for a pound
> Believe me its competition for so
> Trouble in the town when the price drop low
> So when you bounce up[6]

The memorable refrain could well have included Daisy and Chaguanas could easily replace Port of Spain in the next verse:

> Jean and Dinah
> Rosita and Clementina
> Round the corner posing
> Bet your life is something they selling
> And if you catch them broken
> You can get em all for nothing
> Don't make no row, the yankees gone
> Sparrow take over now…
>
> It's the glamour boys again
> We are going to rule Port of Spain
> No more Yankees to spoil the fete
> Dorothy have to take what she get
> All of them who used to make style
> While they taking two shilling with a smile
> No more hotel to rest your head
> By the sweat of thy brow thou shall eat bread[7]

Sparrow's calypso comments on the reassertion of masculine dominance on the departure of foreign male dominance capable of greater masculine machismo.

Similarly, in his story Seepersad Naipaul captures the period of transition for the Indian community occasioned by the American occupation during the War. He mixes the American lingo and lifestyles with the local and points to the cultural crossover in fine detail. At the end of the story Ratni is avenged and Gurudeva is disconsolate. She has found a new love whilst he is alone and loveless. This represents a huge shift in the fortunes of women in the Indian community since it was generally unheard of that a once-married woman would find another partner to love her. Seepersad Naipaul thus portrays a point made previously only by Sarah Morton in her records of hers and her husband's experiences in the Indian communities. He thus recognised and celebrated women's greater independence in the region.

Seepersad Naipaul was also an ardent advocate of education for Indian children. In this he was participating in a widespread post-emancipation attitude in the Caribbean which his son V.S. Naipaul captures in *A Way in the World* in his description of a meeting with his friend's father:

> The lawyer was famous for his first name, which was Evander […] [He] said, 'My father worshipped education. It was his way of giving me ambition. He was not an educated man. But he was born in 1867 or 1870. That's

a long time ago for us. If you look it up, you'll find the name in Homer. Book four or book five.' It was surprising, that this famous man hadn't gone into his unusual name, didn't know that the name came from Latin and Virgil [...] He was a self-made man.[8]

Seepersad Naipaul, another "self-made man" was a constant campaigner for state recognition of non-Christian Schools; a privilege denied the Indian community since the time of their arrival in 1845.

The official policy was that the Canadian Presbyterians were the legitimate agents for educating the Indians; Hindus and Muslims were not. Seepersad Naipaul was very pleased when a joint Hindu-Muslim School was started in Chaguanas in 1929. Sadly this school soon collapsed because of the absence of state or planter support. In the circumstances, the Indians had to send their children to Presbyterian Schools or keep them at home to work on the sugar estates from their teenage years, an outcome famously represented in his son's novel, *A House for Mr Biswas*. Education was the only way out since the work in the canefields was emasculating, and the stratification of male occupational roles to offset emasculatory effects were extreme. V.S. Naipaul captures these issues in *A House for Mr Biswas* in the following scene:

> In another two or three years, when he could be trusted with a sickle, Mr Biswas would be made to join the boys and girls of the grass-gang. Between them and the buffalo boys there were constant disputes, and there was no doubt who were superior. The buffalo boys, with their leggings of white mud, tickling the buffaloes and beating them with sticks, shouting at them and controlling them, exercised power. Whereas the children of the grass-gang, walking briskly along the road single file, their heads practically hidden by tall, wide bundles of wet grass, hardly able to see, and, because of the weight on their heads and the grass over their faces, unable to make more than slurred, brief replies to taunts, were easy objects of ridicule.
>
> And it was to be the grass-gang for Mr Biswas. Later he would move to the cane fields, to weed and clean and plant and reap; he would be paid by the task and his tasks would be measured out by a driver with a long bamboo rod. And there he would remain. He would never become a driver or a weigher because he wouldn't be able to read. Perhaps, after many years, he might save enough to rent or buy a few acres where he would plant his own canes, which he would sell to the estate at a price fixed by them. But he would achieve this only if he had the strength and optimism of his brother Pratap.[9]

The fear of lack of social mobility captured in V.S. Naipaul's depiction is one that informed his family's approach to education. And Seepersad Naipaul encouraged his compatriots to use the Canadian Presbyterian facility in lieu of any of their own. In 1933, the colony's governor, speaking at the graduation ceremony of Naparima Girls' High School stressed the need for women to be educated. Pleased by this injunction Seepersad put his own spin to the Governor's advice as can be seen in the headlines of his report for the *Trinidad Guardian*:

> Unhappy households caused by ignorant wives.
> Governor on need to educate girls.
> Future of Indian race depends on its women.
> Mother-craft and father-craft.[10]

Interestingly, however, at the same time he berated women who were resorting to what he called "bobism" (short hair), wearing clothing in which there is "a minimum of cloth" whilst allowing "a maximum of exposal of the body." He also condemned their lethargy towards reading their own literature.[11] When Stella Abidh returned home to Chaguanas, where she was born, as the first Indo-Trinidadian woman to qualify as a doctor, Seepersad was jubilant. Although he was not invited to her celebratory function, one could say that he "stormed the party" in his official capacity as the *Guardian* reporter for Chaguanas. In a writing style that would be made famous by his son, he claimed that his non-invitation turned out to be a blessing since he did not eat at the banquet and therefore did not have to stop at the nearest cane-field because of the "after-dinner effect".[12] Fortunately for Seepersad Naipaul, he lived to see the positive result of his agitation for the recognition of non-Christian Schools. In 1949, the state recognised a Muslim School and in 1952, Hindu Schools obtained similar parity, both within his lifetime.

There were other issues which caught the crusading eye of Seepersad Naipaul. One was the question of the repatriation of those who had come here as bonded labourers. Part of their *girmit* (agreement) was a return passage to India after the fulfilment of their contractual obligations. Many of these people had been forced to leave India, because of famine or occupational displacement due to the influx of machine-made products from Europe. After indentureship, there was the wish to heed the call of the Ganga, that is, to return to the roots of their nativity. The British Government in India sought to discourage such return since India was seething with anti-British activity. Seepersad Naipaul had the foresight to understand that there were more opportunities for advancement in the New World and that prospective returnees would be unable to re-adapt to Indian society. He therefore sought information about those who had returned and warned others about wanting to return:

> Repatriated Indians bitter homecoming in India. Disillusion and dismay in their homeland. Friends and relatives became enemies. All beg to be brought back to Trinidad.[13]

Seepersad Naipaul was perceptive in his analysis. The story of those who went back is a tale of sadness. In the Caribbean, some had learned to eat beef and had become accustomed to strong drink. To some of their Indian kith and kin, there was the issue of lost caste and then there were also holy men on the banks of the Ganges taking money to cleanse them of their impurities. Soon many were destitute and returned to the Hooghly River, a tributary of the Ganges, to seek a new *girmit* to any colony which would accept them. When recruitment was stopped in 1917, their situation worsened. Seepersad Naipaul, who had found out about these matters, may well have saved many Indians from the trouble inherent to their return to their ancestral place.

Despite Seepersad Naipaul's best efforts, however, there remained those who insisted on going back to India. Ismith Khan, a later Trinidad novelist, tells the story of one of these would-be returnees:

> "I goin back home one day… one day God go find a way for me man… Ah miss my people too bad… Nobody could deny that," Kareem said; he held his milk tin by its lid, using it as a handle, his eyes focused at a point somewhere in mid-space.[14]

For many of those who came to Port of Spain to wait for the next India-bound ship, the wait was long and uncertain, so they became vagrants in the capital city, unable to return to India and ashamed to return to their Trinidad villages. From the safety of his own educated status, in *A Way in the World*, V.S. Naipaul confesses his love for the city with: "I was a country boy, and still am in my heart of hearts. Only a country boy could have loved the town as I did when I came to it. This was in 1938 or 1939. I loved everything about the town that was not like the country".[15] He notes in contrast the condition of those who may have well attempted the re-crossing and gotten no further than Woodford Square, the place which would see the strongest expressions of nationalism a mere twenty years later:

> Always beautiful, always a glorious thing of the town, yet even when I had first seen it, that Sunday before the war when my father took me on a walk through the town centre, this square was one of the places in Port of Spain where homeless people lived. Most of these people were Indians. Many of them would have been indentured immigrants from India who had served out their indentures on the sugar estates and then for one reason or another – perhaps they had become drinkers; perhaps they hadn't been given their promised passage back to India; perhaps they had quarrelled with their families – had found themselves with nowhere to live. These people were without money, job, without anything like a family, without the English language; without any kind of representation. They were utterly destitute. They were people who had been, as in a fairy story, lifted up from the peasantry of India and set down thousands of miles away – weeks and weeks of sailing – in Trinidad. In the colonial setting of Trinidad, where rights were limited, you could have done anything with these people; and they were tormented by the people of the town.[16]

Seepersad Naipaul and some other philanthropists were able to raise sufficient funds to establish a Home for Destitute Indians at Charlotte

Street in the capital city to address the needs of people like these. However, after a few years the house was closed as the majority of Indians decided to stay here permanently and India remained an India of the imagination, not a place of return.

Side by side with this campaign for destitute Indians was Seepersad's agitation for Hindu cremation. During the first hundred years of their presence on the colony, Hindus were prevented from cremating their dead as they had done for thousands of years in the ancestral place. For the Christian rulers, cremation was considered a heathen and polluting practice. Strangely enough, however, cremation was allowed on Nelson Island, one of Trinidad's off-shore islands, which from 1865 was used as a recuperating centre for newly-arrived Indians. If an Indian died there, he could be cremated as in the ancestral place, but once he arrived on mainland Trinidad he had to be buried. Some Indians in Trinidad continued cremation illegally, on rural river banks or beaches. In 1947, the family of an India-born businessman was given official permission to cremate that deceased person. However, an insensitive administration dictated that cremation could only take place at the city's garbage dump, the La Basse. This insult gave added momentum to the agitation by Seepersad Naipaul and his fellow agitators. Members of the colony's legislature took up the issue in 1952, and one year later, in the very year of Seepersad's death, cremation was legalised. He was, as he dearly wished, cremated at El Socorro. Perhaps we can guess what Seepersad would have written about his final farewell: "Just in time. Journalist escapes burial. Naipaul cremated at El Socorro!"

Our final consideration regarding the literary activism of Seepersad Naipaul focuses on his efforts to highlight major aspects of the non-Hindu heritage of the colony. In 1951, he travelled to St. James to witness and to write about the Shiite commemoration of Hosea (Mohuram). He took time to study and then report on the historic origins of this observance and noted that in its Caribbean manifestation, Hosea attracted Hindus as well as non-Indians, who enjoyed the spectacle. Indeed a Muslim woman, Zainab was a principal organiser in 1951.[17] In his earlier *Gurudeva and Other Indian Tales* (1943) he had also described the Hosea ceremonies and highlighted its appeal to all groups in multicultural Trinidad and Tobago. Even Gurudeva, his protagonist, participates in it. Although in his zeal to satirise Gurudeva, Seepersad Naipaul portrays his knowledge to be rather limited, tantalisingly suggesting that so might also the author's be:

> [Gurudeva] confided that he was building a hosey because he had gone and made a vow to Hassan to do so. The old man, without questioning him, understood. Naturally Gurudeva wanted to become the father of a man-child. So he had vowed that he would build hoseys in memory of Hassan and Hussein for five consecutive years.

"You will have to offer them a cock, too," said the old man. "And *maleeda* (sweet-meat). Go ahead, boy; try you' luck."

Gurudeva had no idea as to the real significance of Hosey. In some vague way – mainly from the plaintive songs that the women sang during Hosey days – he gathered that it had something to do with two brothers, Hassan and Hussein. Some said they were the adopted grandsons of Mohammed. He didn't know. They had fought in a war, it seemed, sometime in the dim past, at a place called Kerbala, and were treacherously killed, the one murdered, the other poisoned. They were great fighters who could back a crowd. Of this much he was certain but as to what they fought for, or what the hosey signified or stood for, he neither knew nor cared.

It was enough for him that it culminated in a festival, a passion play with a semi-religious as well as a semi-carnival tang about it, and that it commemorated the fighting talent and subsequent martyrdom of the brothers, who, though purely Mohammedans, with hosey itself an intrinsically Mohammedan affair, had somehow found themselves included in the vast, ever accommodating Hindu pantheon, and occupied fairly prominent niches in the infinite Valhalla of the gods; who could grant boons, even as Shiva, or Kali, or Hanuman could grant boons.[18]

Another cultural celebration which Seepersad Naipaul actively promoted in a very positive manner was the Shouter Baptist activity. In 1917, this group was prohibited from practising their faith because, in a time of war, they were considered subversive. After the Second World War, cultural activists joined Baptist leaders in a campaign for the removal of that prohibition. Naipaul was part of that campaign and started writing in support of the Shouter Baptists in the conservative *Trinidad Guardian*. In a highly supportive but humorous piece called "Shouter Baptists visit China in the Spiritual World", he described the Shouter Baptists in considerable detail (19 February 1950). As a result of this campaign the ban on Shouter Baptists was removed in 1951, two years before Seepersad Naipaul's death.

Seepersad Naipaul was part of a generation of angry young people who energised Trinidad and Tobago between the two World Wars and after. His contemporaries in the movement for change were Albert Gomes, Uriah Butler, Adrian Cola Rienzi, Captain Cipriani and Chanka Maharaj who sought freedom through aggressive trade unionism and active engagement in politics. Seepersad Naipaul's method was the constant and effective use of the Word in the manner of his literary contemporaries, such as C.L.R. James, Alfred Mendes, Beatrice Grieg and Ralph de Boissiere. Both groups did much to lift the burden of colonialism off the shoulders of a crown colony society. In that regard Naipaul was a significant reform leader in his time. Equally important was the foundational role which he played in shaping the future careers of his sons Vidia and Shiva.

In his introduction to the 1976 reprint of the Gurudeva stories, V.S. Naipaul confesses that he cannibalised his fathers' story "They called him Mohun" in the creation of his own *A House for Mr Biswas*. But Seepersad

Naipaul's sharp observation of the conversion methods used by the Presbyterians also formed a constant theme in his sons' writing as well. Mr Sohun, the Presbyterian schoolmaster in *Gurudeva and Other Indian Tales*, re-emerges for example in V.S. Naipaul's work as Chunilal who soon becomes Randolph in "A Christmas Story" (in *A Flag on the Island* (1967)). In Shiva Naipaul's *The Chip-Chip Gatherers*, Ashok the Hindu soon becomes Egbert the Presbyterian. Seepersad Naipaul's bold use of the dialect of Trinidad and Tobago in his stories and journalistic pieces also provided a model for his sons. What was inculcated in the original space became a continuous literary inspiration in their later writings. Seepersad's legacy of the word subsequently flourished in the Naipaulian tradition, which has enriched world literature. Mr. Sohun of *Gurudeva* fame could not solve all the problems of the world, but he could at least give a warning and then wash his hands of the business, like his creator Seepersad has done.

Endnotes

1. Seepersad Naipaul, *The Adventures of Gurudeva and Other Stories* (London: Andre Deutsch, 1976), 27.
2. *The Adventures of Gurudeva*, 30.
3. *The Adventures of Gurudeva*, 32.
4. *The Adventures of Gurudeva*, 104.
5. *The Adventures of Gurudeva*, 122.
6. *Mighty Sparrow at his best*. Vol 1 Hilary R A (LP) 2127. 1967.
8. V.S. Naipaul, *A Way in the World* (London: Heinemann, 1994), 15.
9. V.S. Naipaul, *A House for Mr Biswas* (London: Andre Deutsch, 1961), 22-23.
10. Seepersad Naipaul, "Unhappy households caused by ignorant wives", *Trinidad Guardian*, 11 March 1933.
11. Seepersad Naipaul, "Bobism and the ludicrous fashion of our womenfolk", *East Indian Weekly*, 24 November 1928.
12. Seepersad Naipaul "After effects of a banquet in Chaguanas", *Trinidad Guardian*, 24 July 1932.
13. Seepersad Naipaul "Repatriated Indians bitter home-coming in India", *Trinidad Guardian*, 27 November 1932.
14. Ismith Khan, *The Jumbie Bird* (London: MacGibbon and Kee, 1961), 80.
15. V.S. Naipaul, *A Way in the World*, 11.
16. V.S. Naipaul, *A Way in the World*, 19.
17. Seepersad Naipaul "Hosein is near", *Trinidad Guardian*, 7 October 1951.
18. Seepersad Naipaul, *The Adventures of Gurudeva*, 44-5.
19. Seepersad Naipaul, "Shouter Baptists Visit China in the Spiritual World", *Trinidad Guardian*, 19 February 1950.

6: IN SEEPERSAD'S *GUARDIAN* CIRCLE: J.E. RAMPERSAD AND THE MAKING OF "MCGEE"

ARNOLD RAMPERSAD

On May 12, 1947, a new column appeared on the back page of the *Evening News*, an afternoon tabloid published Monday to Saturday in Trinidad. The new column, "In the Courts Today", did not seem especially promising. At first, it did not even specify an author. Other unsigned columns followed on May 13 and May 14 under the same heading. Then, on May 15, sporting the subtitle "Lucius Cannot Get Any Work", "In the Courts Today" announced itself as written "By McGEE". Who was this McGee? His identity remained a mystery to almost all readers of the *Evening News* even as the column (popularly known simply as "McGee") achieved such a strong following that it virtually sold the newspaper. "McGee" lasted for some thirty years, or until the death in 1978 in Port of Spain of the man who had birthed and developed it into a national institution, Jerome Ewart Rampersad.

The layout and placement of the column were significant. Always printed on the back page, and typically running the length of the page, each line was wide enough for only a few words. Long and slender, it looked like a kind of backbone for the tabloid. And for many people, it *was* the backbone of the *Evening News* and, by extension, of a new approach to the presentation of Trinidadian life, seen from the peculiar angle of crime and the courtroom.

How can a brief essay such as this one recapture the thrill Trinidadian readers felt, especially in its first years, on reading "McGee"? The column was based on a formula. Central to this formula was the unpromising material of petty crime as adjudicated in the lower courts of law; its creator, though, manipulated that formula with virtuosity. He exploited the passion for the dramatic and melodramatic ever present in a country in which a polyglot population valued expressive style and often used the English language with nonchalant brilliance. Like the city's iconic Dry River suddenly swelling after heavy rain, the column exposed a torrent of images of Trinidadian life previously unseen in local journalism, poetry, fiction, or other prose. Every day it appeared, "McGee" offered fresh slices of life served in a lighthearted but in some way memorable fashion. Readers sensed that the mysterious McGee was capturing, almost cinematically, certain inner truths of their lived culture.

Only a patient reading of crumbling newsprint pages in the National Archives can make that point decisively. However, if we look at just a few examples of the column, randomly chosen from late in 1949, when "McGee" had consolidated its hold, perhaps we can get a sense of the column's unique combination of fact and fiction. Let's start arbitrarily on November 17, 1949, two years into the column's life. In "Rebecca Takes The Oath", McGee trains his spotlight on a witness for the defence. To magistrate Fabian J. Camacho's chagrin, Rebecca swears to the court that the evidence she is about to give "might be the truth". "Wait a minute, madam," Camacho jumps in, "I think I am going to adopt your suggestion. It will save a lot of perjury." (The defendant is soon convicted.) Next we have Bruce. He goes to a Chinese restaurant, enjoys a meal of "Chow Min and rice and a beer", but then breezily assures the waitress that "the government would pay for it". Magistrate Victor Ramsaran imposes a bond of $50 – but also orders Bruce to be deported to his native St. Vincent.

Two policemen see Emanuel and George downtown one evening on Charlotte Street, dragging what looks like a wrapped corpse. The suspects explain: "A Chinee man give we this to carry down to the bus station for him." In fact, they have stolen bottles of soft drinks stacked in cases outside a shop. Three months in jail. An illegal immigrant with a lengthy criminal record is caught with stolen property. He begs, he weeps, he implores. He even quotes scripture. "Donald spoke for ten minutes," McGee tells us. "Tears, 'bucket-a-drop', flowed down his bake-flat nose." Eighteen months in prison, then back to Barbados!

Adventurously, McGee accompanies three "commando"-style cops on night patrol down the teeming Eastern Main Road. Just past the edge of the criminal redoubt called John John, "the cops are all eyes." "Stop! Look! Look!" A fellow is toting a load on his head. "Screech! Brakes!" Two doors slam. What do you have there? "Soap. Ah friend of mine just give me some and ah taking it home." All 23 bars? The next morning, he pleads guilty before Mr. Ramsaran. Someone had promised him "ah little piece" of soap. He had never expected such a windfall! He begs the court: "Sir, I would like you to look into the matter because I'm a family man and if I were a rogue and vagabond I would have been here more often, Sir." Intrigued, Ramsaran agrees to "look into the matter". He remands the man into custody (jail) until Monday.

Starting "Elcita Can't Stand The Heat", McGee observes solemnly that animals wear no clothes. Man started off the same way, but "times have changed". However, in the U.S.A., apparently, there are now nudist colonies of people. "We do not know if young Elcita is one of them. But the fact is, she was seen running down George Street [in the heart of the city] shortly after noon yesterday. And do you know what Elcita had on? No? Well… nothing. And we mean nothing!" Constable Mack hustles her off to the police station. The charge is "disorderly behaviour". "What was wrong with you, girl?" Mr Camacho asks solicitously. "I was drunk, sir." But Constable Alves, the court recorder, breaks the bad news – bad for Elcita. She has twenty-nine previous convictions. Fourteen days' hard labour.

"Iona and Muriel had been fighting. You're right… Over an hombre. Iona's hombre." Each had prior convictions for violence. A fine of five dollars for each. Next come Victor and Norman. They were fighting over a woman. Mr Camacho is elaborately impressed: "Well, well, you actually found a woman worth fighting for? Well! Well! Well!" But Baboolal's case is more troubling. He and Bhagwandesh, a couple from St James in the city, had separated after years of living together. Baboolal had been jailed for three months for "half-killing" Bhagwandesh; but in November, according to McGee, he "half-killed her again". Moreover, Baboolal has four previous convictions, all for beating women. "You like to beat up women a lot?" magistrate Ramseran asks. Baboolal knows a rhetorical question when he hears one. Six months' hard labour. "Baboolal smiled", McGee notes. "He knew where he was going and he did not hate the place. Far from it."

"Aldric Absorbs The Atmosphere" unfolds a more complicated case. Money is involved, and a cheque, and civil servants, if minor. To start, McGee holds forth on the rhetorical skill with which the Financial Secretary of the colony recently presented the complex new annual budget, virtually without notes. This case itself involves a cheque that Aldric, a messenger in the Financial Secretary's office, manages to present and cash twice, making himself a nice profit. McGee praises the prosecuting police: "True, Aldric and his capable counsel [Bruce Procope, a rising legal star] tried to scatter the pieces of the puzzle, but they failed. You see it was just another instance of the police having a good case and having it properly presented. Experienced prosecutor Sub-Inspector Gladstone Wilkinson took care of that, you know." Aldric must pay thirty-five dollars in fines and compensation.

"Wilbert Helps Himself" tells of a recent arrival from St Kitts. McGee opens with a disquisition on how a person from St Kitts should be called. Is he a "Kittian"? Or a "Kittitian"? As for Wilbert himself, he had begged a stranger for a penny. The man dips in his pocket and gives him one. This enrages Wilbert. He feels cheated: "Just because ah ask yuh for ah penny yuh gi' me a penny an' yuh have plenty money in yuh packet? … Ah hear plenty money jingling in yuh packet." Shoving his hand into the man's "packet", he makes off with a two-shilling piece (worth twenty-four pence or pennies). An alert policeman snatches him. Camacho puts him on a fifty dollar bond. He also offers some advice: "Don't come back here, eh!"

Three men loiter in a store in Diego Martin, just to the west of Port of Spain. They leave and board a bus. A clerk then discovers that a new shirt is missing. A motorcycle cop, Constable D'Abreau, jumps on his machine and chases the bus. He arrests George. In court, Mr Camacho compliments D'Abreau. George has four prior convictions for violence. This is his first for "dishonesty". Camacho remands him for further study. McGee notes drolly that George must wait a while "to find out whether or not he would be with his friends during the Yuletide holidays."

The *Evening News*, founded in 1935, and its older, richer sibling, the daily *Trinidad Guardian*, founded in 1917, belonged to the British-owned Trinidad Publishing Company. In the 1930s, ambitious young journalists gravitated to these newspapers as older dailies faded. Among these writers were Seepersad Naipaul, born in 1906, and my father, Jerome Rampersad, born in 1917. My father told me once that he had known and liked Seepersad. Although they came from radically different backgrounds, Seepersad and Jerome are crucially linked in my mind because I see certain shared, consequential elements in their writing. Both were reporters, or "journalists", driven by a special interest in capturing in words the lives of "ordinary" Trinidadians – at a time, during WWII and its troubled aftermath, when the country was undergoing radical social change. The major difference between them was that Seepersad sought to express this "special interest" not as a journalist (his "day job") but as a writer of fiction, separate from that "day job". Jerome, however, would seek to achieve essentially similar goals by anchoring his attempts in journalism itself, even as he sought to adapt its norms in order to capture the dramatically evolving reality of Trinidad and Tobago.

In 1943, Seepersad self-published *Gurudeva and Other Indian Tales*. This groundbreaking collection of stories both honours and transcends its Trinidad Indian setting and remains one of the original if still insufficiently acknowledged precursors of the Caribbean literary renaissance of the 1950s. Jerome's column "In the Courts Today", starting in 1947, is also a major if unacknowledged milestone on that road, although *Gurudeva* is literature in the traditional sense, while "McGee" offered itself as journalism. In these efforts both men sought to break the bonds of literary colonialism that had shackled even the most gifted local writers before them. Clearly, like Seepersad's best writing, "McGee" also went beyond journalism into art, and drew on some of the key techniques of fiction. (Jerome's interest in fiction later led him to write "Beulah", a novel of Trinidad life that he entered unsuccessfully in a competition to help mark the arrival of Independence in 1962.)

Their lives were alike in some ways but radically different in others. Seepersad was Brahmin-born, with deep ties to the Hindu world, while Jerome's origins were muddled, to say the least. Seepersad started life dirt-poor but Jerome was born into the middle class. Seepersad's schooling was negligible; Jerome finished high school, a substantial achievement in those days. On the job as reporters, however, they were equal, more or less. Seepersad certainly had seniority, and helped to pave the way for other dark-skinned types like Jerome; but both men worked under expatriate editors or local whites and off-whites who held essentially elitist and racist views of the world. There were exceptions. A British-born editor nurtured Seepersad as a journalist, and a local white (French Creole) boss, C.S. Espinet, penned the foreword to *Gurudeva* in 1943. Nevertheless, both Jerome and Seepersad shared a jaded view of what Seepersad wearily called "these people" (his bosses) in writing to his son Vidia in 1950.

The major difference between them, however, probably had to do with their ethnic origins. People assumed that Rampersad was half-Indian because, while his mother was not Indian, his father, Christopher Rampersad, certainly was. And indeed, with a shock of straight black hair, Jerome looked half-Indian. But a family rumour whispered that Jerome was not Christopher's biological son. The rumour now appears to be true. Popular genetic-based ancestry sites (notably "23andMe") affirm the absence of Indian (South Asian) genetic markers in Jerome's children and their offspring. If there are "Indian" elements, the source is most likely the Carib or "Amerindian" strains that lingered in Trinidad in the area where his mother was born. This was only a part of the muddle that was Jerome's identity. On his birth certificate of September 30, 1917 he is "Geronimo Ewart Hernandez", son of the evidently unmarried Romana Hernandez. (A relative is said to have forced himself on Romana.) The birth certificate suggests both that Spanish might have been her first language, and that she was a devout Catholic. Geromino is Spanish for Jerome, and September 30th is the Feast of St Jerome.

Fortunately for her, Romana soon found a husband. She had some social advantages. A pretty girl, she had a white father, most likely a Venezuelan of Spanish descent. Her husband was Indian, an unusual turn of events, perhaps, but he was not without advantages of his own. Christopher Rampersad was the son of Alfred Rampersad, a major disciple of John Morton, the leader of the Canadian Presbyterian Mission in Trinidad, which targeted Indians for conversion, mainly through the founding of schools. Geronimo Hernandez became Jerome Rampersad. He was the first of fifteen children, with twelve surviving as adults.

Almost certainly, Jerome grew up knowing that his legal father was not his real father, and that his mother both loved him and associated him with personal shame. Romana considered herself "Spanish", although she would hardly have used the term in the disparaging sense in which V.S. Naipaul has done more than once to mean, as he wrote, "a light-skinned Negro". To be called a "Negro" would have infuriated Romana. Her family was part of the proud *coco-panyol* community that cultivated cocoa estates in the cool valleys of the Northern Range, in places such as Guanapo, in the era when cocoa was king and Trinidad cocoa was said to be the world's best. Then disease blighted the trees and left the *coco-panyols* mainly with their bitter pride and their lost glory. An explosive person given to whipping her children, especially after her husband drifted away from her despite the abundance of children, Romana was anti-black. I vividly recall as a child hearing her routinely spit out anti-black slurs.

She didn't like Indians, either, although one had rescued her, and although Ula, her most Indian-looking teenaged daughter, married an Indian – Surujpat "Pat" Mathura. (Ula doubtless met Pat, a journalist, through his friend Jerome.) Glitteringly handsome, Pat was an "old boy" of St. Mary's College and the son of the progressive Indian leader C.B. Mathura. Charming Pat became the youngest mayor ever of Port of Spain. In 1947, (the year "McGee" started and India became free), he launched over Radio Trinidad one of the first two local radio programmes devoted to Indian culture. (The other was guided by Kamaluddin Mohammed, from a Muslim perspective, while Mathura spoke mainly to Hindus.) We listened with pride and mystification as "Uncle" Pat chanted Hindi to a nation largely baffled, and probably repelled, by his "exotic" subject matter.

I believe Romana both loved Jerome and loathed him. When they clashed, she sometimes called him a "nigger". More than once, he spat back that if he was one, she had made him so. For a while, however, he was a dutiful son. Failing in the harsh competition to gain admission to either of the two elite high schools in Port of Spain, St. Mary's and Queen's Royal College, he made do with the striving, Catholic-oriented Pamphylian High School, which mainly served aspiring blacks. Perhaps he taught there briefly after his student days. Then he discovered his love of journalism and the urbane allure of the reporter's life when the decrepit *Port of Spain Gazette* (founded 1825) and, later, the prosperous *Trinidad Guardian* hired him.

At twenty years of age or thereabouts, Jerome blundered into marriage. He started sweet-talking an attractive, whitish, innocent teenager who worked at the Patisserie bakery on Frederick Street. Evelyn De Souza was the only, "illegitimate", child of Lucy Mendes, a striving brown-skinned immigrant from British Guiana. Soon Evelyn was pregnant. Against his wishes, but at her mother's desperate insistence, the couple married. They had three children. The first came in 1938. I was the last, born in 1941. By that point, the marriage was dead, although for years Jerome spitefully refused to agree to a divorce.

By this point, Jerome's character was pretty much set, although the World War II era distended its features, even as it transformed Trinidad. Although belonging to the middle class, he had come to identify most closely with people who were poor, dark-skinned, uneducated, and largely defenceless. Despite his father's coveted government job as a county administrator, Jerome loathed the idea of social superiority. While his mother was devout, he scorned the white-dominated Catholic church. He drank heavily, gambled obsessively, and chased women unscrupulously. As a result, many of his male colleagues and friends admired and even loved him. Exuding a sense of mystery, he mixed a biting, brooding mischievousness with a fondness for violence. He was quick with a quip, like many Trinidadians; but he also seemed ready to kill somebody.

Jerome doubtless modelled this threatening but thrilling persona on the memorable Hollywood "hoods" and "tough guys" of the World War II era such as James Cagney, Edward G. Robinson, and Humphrey Bogart. As a child, I used to watch with dread fascination as he slipped brass knuckles into his pocket before disappearing into the dark. Later, Ric Hernandez, a mature fellow journalist who knew him well, told me that he believed that Jerome's mystique came "partly from the court and police beat" he covered, but also "partly from an air he... carefully cultivated." He presented himself as "a quiet radical, someone who could start a rumble if pushed." With "a brisk way of talking, almost under his breath, and not given to much small talk, he sought to let you know that you did not fool with Jerome." This air of truculence, sharpened by his wide acceptance – once his column took root – by both policemen and some vicious "bad-johns", helped him to intimidate others around him, including some of his bosses at the *Guardian*.

He became an aficionado of professional boxing and wrestling. Through him I came to know the aptly-named "Gentle" Daniel, born Daniel James, then a high-ranking British Commonwealth light-heavyweight fighter from Belmont. To the end of his life, Jerome remained a fan of organised fighting. He prepared, and distributed, without charge, chapbooks on Trinidad pugilists and their schedules. I don't believe he was much of a fighter himself. His forte was beating women. When I was six or seven, I saw him punch a woman (someone I loved, who had taught me to read) so hard that blood gushed from her face and an eye shut down. She had enraged him by taking me to visit my mother without his permission. With me, he was usually silent, even hostile. According to Lucy Mendes, when he first saw me as an infant, drooling in a pram one evening in Memorial Park, he asked her if she thought I was really his child, because I was then very fair-skinned. "Well, Jerome," my grandmother told him, "if he is not yours, he is still ours."

I recall his slaps and, less frequently, his kicks. With my two older sisters, he seemed kinder. With his various nephews, he was always jovial with them when I was around, even as he ignored me. Later in life, with his younger children by another woman, he was more compassionate. Perhaps time had tamed him.

Jerome invented "McGee" by small degrees. By 1945, just as in Seepersad Naipaul's case, the *Guardian* had shifted him to the *Evening News*. For many years, he was a basic reporter, without a by-line. Then, in 1945 (when he was 27), the *Evening News* printed, along with his by-line, a three-part account of a possible agricultural resurgence called "Road Back to Cocoa". It resembles the three-part series on sugar-cane that had lifted Seepersad as a reporter. And as with Seepersad, although the work was fairly mundane, it stirred ambition in Jerome.

A year later he was much livelier when the *Evening News* offered the next story with his by-line. On October 2, 1946, "Jerome E. Rampersad" published a piece called "In This Our Time". Surveying civilisation after World War II, Jerome drew awkwardly on Charles Dickens: "It is an age of war; it is an age of peace. It is an age of inventions; it is an age of inventions to control inventions." And so on. "We live," he asserted, "in the most topsy-turvy era in the history of mankind." Indeed. The ending of World War II in August 1945 had not led to true peace, certainly not in Trinidad. The hasty departure of most of the American military had been followed by acute joblessness, large-scale illegal immigration from other islands, a housing shortage, food rationing, soaring prices, and intense pressures on moral, intellectual, and aesthetic values. And yet there was also hope, or the illusion of hope. The buoyant idea of liberation from European colonialism was sweeping the world, especially with India set to break free of Great Britain in 1947. Indian independence seemed a perfect boon, but, would other changes come so smoothly? The horror of Partition in 1948 suggested not.

Against this backdrop of uncertainty, of hope mixed with threat, Jerome stumbled down the road to "McGee". His quest had begun in earnest the previous year, 1946, with the spicy mixing of local fact and fiction in an article on October 9 in the *Evening News*. His "WEEK-END REGAINED" offered a giddy account of a trip in a taxi to Point Fortin down South. On board are Jerome, "two Barbadian chappies and a fellow Trinidadian." The "chappies" crave booze: "When we got to the Churchill-Roosevelt Highway [the major highway built by the American military] we braced ourselves... Being babies we missed our bottles very much... We asked the chauffeur to stop at the nearest dealer in bottles. Then it was all chat, pass the bottle, chat, pass the bottle, until we reached Point. My friends were in high spirits. A very interesting time was ahead, they prophesied." The rest of the story tells about this harmless adventure.

Two weeks later, on October 30, the *Evening News* printed a similar story called "Five Blind Mice", about "five by-products of Nature who claim to be chappies of mine". Notably, it identifies "McGee" as the author for the first time. The following Wednesday brought "My Cradle Days", again by "McGee". But Jerome was clearly struggling to find his true voice. In a faltering, faux-"Yankee" vein, "McGee" recalls his parents. "Pop would walk on his toes to me, hold my nose between two fat fingers and ask: 'How's papa's yiddle, yiddle, sugar plum today?'" However, one week later, a promising change comes when "McGee" publishes another story, "The Chappie Henson", in the *Evening News*. For the first time, McGee identifies himself as a Trinidadian. Moreover, he knows St Vincent Street (then Trinidad's Fleet Street) well. "This morning," he writes breezily, "I was walking along St Vincent Street minding my own business when I receive a loud thump on my shoulder." A "chappie" named Henson accosts him.

A week later, alluding to a simmering local labour dispute, "McGee" writes flippantly about "The Strike Situation": "I went on strike the other day. I told my employer of my decision to cease work. All he said to me was, 'McGee, I think it's time you go on strike. Strike the typewriter with your two index fingers. That's all I request of you'." Two telling points here: First, my father always typed using two fingers only. Secondly, labour relations, especially at a local newspaper, were normally serious matters to my father. Why was he joking here? Especially since this "McGee" is now said to be working at the *Guardian*.

And what's with the name "McGee" and other references by Jerome to "McTarvish", "McNought", "McLooney", "McVigor", and the like? Is "Mc" a specific allusion to Irish or Scottish culture? Is it British in origin? Or did it come to Jerome from American sources – newspapers, comic strips, and the like – that had flooded into the island with the War. Why did he want to take this particular name? Of course, pen-names have been invaluable to serious writers, such as "Mark Twain" (Samuel Clemens) in the US and the essayist "Elia" (Charles Lamb), in England. But one must also consider calypso. In Trinidad, a devoted calypsonian is born again, self-baptised, self-named. In this way, Raymond Quevedo, for example, became "Attila the Hun" – the composer of the glorious 1934 calypso "Graf Zeppelin" about its visit to Trinidad. Taking a *nom-de-plume* affirmed Jerome's mastery over a new world he was creating. "Mc" obviously meant for him a regular bloke, someone with "classic" Irish properties, if seen mainly in caricature – fun-loving, a drinker and a talker, a bit of a rascal but decent at heart. Note also that Jerome's pen-name was not aggrandising like Tiger, Lion, Attila, or Lord Kitchener. Rather it is diminutive. The next great calypsonian – perhaps the greatest of all – would do the same in 1956, when Slinger Francisco became "The Mighty Sparrow".

America was the most likely source of Jerome's "McGee", with one writer, Damon Runyon, crucial here. Runyon, who had just died in December 1946, had been the highest paid journalist in the U.S., as well as the beloved author of *Guys and Dolls* and other literary productions. Celebrated for his aggressive twisting of English (he loved to invent words, such as "gazillion") and for columns and essays about crime and tough guys, as well as sport, he was the supreme journalistic hero to Jerome, who openly admits his indebtedness in at least two places. For example: "*Look out, Damon Runyon,*" he writes flatly just before launching his column, "*here I come!*"

Under these influences, "McGee" published at least six other pieces in the *Evening News*. Then he lapsed into silence. Next, without naming "McGee" or Jerome, on May 12, 1947 the *News* published a piece called "In The Courts Today". Jerome was getting close now, even if he was still largely in the dark about where inspiration was taking him. Similar pieces, also unsigned, followed on May 13 and 14. All of them sported subtitles but identified no author. Finally, on May 15, 1947, came "In the Courts Today", with the subtitle "Lucius Cannot Get Any Work" – and the attribution "By McGEE." Undoubtedly, Jerome had started "In the Courts Today". He had proposed to the "bosses" to visit the magistrates' courts near the *Guardian*, and then write up in his own style what he had seen and heard there. Sensing that he might be on to something good and profitable, the "bosses" let him sign it as he saw fit.

McGee was born.

What are the key elements of a typical "McGee" column? Over its three decades they barely changed. Central to the formula was the narrator, McGee. Taking no prominent part in the action, he typically opened the column with droll observations about the world around him. Then he moved on quickly to identify the cause of the trial, or the first trial, he would cover that day.

As a narrator, Jerome saw McGee as a kind of insouciant Trinidadian, decently educated but definitely unaffected. Years later, some readers would recall the column as written in the vernacular. This error would have pleased Jerome. It pointed to the success of his crucial decision to report the words of Trinidadians (or other Caribbean folks) just as they had been spoken in the courtroom, and to have his narrator speak in a way absolutely familiar to Trinidadians. In that way, he placed the average Trinidadian's English on a par with the King's. This honouring of the vernacular was virtually new to local journalism. It is also of a piece with Seepersad Naipaul's use of the vernacular in *Gurudeva*. Jerome loved the language that the people had created, just as he loved the people. Inspired by the peculiar literary dynamic that arose from American democracy, Jerome placed a love of the common people at the heart of his column, just as Seepersad emphasised the "ordinary" Indo-Trinidadian. McGee seeks to be fair to everyone – to Blacks (who predominate), Indians, Whites, Chinese, Portuguese, and others in Trinidad's ethnic hodgepodge.

McGee was also committed to facts. He was strict about using real names, from the lowliest defendant to the most exalted magistrate, although typically he used only the accused's first name, no doubt to prevent embarrassing the unfortunate. Just as carefully, McGee respected the police. He identified each by name and rank. In these courts, police gave evidence about the crime in question but also prosecuted the case. This sometimes pitted them against well-trained, suave defence attorneys. If McGee had a bias here, it was in favour of the comparatively humble policemen. He showed them as competent and humane. As a result, Jerome was always welcome in the busy canteen at police headquarters on St Vincent Street.

A crucial element of the column is its anchoring in the "lowest" courts, where defendants were usually working-class or poorer. Thus, McGee avoided heinous or complex crimes, which were adjudicated in the "higher" courts. Humour, not violence, was central to the column. The *Evening News* understood and exploited elsewhere the news value of a sensational murder case; but McGee's world was almost benign. Minor but ingenious thefts, colourful drunken behaviour, episodes of men beating men (but not too badly), or men beating women, or – best of all as theatre – women beating men, were his preferred material. Illegal immigration from the other, poorer islands, profiteering in a time of food rationing, and the mistreatment of working animals, also provided good stuff. The relative mildness of these offences allowed for both comedy and compassion.

Nevertheless, comedy and compassion could not alter the fact that the column made entertainment out of crime. Moreover, it did so at a time when crime was rising at an alarming rate. With an economy damaged by the end of the war, people were suffering. The *Evening News* did not dwell on this fact. Advancing a "Chamber of Commerce" optimism, it played down the issue of poverty. And yet the conditions for an island-wide crisis concerning serious crime were taking root. Ironically, it took a new British governor, Sir John Shaw, to yank back the veil in 1946. In July, as the highest British official in Palestine, he had barely survived the bombing of the King David Hotel that killed 91 people. And yet Trinidad shocked him. "I have seen things that are a disgrace," the *Evening News* reported him saying. "I have visited the slums twice," he elaborated, and found them "a disgrace to a civilised society."

What was McGee's relationship to this genuine "disgrace"? Gordon Rohlehr has pointed out that the decade of 1946 to 1956 (the golden years of the "McGee" column) was characterised locally by social conflict of every kind. Young criminals became an unprecedented menace. In 1946, the year before "McGee" started, a proposed bill sought to bring back the flogging of convicted criminals. Supporters of flogging with the dreaded "cat 'o nine tails" included both the prosperous and the poor, who were often the main victims of crime. "Shocking cases of rape, robbery with violence and maiming have been all too prevalent here of late", a leading attorney wrote in the Port of Spain *Gazette*. He alluded to an expanding class of young criminals "for whom discipline has no meaning and prison few terrors," and for whom flogging was "the only remedy".

The "McGee" column was surely shaped in part by this controversy. It is unclear whether or not Jerome supported the bill. Perhaps he opposed it but saw all sides of the issue. Fortunately, flogging was not an option as punishment in the magistrates' courts. Freed of such heavy responsibility, the magistrate could look at the plight both of the victim and the accused, when extenuating circumstances seemed to be present. McGee paid full attention to the magistrate. His individual style, his volubility or his reticence, his sense of humour or his lack of one, were all important to McGee. Jerome's favourite magistrate was undoubtedly Fabian J. Camacho, Antiguan-born and presumably of Portuguese extraction. Most likely he was white or whitish, but he was very much a local. (Speaking to me, the veteran lawyer H.A. Selby Wooding spontaneously recalled Camacho as "humane".) Camacho could be strict. Beat a woman or strike a policeman and you were going to jail. Otherwise, he was often willing to give poor people second and third chances. Quick-witted, he had the teasing way with words that Trinidadians loved. Thus Camacho – and McGee – affirmed humane values in a court system that imposed discipline on a society marked by gross economic, social, and racial inequities.

In the column, the role of the defence attorney – when there was one – was usually perfunctory. Many defendants at this level could not afford counsel, or hiring counsel made no financial sense. Defendants in general had to speak for themselves. Most were intimidated but others were not. People from Tobago were often depicted as so timid as to be almost mute, but Trinidadians could put on a show. An old Indian woman from the country looked cowed but then (to McGee's delight) refused to shut up. Some defendants were ingenious in their defiance. One man, charged with using obscene language in a rum shop, insisted that he had done nothing of the kind. He has simply stated in the rum shop that he wanted some liquor "FOR CURIOSITY'S SAKE". Staring down the magistrate, he loudly repeated the magic words: "FOR CURIOSITY, YOUR WORSHIP, FOR CURIOSITY!!"

With a large docket of cases, magistrates had to act swiftly. Although they listened to prosecutors' recommendations or to pleas from the accused, the final decision was theirs. They acquitted some defendants. A large number were found guilty but sent home unpunished except for a form of probation that noted their guilt. Sometimes the magistrate imposed a small fine. Most of the guilty could ill afford it. A few went to jail.

Many defendants and witnesses were women (and McGee seemed to delight in their presence), but men outnumbered women in every area. But again, 1947 saw a historic change. Mrs. Gladys Ramsaran became the first woman magistrate, just as in 1932 she had been the first woman admitted to the local bar. (Her husband, Victor Ramsaran, was himself a magistrate.)

"In the Courts Today" by "McGee" became a sensation. In calypsos, "ordinary" Trinidadians had been depicted vibrantly, but the "cultured" world of newspapers typically had excluded them. Appropriately, calypsonians openly saluted the column. The high point, here, came in 1949 with the recording "McGee," composed and sung by the celebrated Rupert Grant, or "Lord Invader". Invader's "Rum and Coca-Cola" (1943) had become internationally known when the famed Andrews Sisters successfully recorded the calypso in the US, but gave Grant no credit, much less royalties. (He sued and won his case.) In 1949, his "McGee" spoke both to the column's popularity and its controversial side. Lord Invader lives in (comic) terror of being written up as a defendant in "McGee". He would then be a hapless object of ridicule across the land. Invader thus acknowledged both McGee's skill as a writer and the breadth of his fame. Although the magistrates (he mentions Camacho) do not scare him, McGee leaves him quaking:

> For if you have a case whether win or lose,
> Your name must appear on the evening news
> Because that man they call McGee
> McGee McGee McGee writing bout everybody
> So I'm trying to live peacefully
> Because I don't want McGee write about me.

Its dominant refrain, the last three lines are repeated throughout, but other comments are also telling. While he praises McGee "wholeheartedly/ For his intelligence and ingenuity", Invader also makes the crucial point that "The way he writes you can see he's not prejudice". A column about poor people and crime invited displays of snobbery and racism. McGee made no such mistake, Invader believed – although some thin-skinned people took umbrage at it. "The ordinary class of people was very displeased", he sang; "they said they [McGee] never wrote about the aristocracy" committing crimes. Disputing this criticism, Invader cites examples of McGee taking on "respectable" people, as in reporting on the alleged legal troubles of the eminent lawyer H.O.B. Wooding (who later became Chief Justice of Trinidad and Tobago). Invader could also have cited McGee's ribbing of another major lawyer, Henry Hudson-Phillips, because of his known verbosity. And McGee occasionally wrote about white defendants – although they were usually foreign seamen who had drunk too much rum and missed their ships. In any event, Invader's main point is clear: *"I'm trying to live peacefully / Because I don't want McGee write about me."*

In addition to Invader, at least one other major singer referred in a song to McGee. This reference drew McGee intimately into the calypso world. However, a degree of mystery surrounds its dating. In 1937, the celebrated "Growling Tiger" (or "Tiger") saw his "Lazy Man" become a hit. Tiger structured the calypso as a verbal duel between a man (the lazy man) and the peppery Elaine, his landlady and one-time lover. According to a transcription ascribed to 1937, Elaine reminds him scathingly about how poor he had been when they first met. "You had one old khaki pants in yuh name", she sings, "Knocking round the town / Yuh big toe was showing in your watchekong" [cheap "gym" shoes]. She then adds: "Ah never see a man more ungrateful than that / Is Mr McGee who di[d] give him the ole felt hat…"

But how could this "Mr McGee" be Jerome, when the calypso, "Lazy Man", appeared first in 1937, and Jerome's column started in 1947? In 2015, the music expert Ray Funk insisted to me that Tiger's "Mr McGee" must be someone else – "unless your father knew Tiger then and Tiger gave him the nickname, but it was a private nickname between them until he took on the sobriquet a decade later." Clearly, however, Tiger wouldn't have used the name "McGee" in a calypso unless he was sure his audiences would recognise it. No "Mr McGee" was prominent in Trinidad before the *Evening News* in 1947. Tiger, like so many calypsonians, fiddled with his lyrics over the years, especially for recordings, and obviously added the McGee reference after 1947.

In fact, my father knew Tiger very well. As a little boy I, too, knew Tiger well. The men could have met in the early 1940s, or even before then. They loved boxing. As Neville Marcano from Siparia, before he turned calypsonian, Tiger had been the Trinidad flyweight champion. He was also race conscious, as when he combined the two interests in his 1937 calypso "Beat Them, Cuff Them, Joe Louis". But he and my father shared even more. For a while, I saw Tiger almost every day at the house on Belle Eau Road in Belmont where I lived with my father, my two sisters, and at least four grown women. One, Myra, was Tiger's lover. They had a child, Michael Lancelot Marcano, a charming toddler who was like our little brother. Tiger often woke up at our house, where my father lived with Myra's sister Edith, a schoolteacher. Childless, Edith acted as a mother to his three children. She had known my father even before he married my mother in 1938. We shared the house with Edith's wonderful, humble mother, Eliza "Dado" Thomas, and three of her daughters, including Edith and Myra.

This is more than a question of coincidence. The "McGee" column is closely linked to the content, style, and popularity of the calypso. McGee walked a tightrope between honouring the poor by telling their stories humanely and also satirising them. Most calypsonians walked a similar line. In many respects, *Gurudeva* also partakes of the liberating calypso world. Even before he moved to urban St James, Seepersad found "creole" culture of the type on which calypso is founded, fascinating. Jerome was inspired by men like Lord Invader and Growling Tiger as much as by foreigners such as Damon Runyon. As for Tiger and the gift of a "felt hat" from "Mr McGee", my father wore hats every day in those years, as did many men of his station, including Seepersad, as photographs of him show. Handsome Tiger was a dapper fellow. I can easily imagine my father giving him a classy hat as a present.

Jerome Rampersad was hardly the first middle-class or lower-middle-class writer to champion the Trinidadian black poor, or the poor in general. In this he was in the company of men like C.L.R. James, Albert Gomes, Ralph de Boissiere and Alfred Mendes. However, he was arguably the first and only one to take as his main angle of vision the criminal class or, more accurately, poor people caught up in crime at some point in their lives. Should his column be considered "art"? Does he deserve admission to the company of "creative" writers such as James, Gomes, de Boissiere, Mendes, and Seepersad Naipaul? "McGee", like *Gurudeva,* which must have impressed Jerome, was one of the prime anticipators of the Caribbean literary renaissance of the 1950s that was led by Sam Selvon, V.S. Naipaul, Roger Mais, George Lamming, and others. The strained relationship between these writers and their precursors is no more pathetically played out, perhaps, than in V.S. Naipaul's difficulty in dealing with the book *Gurudeva,* which he had helped to produce as a precocious boy. However the similarities between Samuel Selvon's work, V.S. Naipaul's early and the "McGee" columns would suggest that Jerome's column was indeed art which influenced the work of these future stars. His impact on Selvon may have been even more immediate since Selvon also worked for the *Guardian,* where their paths inevitably crossed.

The native fertility of Jerome's column is clear when one browses the pages of the *Evening News* and the *Guardian* from the late 1940s. The 1940s in Trinidad was a decade of excitement but also of cultural confusion and even desolation. By 1941, when Yankee money, manners, and mores flooded the island along with the displayed might of the US armed forces, the indigenous cultural promise of the 1930s virtually collapsed. World War II made assertions of cultural nationalism, political protest, and racial and ethnic pride – all vital to forging a new kind of art – seem at best insular and at worst almost treasonous. The new US-inspired wealth made social protest appear somewhat pointless. Global war stimulated Trinidad wildly in many ways but also – except for the calypso and the emerging steel band – drained it of inspiration in art. This was especially so in literature.

The newspapers played a critical role here – and played it badly. While the *Guardian* exuded a fake cosmopolitanism, the *Evening News* seemed populist – but that view was largely an illusion. Ken Ramchand is right in pointing out its democratic elements, but those impulses were largely inherent in the tabloid form, until 1947 and the rise of "McGee". True, as Ramchand says, the *Evening News* became for a generation "the most culturally significant and wide-ranging local paper… the paper most read by the ordinary people of the island." But it was democratic in a superficial way until 1947 and the rise of "McGee".

To read its pages from 1946 and 1947 is mainly to see racism, snobbery, and literary incompetence. On April 25, 1947, for example, an essay ("Life of a NOBODY") by one John Lansard rails against "these pitiable creatures that hang out in the shady slums of Port-of-Spain." Steps must be taken "to eradicate them from our social set-up." Lansard sneers openly at the dandyish "saga-boy". "What books does he read?" Lansard asks. "Of course he doesn't work. His philosophy is typical of fellows like himself that 'work en't sweet'." Responsible readers have "to save fellows like [him] for their sake and ours, and for the sake of the prestige of the colony." Racism ruled both newspapers. In 1947, virtually every image in the *Evening News*, whether tied to news or sales of merchandise, featured whites almost exclusively. The white woman ruled; the black or brown woman is virtually nonexistent. Only in sports is there a flashing of darker skin colour, or veiled hints about discontent about the role of "pigmentation" as a sports editor put it cautiously at one point.

But the aesthetic crisis is best exemplified in the "fine" writing the *Evening News* favoured. For many weeks in 1947, for example, it ran serialised chapters by the genteel American fiction writer Kathleen Norris. She and similar authors explored social milieus and themes far removed from Trinidad. But even promising local writers were creatively adrift. The reality of Trinidad seemed to mean nothing to them. In a reflective piece called "The Life of Day", for example, one essayist writes: "I know the day, each passing hour that comes and goes from dawn till dawn then dawn again. From the dead hours of midnight, when the earth is deep in sleep, to the blatant heat of noon, there is not an hour which has slipped past me, though I confess to no nocturnal toiling while my companion slept." He goes on: "Wonderful is the day with its lustrous stars and marvellous moon." When he uses Trinidadian English, he is clumsy and patronising, as in "THOUGHTS": "Some people console themselves with a hollow philosophy whenever they become the victim of circumstances, saying that what has happened is for the best, or to put it in the local parlance, 'what is to is must is'."

Who is this young Trinidadian writing so fatuously just as "McGee" starts? He is, the *Evening News* tells us, "Samuel Selvon". In a few short years, he would thrive as "Sam Selvon", as he began to work the ground broken in the same *Evening News* by "McGee" and earlier by *Gurudeva*. Other factors, of course, sparked the eruption of the local democratic imagination. None was more important, probably, than the tour of England in 1950 by the West Indies cricket team, when it defeated England for the first time on English soil. Its bowling hero, almost unplayable at times, was a hitherto obscure Indian lad from rural Trinidad, Sonny Ramadhin. He might have stepped straight from the pages of *Gurudeva*. With no first name on his birth certificate, people had simply called him "Sonny", from the word "son" on the certificate. Returning from England a Caribbean hero, he was eagerly photographed by Seepersad, who doubtless saw in him a rare triumph of

Hindu Indian manhood in a culture that devalued Indians. Virtually no one connected Ramadhin to *Gurudeva*, Seepersad's ignored paean to local Indian culture, but Lord Invader saw the link between McGee and Ramadhin. When the Sa Gomes recording company put out Invader's "McGee" in 1951, on the flip side was Invader's even more popular "We want Ramadin [sic] on the ball."

Stepping "down" in class had been a rite of passage for the Trinidad writer seeking to depict the local masses. In 1930, Alfred Mendes, white but a democrat, had moved for six months to a barrack yard, the quintessential space of poverty in Port of Spain, near Park Street. He aimed to hone his literary skills there. "What I did... to get the atmosphere," Mendes wrote about poor urban blacks, "to get the sort of jargon that they spoke – the vernacular, the idiom – what I did was: I went into the barrack-yard that was then at the bottom of Park Street just before you came into Richmond Street, and I lived in it for about six months. I did not live completely there, but I ingratiated myself." He was not alone. C.L.R. James, a brilliant, brown-skinned boy from Tunapuna schooled at elite QRC, his brain and being steeped in British literature, had made a similar move. The hero in his deft novel *Minty Alley* (1936) ventures as an outsider into barrack-yard life. There he is caught up in a sexual relationship. In the end, however, he returns to the safety of his middle-class loyalties just as Mendes had done.

Jerome Rampersad, maturing in a Trinidad and, indeed, a world grown atomic in its sense of freedom, pushed past such compromises. It is no accident, I think, that the "McGee" column was born in May 1947, weeks after the birth of Valda Toussaint. Valda was his third daughter, his first child with Josephine Mary Toussaint. Josephine was a beautiful, intelligent, but poor young woman living in tight quarters on Upper Duke Street, in the dicey area called "Behind the Bridge". Unlike Mendes and James, Jerome did not "slum" a while and then scurry home. He and Josephine never married but would have six children together – compared to the three he had fathered with my mother and the four that would come from his second marriage, which came in 1952. Out of this relationship with Josephine would come Cheryl Toussaint O'Neil, a university-educated communications specialist who later worked in a newsroom with our father; and Roger Toussaint, celebrated later as a visionary trade union leader of transit workers in New York City. (The children differ somewhat about Jerome's confidence in visiting them. One recalls him "slipping into" their home "under cover of the night. He shared the same shame that was visited upon him by his family." But another is sure that not all of their father's visits were at night, and that in the morning "he left in what I would consider broad daylight.")

For a while, obviously, Jerome maintained parallel romantic or sexual relationships with at least two and sometimes three different partners. But

– in his erratic fashion – he tried to honour his obligations to his Toussaint children. In 1965, he moved with some of them into an apartment he rented on Jerningham Avenue in Belmont. But he sometimes beat Josephine, which embittered at least one son. Eventually the Toussaints all moved out and left him behind.

Jerome's second wife, Mutrice Greaves, was an intelligent, disciplined, generally stern, brown-skinned woman from Belmont. Her brother was a friend and co-worker of my father's. Living with Edith and our often absent father, my two sisters and I knew nothing of her until one morning in 1953 when a man arrived at Edith's bringing with him an empty suitcase. He had come to take us to join our father and his bride or bride-to-be. We left with him. We were to live together in a rented, charming if run-down vacation house a few yards from the sea in Point Cumana (an area celebrated in Invader's "Rum and Coca Cola"), to the west of Port of Spain. There we met our father's new wife Mutrice.

Later that year, the couple had their first child, Mary. We liked Mary, but Mutrice looked at us coldly. The chill persisted. After a difficult year, this arrangement ended. Improbably, we three children returned to live with Edith. My father's second marriage broke up after he and Mutrice had four children. Then their mother, acting without his knowledge, and no doubt fed up with him, emigrated to the U.K. I think the children, with one exception, never saw or spoke to him after that point. They came to loathe him.

Why Jerome never married Josephine, I don't know. The same might be asked of his relationship with Edith. Nonetheless he had boldly crossed certain major lines in Trinidad. He had defied the walls between prosperous and poor, black and Indian, half-Indian and Spanish and Portuguese. These lines, he believed, disfigured the soul of Trinidad. In this respect he was radically unlike Naipaul, who became cosmopolitan but remained conscious of himself as a Hindu of Brahmin caste. "Negroes" or mixed-race "coloured" people in general, were for him (as far as I can tell) beyond the pale. To be sure, there were reasons enough why Seepersad, as an Indian in Trinidad, should have felt alienated in this way.

In 1958, fed up with Jerome's pro-trade union agitation, the Trinidad Publishing Company fired him. He became involved in various ventures. He founded a weekly newspaper, the *Sun*, but it soon died. He took a job at the *Nation*, the weekly newspaper of the ruling People's National Movement, where he helped its high-strung editor, C.L.R. James put out the *Nation*. All the while, Jerome enjoyed the respect he deserved as a veteran, creative journalist. Thus, when a job became open in the newsroom at Radio Guardian (or 610 Radio), which the Trinidad Publishing Company founded in 1957 as a rival to the monopolistic Radio Trinidad, no one in power objected to his hiring. The chief news editor was the debonair Yusuff Ali, who liked Jerome. In 1960, when Ali stepped down, Jerome replaced him. He did very well as the boss of a staff of four or five solid reporters who prepared newscasts culled mainly from *Guardian* material and from our chattering Associated Press teletype machine.

By this time, of course, the incomparable Seepersad was dead, and his *Gurudeva* virtually, and unforgivably, in my opinion, forgotten, As Vidia struggled toward his unquestionable literary greatness, for various reasons he was less than helpful in advancing the cause of his father's own considerable accomplishments as a writer.

I was often in my father's 610 Radio newsroom, where I saw that he was clearly admired and even loved. Early in 1961, without revealing that I was his son or telling him of my application, 610 hired me as a trainee radio announcer. I stayed there for slightly more than a year. In that time, I interacted cordially if somewhat remotely with my father. His talented staff, which included John Babb (later a major newspaper editor), seemed to adore him – although Jerome tolerated no slackness. (Once, Babb later told me, Jerome exploded at an incompetent trainee and threw a typewriter at him – a portable machine, I assume.) Then, in 1969, the government bought the station as part of a planned national broadcasting service. But as the nation weathered a succession of political storms, press coverage of politics began to irritate Prime Minister Eric Williams. In 1975, his proxy suddenly fired Jerome in a purge of writers that included Raoul Pantin (who had married one of my older sisters) and even Tony Williams (the PM's brother).

After 1958, when the TPC fired him, who was writing "McGee"? Since the TPC owned the McGee column, Jerome could not take it elsewhere on his own. It stayed in the *Evening News*, where it was composed by various people over the years, including Jerome – when the "bosses" saw fit for him to write it. The time would come when his connection to the column would be comprehensively denied. In 2007, in challenging some point made by the columnist Professor Selwyn Cudjoe, a letter to a local paper asserted that the "McGee" column had been entirely the work of a once well-known journalist, Patrick Chookolingo. Founder in 1970 of the muckraking weekly scandal-sheet *The Bomb*, "Chooko" had also been a veteran employee of the *Guardian* group. When Chooko asked my father to help him launch *The Bomb*, Jerome pitched in. But they were never close friends, and Chooko definitely was never "McGee".

Other writers, at the discretion of the "bosses", could fairly claim to have been "McGee" from time to time. Almost all were outstanding Trinidadian journalists, happy to don the mantle as Jerome's replacement; but there is no agreement on who did so and when. If Lennox Raphael claimed he succeeded Jerome as "McGee", Vernon Khelawan begged to differ: "When Jerome left the *Trinidad Guardian*, the 'McGee' column was then written by

John Grimes and after him by myself." After Khelawan came, apparently, Ewart Rouse, who recalled that "it was fun writing it." He did so "for at least a couple years until I left Trinidad in early 1969." John Babb recalls that a certain young woman became "McGee" at one point, but never got the hang of it and soon quit. The uncertainty surrounding these "McGee" writers, and even the isolated denial that Jerome was *ever* McGee, all contribute to a curiously fitting mythic element about the column – that is, when the column is remembered at all, given journalism's ephemeral essence. "McGee" touched not only its readers but also the lives of a community of writers whose duty was to offer a vital angle on local life. At its best, it commanded attention by the power of its comic, compassionate, and democratic charm.

According to Alfred Aguiton, Jerome never recovered from his purging in 1975. Living often alone in near poverty in his apartment on Jerningham Avenue, he depended largely on the kindness of family and friends, as well as – possibly – dribbling payments from the *Evening News*. Taking pity on him, apparently, its editors asked him at some point to resume writing the column. If they did hire Jerome (and it is likely they did so), they probably paid him little. Aguiton saw him as a broken man.

The end came suddenly in 1978. Kenny De Silva was a friend and admirer of Jerome's since 1959, when he joined 610 Radio as an office boy. De Silva was rising high in the world of sports, entertainment, and business in Trinidad, but remained loyal to Jerome. He stopped by the apartment on Jerningham Avenue one afternoon. Using a key that Jerome had given him, he let himself in. De Silva called out but heard no answer. He found Jerome lying on his bed. He was wearing shorts and a merino undershirt. On his chest was an open bag of Crix biscuits. A heart attack, apparently, had killed him.

But someone else was in the apartment. Garvin Rampersad, one of Jerome's four children by his second wife, Mutrice, had come from London to stay indefinitely. He had grown up in England. A brilliant student with a passion for philosophy, Garvin possessed a brilliant mind but was scarred by mental illness and an occasional tendency toward violence. After a scary incident in England, his mother shipped him back to Trinidad to live with his father. It didn't work out: "I came not to like my father," Garvin would write, "who... never smiled." When Garvin spoke of loving the study of philosophy, Jerome dismissed the field as trivial, fitting for a mere teacher. So Garvin would assert in a memoir appended in 2011 to his book (published in London) *The End of Existence: Membership and Metaphysics*. When Garvin acted up one day, Jerome threatened to have him committed to the mental hospital in St. Ann's. The next day, while Garvin was out, "I brooded on this threat and wished for my father's death." When he came home, Jerome was lying on his bed. Garvin assumed he was asleep. "I went to my room." Then Kenny De Silva showed up.

Jerome's funeral at Rosary Church on Park Street in April 1978 was heavily attended. Grown men wept, I am told. The *Evening News* published an obituary, along with a photograph of him. For the first time ever, it admitted that Jerome Ewart Rampersad indeed had been – at least for some time – McGee, its most popular columnist. "Rampersad's last 'McGee' column," the *Evening News* noted, "appears on Pages 8 & 9."

7: OUR ST JAMES

ROBERT CLARKE

The Naipaul family lived in this house at 26 Nepaul Street, St James, from 1946 – some for longer periods, others for shorter. The most celebrated of the family, one Sir Vidia, lived here for four years while at Queen's Royal College (QRC), before leaving for Oxford University in England just before his eighteenth birthday. Another member of the family, father Seepersad Naipaul, a journalist at the *Trinidad Guardian*, lived there for seven years between buying the property and thus escaping the overbearing influence of his wife's in-laws, and his death at the age of forty-seven. Mother, Droapatie Capildeo, of the Capildeo clan from the Lion House in Chaguanas, lived there for over four decades, well beyond her husband's passing.

But it is Shiva, the third writer in the family, who has left us the best portraits of a fictionalised St James. He spent his formative years there, from the age of one well into his teens and beyond. So perhaps it is fitting that we should begin with him. Or rather, my imagined version of his five-year-old self:

From the second storey of 26 Nepaul Street, Shiva heard the first rap-pap-pap of the Hosay tassa. He tumbled down the staircase, past the oil portrait of his father, journalist Seepersad Naipaul, snatched a piece of roti from the tabletop bowl, gave Gyp the family dog a friendly kick and bounded into the yard. From the light of the bare incandescent bulb, through the leaves of the cassia, he spied cousin Deo, shoo-shooing by the gate with the Muslim drummer boy. Good thing Pa ain' reach from work, he thinks.

So would this be historically accurate? There was a dog called Gyp, and an oil portrait of Seepersad – a curious indulgence that cost him $52 when money was tight – and a cousin named Deo, who scandalised the senior Naipaul by dating outside her religion. There was a cassia tree, and a shade tree that Gyp died under after being struck by a motor-van on Nepaul Street. There was a rich scarlet bougainvillea and several orchids that Seepersad had taken up as a hobby. There was roti and there was rice; neither of which may have been missed by Vidia off in England. And beyond the front wall, there was a street.

Nepaul Street was home to Indo-Trinidadians. It was they who had begun the settlement of St James, transforming it by degrees from former cane lands to residential community and suburb of Port of Spain. But by the late 1940s it had already assumed its multi-ethnic character.

"By the time I was born," writes Shiva, in the preface to his book of short stories *Beyond the Dragon's Mouth*, "the living link with the sugar cane estates of the Caroni plains had been effectively broken. About that other life I knew virtually nothing. I was a town boy through and through."

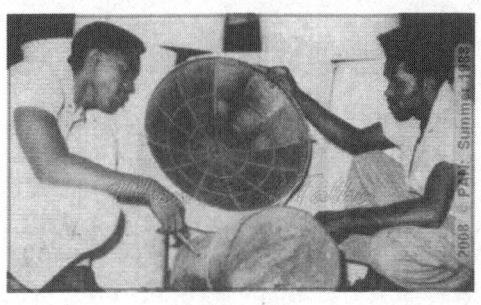

A stroll down the town boy's street would have led him past the home of pan pioneer Anthony Williams, and perhaps it was unsurprising that, by the age of six, Shiva was beating pan – news of which Vidia in London found "distressing". It may have been a passing fancy, rather than a life-long pursuit, but there was no lack of options for an aspiring pannist in St James in the 1950s: North Stars on Bombay Street, Five Graves to Cairo in Belle Vue, Tripoli at the corner of Ethel Street and Mucurapo Road.

From the second storey window of his snug box-shaped home, Shiva could see the Rialto cinema at the corner of Agra Street and the Western Main Road, where nine cents would get you a wooden chair in Pit for a double feature of the Westerns that proved so influential in the naming of St James pansides. Occasionally the theatre was plunged into darkness as the film reel snapped and from the gritty depths, the first shout rose, aimed at the poor projectionist: "Bascombe, your mother-so-and-so!" That gem from one of the denizens of Pit, a contemporary of Shiva's.

But it is in Shiva's stories that you are invited into *his* St James, just as you were introduced to the characters of Woodbrook through Vidia's *Miguel Street*, written from observations made from the safety of his grandmother's yard while living at the Capildeo house at Luis Street, Woodbrook. In Shiva's "The Beauty Contest", Doon Town stands in for St James.

> There were two hardware shops in Doon Town, and the Oriental Emporium, proprietor R. Prasad, was one of them. There was nothing remotely oriental about the place, but the name had been given by Mr.

Prasad's father (a man noted for his flights of fancy) and no one cared enough to change it. The other, just a few doors away, was the more aptly named General Store, proprietor A. Aleong. Though selling the same goods they had competed amicably for many years, and Mr. Prasad appeared to derive a certain pleasure in telling his customers, 'Me and Mr Aleong is the best of friends. Not a harsh word in ten years.'[1]

It is a story about suburban development, American cultural imperialism, and a parochial shopkeeper spurred on by an ambitious wife to ever more ridiculous competitive feats. In it you recognise a St James that exists even today: "It was the custom in Doon Town for shops to bring their goods on to the pavements, where the bulkier items were displayed."[2] I don't need to show you a picture for you to know that this is true.

Mr Aleong, whose son has returned from studying business management in America, takes the goods off the pavement and puts up a sign: "Pavements were made to be walked on."[3] He erects a neon sign with flickering lights and the image of a man dressed cowboy style, saying: "*Darn me if this ain't the finest store in town.*"[4] Of course, he captures the market.

> 'Man, I know what you could do,' said Prasad's wife one day, visibly excited. [...] 'You could enter someone for the Miss Doon Town contest. Imagine you get a really nice girl, Miss Oriental Emporium – you know they have to say who sponsoring them in a sash across they chest – and if she win Aleong go come crawling back to you. He'll keep his tail quiet after that.'[5]

Disaster ensues. Miss Oriental Emporium portrays Isis, Egyptian fertility goddess. By custom, the more exotic your Carnival Queen the better. But Aleong, recently an upsetter of tradition and embracer of foreignness, has his queen go local: Miss General Store as Fruits and Flowers.

> Mr Prasad stiffened. The audience digested the significance of this before bursting into rapturous applause. Miss General Store wore what was basically a grass skirt, hidden behind bunches of hibiscus, oleander and carnations. Her bosom and back were encased in banana leaves overspread with wreaths of fern and more flowers, and on her head she balanced a fruit-filled basket from which hung chains of roses reaching to the floor. People rose from their seats and applauded. Someone threw a straw hat on the stage.
> 'Original!'
> 'Fruits and flowers, a local thing.'[6]

Aleong is elected mayor, the General Store grows into a chain, and Mr Prasad enjoys recounting the memory of his close friendship with the Mayor.

The inherent tension of racial and religious diversity is also among Shiva's themes. In "The Tenant", Pankar the jeweller buys a house on the up-and-coming Western Main Road. There his wife Dulcie gives birth to a deformed baby, and pegs her misfortune to her husband's growing proximity to their tenant – a tall, dark woman of half-Indian, half-Negro extraction – widely believed to be an obeah woman. Dulcie abandons the house, Pankar's jewellery store prospers, and Eugenie Radix, tenant-cum-common-law-wife-of-a-sort, replaces her garlands of hibiscus and oleander with "necklaces of an intricate and occult design." Again, disaster. The business fails dramatically and it seems that Pankar will abandon Radix. But he is deep in her thrall.

In "A Man of Mystery", Grant Street could easily be replaced with the name of half-a-dozen St James streets. It is in the process of being commercialised and gentrified, but retains its communal character.

> Grant Street lived an outdoor, communal life. Privacy was unknown and if anyone had demanded it he would have been laughed at. [...] The constant lack of privacy had led ultimately to a kind of fuzziness with regard to private property. No one was sure, or could be sure, what belonged to whom or who belonged to whom. When this involved material objects, like bicycles, there would be a fight. When it involved children, more numerous on Grant Street than bicycles, there was a feckless tolerance of the inevitable doubts about paternity.[7]

In the story, shoemaker Mr. Green, described as spectacularly black, is taunted for dressing in a cork hat and starched white tropical suit while taking the neighbourhood children for walks: "Make way for the Governor, everybody make way for the Governor."[8] His jaunts from Grant Street lead him to the Queen's Park Savannah, the Zoo, the Botanical Gardens. The Greens, in some ways are different from their neighbours. Apart from the tropical suit, Mr Green's wife paints – ships in stormy seas – and is often seen carrying books. But in many ways, they are the same.

> [T]he Greens did come to have one thing in common with their neighbours: they shared their unchanging way of life. In that life, no one ever got richer or poorer; there were no dramatic successes or, for that matter, dramatic failures; no one was ever in serious trouble. Basically, they were cowards. Now and again Grant Street spawned a prodigy, a policeman for instance, but that was considered an aberration and did not happen often.[9]

This is a caricature of St James, to be sure. But as Vidia said of the biographical elements of *A House for Mr Biswas*, whose protagonist, Mohun Biswas, is heroic and pitiful as he strives for a house of his own: "It's not a portrait. Fiction is one thing and real life is another. My father is a much more serious man than the novel makes out. To make him a very serious man, in this novel, it would not have worked." In other words, characters have been altered for dramatic effect.

Shiva's and Vidia's mother, Droapatie, has her own St James. She was one of seven sisters and two brothers of the Capildeo clan. She had come from the Lion House of Chaguanas (Hanuman House in Arwacas in the novel). For Droapatie the move to St James involved the greatest change of circumstance, away from the emotional and family support of her sisters. Her St James revolved around the home, where her three-burner stove and wash tub reside. One of her daughters says that she loved J'Ouvert, and would be out on the road every Carnival Monday morning at four a.m. But it was the Ethel Street Hindu temple that was her main domain.

Listed among the founding members, Droapatie's contributions, a shilling here, a few cents there, helped build the impressive structure that took shape in 1962.

Before that, Hindus had prayed at home or in a tiny kootiah, no more than a hut really, near the very same site.

There were big names among the temple donors – multi-millionaire Port of Spain businessman Jang Bahadoorsingh; Droapatie's brother, attorney Simbhoonath Capildeo; Bhadase Sagan Maraj of the Maha Sabha – but the mandir's construction was driven by the working class Hindus of the community.

Imagine a Sunday morning puja, an offering of sweet-smelling smoke rising from the hawan bowl as flames devour the ghee and guggul-sap. The younger temple-goers show the older women respect for their seniority and knowledge of the rituals; they are referred to as *mausis*, or aunts. Droapatie Naipaul is *Bhola Mausi*, a light scarf draped over her head as she performs her aarti. She is remembered as being there every Sunday from 1962 until her passing in 1991.

Inside the dome of the mandir   A marble murti imported from India

The temple expanded around her, with marble murtis imported from India and a congregation drawn from well beyond St James. "People used to come in abundance because this was the flagship of the Caribbean," says Ralph Lakhan – a member of the Lakhan family, as instrumental as any in the temple's establishment and upkeep. "There were fewer temples then." In the late 1970s, the temple was expanded and smaller mandirs were built towards the back – to Kali, Shiva, Hanuman and Rama. Once again, Shiva and Vidia's uncle, Simbhoonath Capildeo, was a major donor. His wife and then his daughter-in-law, Shakti Capildeo, now manage the temple affairs.

Droapatie's temple is a truly Trinidadian structure.

The original mandir was designed by a British expat, architect John Newel-Lewis.

The smaller temples were designed by Chinese Trinidadian, John Yip Young; and it was built by a Muslim contractor named Shaffeek Shah. Afro-Trinidadian masman and copper sculptor Ken Morris made Hanuman's mace, which tops Hanuman's temple, and Kali's sword, which tops hers.

And then there is Vidia, raised in the faith but an atheist himself. His knowledge of Hinduism originates from his mother and her extended family. It is best displayed in his short story "My Aunt Gold Teeth", where the narrator is effortlessly specific about the objects of ritual required for the healing of Gold Teeth's sick husband: a brass jar of fresh water, a mango leaf, a plate full of burning charcoal. Gold Teeth, of course, actually existed; she was a family friend. Her death is recounted to Vido in a letter from Pa, written from the Nepaul Street house. "Gold Teeth Nanie died last Sunday night at the Colonial Hospital and was buried the following day."[10] Whether she was indeed an addict of Christianity as described in the story, who brings misfortune on herself by adding Christian charms to her arsenal of Hindu icons, I cannot say. Nor can I confirm that she had sixteen gold teeth as related in Vidia's story.

As much as Vidia was happier close to the metropolis and did not often long for "insipid" Trinidad, he did have moments of yearning for the familiarities of home. In the collection of letters *Between Father and Son*, on 7 March 1952, he writes: "I feel nostalgic for home. Do you know what I long for? I long for the nights that fall blackly, suddenly without warning. I long for a violent shower of rain at night. I long to hear the tinny tattoo of heavy raindrops on a roof, or the drops of rain on the broad leaves of that wonderful plant, the wild tannia. But in short I long for home, or perhaps, the homely atmosphere. And I miss my bicycle rides, and the sea, and the pit at Rialto, and the sort of cigarettes I used to smoke, to everyone's scandal."[11]

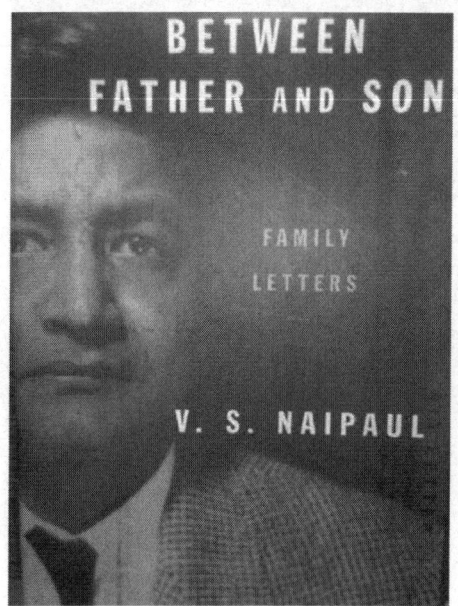

He would ride from St James to Point Cumana to swim, in what was likely a solitary endeavour. A year later, on a glorious Saturday evening at an Oxford library, he remembers distinctly "the road home, the Oval and all the signs and the Oval Café and those Chinese shops and the Police Barracks and The Post Office." Plot the route: In his memory, he is riding East to West, from QRC to Nepaul Street. "Every thing", he writes, "is absolutely clear in my mind."[12]

Seepersad's St James is, again, the home of an observer. But he also knew much of the rest of the country through his time at the *Trinidad Guardian*. He writes to Vido from Nepaul Street, plotting their correspondence, already well aware of his son's immense talent and the possibility that their letters might, one day, be assembled as a book. "My letters then would not

be just preachings," he says, "but descriptions of people and incidents in these parts... A katha, a Bhagavad, a calypso night, a shango; a chat with Baboolal, a chat with Rapooche." Vido is introduced in this way to every tradition through their correspondence.

"Today was Hosey. Everybody went to see the things, except me. But I did have a look from upstairs, and as the tadjiahs were passing the Rialto, I went across and took two snaps of hoseys and the moon."[13]

Seepersad lives among a welter of religions and races – Shango, Hosay, Muslims, Christians, Chinese, Portuguese – but his exposure does not relieve him of prejudice. Two cousins, Deo and Phoolo, are living in his house with his daughters. He fears that their "lamentable perversity" may rub off.[14] "These girls have become so ultra-modern that they make no distinction between Negroes, Mussulmans or any other people. Deo says, without the semblance of a blush, there's nothing bad or ugly in a Hindu girl marrying a Negro boy. Her actual words: 'What does it matter as long as you can be happy?' As to Muslims: 'Why, they are only human.'"[15] Vidia agrees that it's a sad state of affairs, and then goes and marries a white woman.

But within his house, now a home, Seepersad/Biswas is content. Free of the Capildeos (aka Tulsis), he is man and boss. There is space and privacy. Around him, there is a community, sometimes alien, often intriguing. To some extent, as Ken Ramchand notes, the move from the country to the town is an evolution of Indians to

Trinidadians, through the process of becoming more exposed to the rest of society. It was so for Shiva, a Town Boy through and through.

Returning home from hospital after his heart attack not long before he died in 1953, Seepersad Naipaul wrote of his domestic bliss: "[W]hat a neat little home we have in 26. I had never seen it in this way before. The girls are to be commended for this, though they are rather quite apathetic in other ways."[16]

The Naipaul House and the lives it contained are quintessential parts of our St James – cheek by jowl we live and our relations are generally cordial, despite the dark recesses of some of our petty biases.

Endnotes

1. Shiva Naipaul, "Beauty Contest" in *A Man of Mystery and Other Stories* (London: Penguin, 1995), 1.
2. Shiva Naipaul, "Beauty Contest", 2.
3. "The Beauty Contest", 2.
4. "The Beauty Contest", 1.
5. "The Beauty Contest", 5.
6. "The Beauty Contest", 10.
7. Shiva Naipaul, "A Man of Mystery", in *A Man of Mystery and Other Stories* (London: Penguin, 1995), 12.
8. Shiva Naipaul, "A Man of Mystery", 15.
9. "A Man of Mystery", 16-7.
10. V.S. Naipaul, *Letters Between a Father and a Son*, ed. Gillon Aitken (London: Abacus, 1999), 113.
11. V.S. Naipaul, *Letters Between a Father and Son* [1999], (London: Abacus, 1999), 174.
12. V.S. Naipaul, *Letters* [1999], 43.
13. V.S. Naipaul, *Letters* [1999], 31. (katha corrected from Kamla, and Bhagavad from Bhagwat in 2009 edition).
14. V.S. Naipaul, *Letters* [1999], 135.
15. V.S. Naipaul, *Letters* [1999], 134.
16. V.S. Naipaul, *Letters* [1999], 247.

8: STRANGERS IN THE HOUSE: CINEMA, SEXUALITY AND POLITICS IN V.S. NAIPAUL'S "TELL ME WHO TO KILL"

ANDRE BAGOO

> In the afternoon, I had my favourite drug – the cinema.
> – V.S. Naipaul, letter to Kamla Naipaul, September 6, 1949

V.S. Naipaul's short-story, "Tell Me Who to Kill", can be viewed as classic film noir. Its references to popular American cinema of the 1930s, 1940s and 1950s are not decorative. In addition to setting the mood by generating suspense, they embody central themes. Film references in this story serve to deepen our understanding of the main character. They reflect anxiety about sexuality, national identity and freedom in a world grappling with globalisation. If a dead body must appear in a film noir, Naipaul produces one for us. The narrator roams the pages of this story, walking like a zombie in the realm of the undead, becoming the author's melancholy commentary on the nature of our world. He is at once the villain, the *femme fatale* and the innocent hero.

"Tell Me Who to Kill" appears in Naipaul's 1971 book, *In a Free State*. The book is a "sequence" of short pieces. There is a prologue, two short stories, a novella set in a fictional African state, and an epilogue. Whether this adds up to a novel is debatable: the parts are not overtly linked, though they share similar themes. Nevertheless, the uncertainty over the work's form mirrors the author's ambivalence to the idea of freedom – in a national and personal sense – an ambivalence that seems to be the subject at the heart of so much of Naipaul's work.

References to films from the 1930s to the 1950s are the dominant motif of the forty-four-page story. The protagonist alludes to Alfred Hitchcock's *Rebecca* (1940), *Rope* (1948) and *Strangers on a Train* (1951). There are also references to *Waterloo Bridge*, a 1940 film directed by Mervyn LeRoy starring Vivien Leigh and Robert Taylor, and *Jesse James*, a 1939 western with Henry Fonda. On the one hand, these references give us a sense of time, of the period the characters inhabit. Naipaul wrote *In a Free State* between August 1969 and October 1970 and therefore the protagonist's references to films of decades past may hint that he is out of place, at odds with contemporaneous events: left behind in a realm of escape and fantasy. Because there are no overt markers of the period in which the story's action is meant to be set, and because the time span of the films is so wide, the effect is of time's suspension. The main character's life is half-lived, the world has frozen. But Naipaul's choice of films, I will argue, goes further. The movie allusions clearly allow us to understand the character's points of reference and even educational background. Additionally, each also plays a specific role in the narrative, stemming from the plot and the issues that arise.

"Tell Me Who to Kill" is, at its most basic level, a film noir centred on a wedding story. Set in England, the filmic journey follows an unnamed protagonist who has migrated from Trinidad to support his brother, Dayo, who is pursuing further education. After years of struggle, Dayo is getting married, and the narrator is journeying to the wedding ceremony in the company of a male companion, named Frank. It is clear that the main character struggles with life as an immigrant in England. His life is defined by the limits of race and class, as well as the fact that he is a product of colonialism who has come to the colonial motherland and found it not quite as motherly as he has imagined. He tells us of his ambition to defy the expectations of his East Indian family in Trinidad, to fund his brother's education and to become someone with money and power. But all of his plans come to nought. They are sabotaged by his own poor decision-making (he invests his life savings recklessly); his depressed mental state; as well as external forces. In one instance, a group of white thugs attacks the business-place he opens with his life savings. The story's central character relies on the idea of the abstract freedom of the individual to make a way in the world, but he finds that the world is more complex, more forbidding and more at odds with his dreams. He is cut down almost completely, at one stage exasperatedly saying, "[N]ow the dead man is me".[1]

All of the film references serve to enforce an atmosphere of dread and unhappiness and to build suspense. Consider the first mention of a film; it helps us build a psychological profile of the narrator:

> And it is as though you are frightened of something it is bound to come, as though because you are carrying danger with you danger is bound to come. And again it is like a dream. I see myself in this old English house, like something in *Rebecca* starring Laurence Oliver and Joan Fountain. It is an upstairs room with a lot of jalousies and fretwork. No weather. I am there with my brother, and we are strangers in the house.[2]

The doom and gloom of Hitchcock's movie is easy to imagine transposed onto the narrator's life or at least his sense of his life. The film version of Daphne du Maurier's novel *Rebecca* is a love story which follows a woman who marries a man, only to find out that she will always be in the shadow of his first wife who died in mysterious circumstances.

The reference to fretwork and jalousies is a refraction of the gingerbread houses of Trinidad from which the narrator originates. Importantly, *Rebecca* is a black and white film featuring many twists and turns and sinister elements which conspire to deceive and smother the woman. The sense of unseen danger, of helplessness, may be transposed to Naipaul's protagonist. Houses are always important symbols, particularly from the author of *A House for Mr Biswas*, but the line, "we are strangers in the house"[3] echoes the title of another suspenseful Hitchcock film, *Strangers on a Train* (1951), where two men plot murder. The narrator does not spell Laurence Olivier and Joan Fountaine correctly, in a possible indication that his points of reference are somewhat casually stored in his memory; he is not concerned with specific details of film production, but rather their more immediate aspects such as plot outlines and striking images. Here is an everyday man. It is also important that *Rebecca* is set in England – a Hollywood rendition of what is English, a detail which we shall see is key in understanding how films may have served the narrator as a preliminary form of travel away from Trinidad.

Another early film reference shows how the protagonist has used movies to map London's urban landscape. His vision of what the city is supposed to look like has come partially from *Waterloo Bridge*, named after the famous bridge off the Strand:

> I used to have a vision of a big city. It wasn't like this, not streets like this. I used to see a pretty park with high black iron railings like spears, old thick trees growing out of the wide pavement, rain falling the way it fall over Robert Taylor in *Waterloo Bridge*, and the pavement covered with flat leaves of a perfect shape in pretty colours, gold and red and crimson.[4]

Waterloo Bridge is a black and white film about a ballerina – played by Leigh – who falls in love with a man and sacrifices her job for him. But he goes off to war, dies. She turns to prostitution to make a living. But then it turns out that he has not died; he returns and is revealed to be wealthy and wants to marry her. She feels she cannot do so given her past life as a prostitute. In the film's climax, she kills herself on Waterloo Bridge by throwing herself into oncoming traffic. This bleak world where love and free will are trumped by fate is precisely the same world in which Naipaul's story operates. Because the film is black and white, the narrator's impression of a pavement with leaves, "in pretty colours",[5] demonstrates a misremembering and a tendency for over-idealisation. More generally, however, we wonder if the narrator's story will follow a similar tragic trajectory as he journeys to the wedding.

All of the films are suspenseful, they often feature characters in love or with secrets or both, and these secrets in different ways threaten to engulf and destroy them. This is true of *Jesse James*, and, very true of *Rope*, which of all the films is the one which most appears in this short story. In an extended fantasy sequence, the narrator imagines something tragic happening, something which must be concealed and covered up by him and by his beloved, his brother, Dayo. As with most Hitchcock films, this tragic incident appears to come out of nowhere or embroils an ordinary person who must move from a banal situation into one of extraordinary peril. In a dream sequence, the narrator takes us to a place somewhere proximate to the house in *Rebecca* and tells us "a quarrel, a friendly argument, a scuffle"[6] involving a friend of Dayo results in a murder. The details are only telegraphed, we learn that the boys "are only playing, but the knife go in the boy, easy."[7] The narrator says:

> And the body is in the house, in a chest, like in *Rope* with Fairley Granger. It is there at the beginning, it is there forever, and everything else is only like a mockery. But we eat. My brother is trembling; he is not a good actor. The people we are eating with, I can't see their faces, I don't know what they look like.[8]

The second *Rope* reference occurs at page 95, with the reappearance of "Fairley Granger" – or Farley Granger – whose hairstyle is compared to Dayo's. Then the imagined encounter with the friend of Dayo – now described as a college friend – recurs and again death comes. Again when a penetrating knife goes in, "it is an accident" and, "The body is in the chest, like in *Rope*, but in this English house."[9] The entire story ends, in film-reel fashion, with a panoramic sweep of several images that have dotted the narrative and a fourth and final reference to *Rope*:

> I have my own place to go back to. Frank will take me there when this is over. And now that my brother leave me for good I forget his face already, and I only seeing the rain and the house and the mud, the field at the back with the para-grass bending down with the rain, the donkey and the smoke from the kitchen, my father in the gallery and my brother in the room on the floor and that boy opening his mouth to scream, like in *Rope*.[10]

The male protagonist's relationship with Frank is key. Near the story's climax, when both men must present a public face to the world in a church setting, we get a clearer idea of the dynamic between them:

> Frank touch me on the arm. I am glad he touch me, but I shrug his hand away. I know it isn't true, but I tell myself he is on the other side, with the others, looking at me without looking at me. I know it isn't true about Frank because, look, he too is nervous. He want to be alone with me; he don't like being with his own people. It isn't like being on a bus or in a café, where he can be like a man saying: I protect this man with me.[11]

Earlier, at the start of the story, Frank is described thus: "Tall, thin, going a little bald. But happy. Happy to be with me, happy when people look at us and see that he is with me. He is a good man, he is my friend".[12] This is not quite a bromance: it seems more intense than that. Yet, we need not determine the question of whether both characters are gay. At the very least their relationship is a homosocial one. It challenges heterosexual notions of the limits of interactions between persons of the same sex. That challenge, I argue, is a central political aspect of this story, running parallel with other themes of identity. It is why the references to *Rope* are repeated so often.

Rope was loosely based on a play which had been inspired by the real-life murder of 14-year old Bobby Frank in 1924 by University of Chicago students Nathan Leopold and Richard Loeb, who shared a homosexual relationship. The film – which opens with a victim being strangled – arguably contains coded references to homosexuality and the criminal enterprise it covers may work on a metaphorical level as a reference to the committing of forbidden sexual acts. Sex, love and marginal identity conflate, and are rendered, in a manner reflecting taboos of the time, as crime. Something of the muted, coded nature of *Rope* hangs over "Tell Me Who to Kill". The intensity of the unnamed male narrator's devotion to his brother, as well as the intensity of his work ethic, his apparent sacrifice of all things sexual as he tries to live life as a migrant, reflects his half-dead status. But there is one moment in the text when sexual realities irrupt. One day, growing resentful of Dayo – who has simply been drifting from course to course – the narrator has another dream.

> I wake up early one morning with a wet-dream. It was the second wet-dream I had; the first happen when I was a boy. It leave me exhausted and dirty and ashamed. I want to go to Dayo and beg him to forgive me, because this, the thing that just happen to me, is something I never did think about for him. I feel I let him down, that I betray him in my heart, and I feel I would like to go to him and make up and talk as in the old days. I feel I must show him that I always love him.[13]

What is happening here? This incident comes after the narrator repeatedly describes Dayo as beautiful. Is there a sexual aspect to their relationship? There isn't much to explicitly support that. But what is clear is that we are dealing with a eunuch-like ascetic. The narrator's entire sexual life seems suspended. It does not conform to mainstream, heteronormative dictates. This submergence is a reflection of the intensity of all the forces acting upon him. Though the wet-dream catches him by surprise, it makes sense, as he has suppressed and sacrificed so much, including sexual impulses, to embark on the journey he has made.

Just as he seeks to transgress boundaries of all forms – national, race, class – there is a coded, unspoken, and all-powerful line which he seeks to cross, but cannot speak of. The presence of Frank, and the narrator's specific references to films, however, tell us the tale that is not being told by the unreliable first-person narrator. That the story ends at a wedding is important. The two male characters are not at ease in this public assertion of heterosexual norms as represented by the marriage of Dayo to his bride. This wedding is more like a funeral, as the narrator says, and it features a character who might as well be the fugitive at the wedding, also featured in *Jesse James*.

It is useful to picture what might have been foremost in Naipaul's mind during the composition of "Tell Me Who to Kill". In his biography of V.S. Naipaul, *The World is What it Is*, Patrick French gives us a glimpse of Naipaul's life during the period of composition of *In a Free State*, the book that contains this story. During this period, Naipaul interviews the gay artist David Hockney and writes an essay for the *Telegraph Magazine*. It is a piece Naipaul has never had reprinted in his numerous collections of journalism. According to French, "a sensual undercurrent runs through the article". Says the biographer:

> In his writing, Vidia would almost always describe men in greater physical detail than women. He was ever captivated by the beauty of the male body, but the idea of sex between men, and in particular anal sex, frightened and fascinated him. His reaction to Hockney's visitors appears to have been less a direct sexual attraction than a sense of excitement at the proximity of sex, and an awareness that he was attractive to gay men.[14]

French asserts that in the novel *Magic Seeds*, Naipaul tries to address or explain his own impulses through the fictional character of Roger who says:

> The idea of sex with a woman, exposing myself to that kind of intimacy, was distasteful to me. Some people insist that if you're not one thing you're the other. They believe that I'm interested in men. The opposite is true. The fact is all sexual intimacy is distasteful to me. I've always considered my low sexual energy as a kind of freedom.[15]

Gay characters – whether implied or otherwise – are not unusual in Naipaul's work. The novella at the heart of *In a Free State* contains a clearly gay character, though that character's attitude to his sexuality is less clear. Gay characters also appear in *Guerillas*, *A Way in the World*, and in *The Enigma of Arrival*. Many of the strands of "Tell Me Who to Kill", including its homoeroticism, are taken up and amplified in *The Enigma of Arrival*. That novel features a mysterious landlord with whom the protagonist is obsessed, yet whom we see only twice. The landlord writes homoerotic poetry and sends it to his tenant. There is also another character, Alan, who is presumably gay, who visits the premises of the landlord often, though his relationship with the landlord, who is ailing, is not spelled out.

We are not here concerned with the politics of V.S. Naipaul's sexuality. Rather, what I would like to point out is the fact that we are dealing with a writer who – despite once dismissing the novelist E.M. Forster as a "nasty homosexual" – is very much aware of gay issues, who peoples his work with gay figures and who creates complex characters who – whatever sexuality we may wish to ascribe to them – are at odds with narrow notions of heteronormative life. "Tell Me Who To Kill" fits this bill, with a main character who is marginal in every possible way, including in terms of sexuality.

In some respects, Naipaul's novel *The Enigma of Arrival*, which was published sixteen years after *In a Free State*, takes up key elements of "Tell Me Who to Kill" and elaborates on them. It is typical Naipaul, taking autobiographical elements and infusing them with fiction. There is a moment in it when the narrator – a writer who resembles Naipaul – looks back at the composition of an earlier book which may very well be *In a Free State*. The enigmatic narrator – who, like the protagonist of "Tell Me Who to Kill" is also unnamed – discusses the writing of a book with "a story set in an African country, once a colony, with white and Asian settlers, and now independent… the story of a day-long journey made by car by two white people."[16] Just as the central character in "Tell Me Who to Kill" migrates to England on a ship called the *Colombie*, the protagonist of *Enigma* travels to England on the *SS Columbia*. The *Enigma of Arrival* contains much discussion on the role of American popular films on the protagonist's life, a discussion which I feel illuminates the earlier short story:

> I lived imaginatively in the cinema, a foretaste of that life abroad. On Saturday afternoons, after the special holiday shows which began at one-thirty (and which we simply called 'one-thirty' rather in the way other people might speak of matinees), it was painful, after the dark cinema and the remote realms where one had been living for three hours or so, to come out into the very bright colours of one's own world.[17]

Later, after moving to England and experiencing life there, things change.

> I had thought of the cinema pleasure as a foretaste of my adult life. Now, with all kinds of shame in many recesses of my mind, I felt it to be fantasy… And when, ten or twelve years later, I did return to the cinema, the Hollywood I had known was dead, the extraordinary circumstances in which it had flourished no longer existing; American films had become as self-regardingly local as the French or English; and there was as much distance between a film and me as between a book of painting and me. Fantasy was no longer possible. I went to the cinema not as a dreamer or a fantast but as a critic.[18]

The openings of both works are even echoes of each other. "Tell Me Who To Kill" starts with a memorable description of a landscape dominated by rain:

> Just like my brother. He choose a bad morning to get married. Cold and wet, the little country parts between towns white rather than green, mist falling like rain, fields soaking, sometimes a cow standing up just like that. The little streams have a dirty milky colour and some of them

are full of empty tins and other rubbish. Water everywhere, just like back home after a heavy shower in the rainy season, only the sky is not showing in the places where the water collect, and the sun is not coming out to heat up everything and steam dry it fast.[19]

The narrator seeks to describe the English landscape, and is pulled, almost inexorably, back to the landscape of his home by way of comparison. Though Trinidad is never explicitly mentioned in the story, some evidence in the text supports the idea that this is the narrator's home: there is the particular dialect deployed, certain descriptions of rainfall and seasons, descriptions of vegetation and the descriptions of social and cultural dynamics of an English-speaking East Indian community. But the lack of any mention, the overt erasure of Trinidad from the text to the extent that plausible arguments for Guyana and perhaps parts of India may be made, demonstrates how this narrator has sought to erase his past because it is too painful.

In opening of *The Enigma of Arrival*, the same rainy English landscape is almost discovered afresh, and rendered more positively in a work where characters are somewhat more specific about their origins:

> For the first four days it rained. I could hardly see where I was. Then it stopped raining and beyond the lawn and outbuildings in front of my cottage I saw fields with stripped trees on the boundaries of each field; and far away, depending on the light, glints of a little river, glints which sometimes appeared, oddly, to be above the level of the land...
> The river was called the Avon; not the one connected with Shakespeare. Later – when the land had more meaning, when it had absorbed more of my life than the tropical street where I had grown up – I was able to think of the flat wet fields with the ditches as 'water meadows'.[20]

The land is re-christened, things are seen from a new perspective. That said, the two characters in these separate pieces share the same sensibilities. One is arguably an older, more articulate version of the other. The language of the earlier story is standard English yet unmistakably Trinidad dialect (the very title of the story hints at this, being "Tell Me Who to Kill" and not "Tell Me Whom to Kill"). In *The Enigma of Arrival*, the second character's language is different; he is more formal, more articulate about things like cinema and his references have a self-consciousness absent from the earlier character. If the story's narrator is a younger, rougher version of the novel's character, then the way film functions in the story is more innocent, meant to evoke an almost visceral response from the reader, and has even more psychological import because of this rawness. Film references are also used elsewhere in Naipaul, characters in *Miguel Street* emulate film heroes; "A Flag on the Island" was meant to be a "fantasy for the silver screen". But in this short story the intensity and focus on movies marks it as unique. Properly understood, it is an intersemiotic work: a mood poem embracing film and text. Its hybrid nature mirrors the complexity of the modern individual who crosses boundaries, whether of nationality, race, class, or sexuality. It is a story of brothers, fathers, lovers and villains; a mystery with an unstated trauma at its heart, awaiting its sequel.

Endnotes

1. V.S. Naipaul, "Tell Me Who to Kill", in *In a Free State* (London: Andre Deutsch, 1971), 63-108, 77.
2. V.S. Naipaul, "Tell Me Who to Kill", 68.
3. V.S. Naipaul, "Tell Me Who to Kill", 68.
4. "Tell Me Who to Kill", 77.
5. Ibid, 78.
6. Ibid, 68.
7. Ibid, 68.
8. Ibid, 68-9.
9. Ibid, 102.
10. Ibid, 107-8.
11. Ibid, 104-5.
12. Ibid, 65.
13. Ibid, 95.
14. Patrick French, *The World Is What It Is: The Authorised Biography of V.S. Naipaul* (London: Picador, 2008), 287.
15. French, 287-88.
16. V.S. Naipaul, *The Enigma of Arrival* (London: Viking, 93), 93.
17. V.S. Naipaul, *The Enigma of Arrival*, 108.
18. V.S. Naipaul, *The Enigma of Arrival*, 124.
19. V.S. Naipaul, "Tell Me Who to Kill", 65.
20. V.S. Naipaul, *The Enigma of Arrival*, 11.

9: SHASTRI MAHARAJ: A GRAIN OF MUSTARD

J. VIJAY MAHARAJ

The twelve paintings by Trinidadian artist, Shastri Maharaj, presented in this essay have been selected from the fifty presented to an audience in Chaguanas after a tour of the Lion House, etched in memory through its fictionalisation as Hanuman House in *A House for Mr Biswas*. Maharaj began with the painting entitled *Fyzabad* and spoke about its representation of the rural location up to today of the descendants of the indentured labourer from India, and of the odd combination of poverty and richness in the lives they live in this setting. As the Naipauls did in words, for these areas like Chaguanas and Fyzabad beyond the Caroni Bridge and Mosquito Creek, so did Maharaj in paint.

Fyzabad

Maharaj pointed out that just as Chaguanas was to the sugar belt so is Fyzabad to the oil belt and both to the economic well-being of the nation. The major oilfields of Fyzabad were established in 1919 soon after indentureship ended, although new wells continue to be drilled in the area. Reminiscent of the pre-indentureship past, it recalls the city of Faizabad on the banks of the Sarayu in the municipality of Ayodha in the state of Uttar Pradesh in India from which many of the indentured came. But it is also representative of the industrial expansion that brought them here and their desire to exceed its capital machinery by retaining reminders of the past, signified strongly not just in the title but in the jhandis or puja flags foregrounded in the painting, the harmoniousness of the buildings with their environment and the absence of any value for the oil which makes the place commercially viable. The closeness of one of the buildings to the road and its suggestion of movement beyond Fyzabad is however a statement on the necessary focus on the future of the absent residents of this rural idyll. Its necessity is apparent in the removal of the idyllic frame in paintings like the one entitled *Cane*.

Cane

Maharaj's engagement with things pertaining to Indo-Caribbean lives has given him, as has happened with the Naipaul family, a reputation for ethnic parochialism and narrow-minded ethnic interest. Maharaj himself has persistently objected to this. He has said: "For three months from 20th October 2011 to 19th January 2012, I travelled through India, and finding or discovering my roots and ancestry was never on the agenda. It was reassuring to know that I was outside of that loop of people that were eager to meet with their ancestry. All of India was my ancestry."[1] For the members of the audience familiar with them, academic evaluations of his work may have made this a moot point in this particular setting.

Leon Wainwright, for example, in "Indian Art' in Trinidad?: Ethnicity at its Limits", discusses his work in terms of a diasporic Indian art but finds it also evocative of the artist's negotiation with nationhood and visual imaging.[2] Wainwright notes the conflict this location brings to the artist seeking personal, perceptual and aesthetic autonomy. Maharaj recognises however that autonomy is dependent on interpersonal relationships and many of his paintings attempt to capture the camaraderie of inter-racial and inter-ethnic relations in Trinidad and Tobago as the following painting, entitled *Neighbours*, illustrates.

Neighbours

This painting evokes a spiritual atmosphere encompassing the encounter with the other. Frequently sounding like Wilson Harris insisting that it is his "deeply considered" opinion that the "ground of accommodation" is an "art of creative co-existence… pointing away from apartheid and ghetto fixations and is of utmost importance and *native* to the Caribbean",[3] the artist talked about his paintings that touched on this theme in exactly these terms, albeit in a significantly different way. This is reflective of a common view among Indo-Caribbeans that the journey to the New World and the acceptance of unity in diversity were fated. Maharaj has, however, addressed a similar theme in other paintings he has done, that speak less to spirituality than to the violence of the labour system in which the multiracial, multicultural encounter occurred, as for example in *The Meeting* and *Conversation*.

The Meeting

Conversation

Maharaj's entanglement of life, religion and labour is of course also evident in the poetry presented by Raymond Ramcharitar reproduced in Chapter 12. Like Ramcharitar, and the Naipauls before him, Maharaj also draws upon the mental landscape and language of the gods which he inherited, thus rendering their works unique kinds of memory projects, or postmemory, as Marianne Hirsch would have it.[4] But in many of the paintings in which he does this, he does the reverse of what he did in *Neighbours*. In *Ritual* for example he uses the iconography of Hinduism and mixes it with that of the Shouter and Spiritual Baptist religions and renders the worshipper's ethnicity and race deliberately ambiguous. In *Surrender*, on the other hand, there is even less to specify race, class, ethnicity or other sociological categories of personhood. There is only the suggestion of the idea that out of diversity and commercial greed, there must be an eventual surrender to something larger and

Ritual

more encompassing. In terms of contrasting colours and contrasting ideas, no painting in the presentation matched this one for its vivid depiction of the chaos and divergences of our co-existence.

Surrender

This decided turn towards abstraction in Maharaj's work has been discussed by many. Bernadette Persaud, for instance, on whose work his may be seen as having an impact, or with whose work his own shares many similarities, has pointed this out. This was particularly noted at the conference in relation to the greater power and control over the range of the colour canvas that he begins to employ and in the fact that, like Wasily Kandinsky, aka Vasily Vasilyevich, he can be pinned down to no particular style or school. Persaud has stated: "The art of Shastri Maharaj speaks to…the human condition: a condition inscribed with the contradictions of Time and the enigma of transcendent Time".[5] There is certainly evidence for this in paintings such as *Within Maya* and *Tenement Yard*.

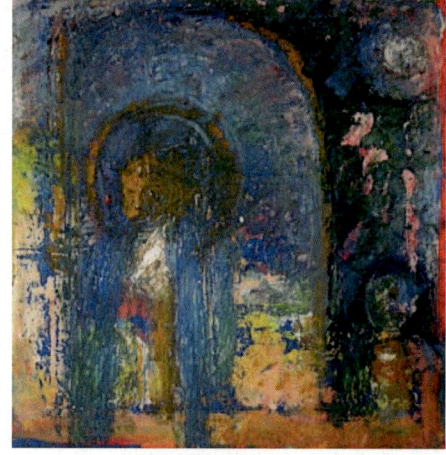

Within Maya

Tenement Yard

Patrick Colm Hogan argues that there "are considerable continuities between verbal narrative and representational painting" and "narratological discourse analysis" can be performed on paintings in order to reveal interesting cultural insights, when "theoretical issues [such] as what an implied painter may be and what relation the implied painter may have to a narrator in painting" are addressed.[6] The theoretical issues addressed at the conference exceeded these and set up a continuation of the narratives shared at the conference as well as those written by the Naipaul men into the real world. Perhaps in the context of the conference it was not surprising that many in the audience also saw in Maharaj's work evocations of the world of *A House for Mr Biswas*. The calf that killed Raghu took on

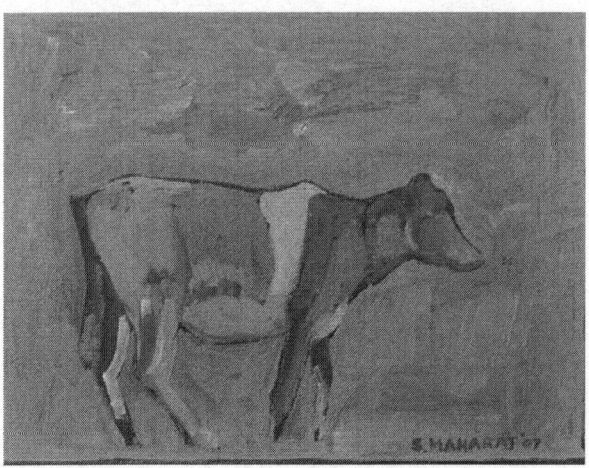

Blue Cow

uncanny connotations of the rolling calf of mythology in Maharaj's *Blue Cow*. The pastoral was perceived in, no surprise here, *Pasture* and the Tulsi sisters in *Four Women*.

Pasture

Four Women

As Maharaj pointed out the conference may indeed have been a grain of mustard of a similar type to the disembarkation from the *Fath-al-Razack*.

Endnotes

1. Shastri Maharaj quoted in Bernadette Persaud, "Shastri Maharaj: History, Myth and Beyond", in *The Arts Journal: Critical Perspectives on Contemporary Literature, History, Art and Culture of Guyana and the Caribbean* (Memory and Experience: 170 Years On) 4, no. 1-2 (2008): 91-111, p 106.
2. Leon Wainwright, "'Indian Art' in Trinidad?: Ethnicity at its Limits", *Journal of Creative Communications 2*, no. 1-2 (2007): 163-188.
3. Wilson Harris, "The Limbo Gateway", in *The Postcolonial Studies Reader*, ed. Bill Ashcroft, Gareth Griffiths and Helen Tiffin (Oxford: Routledge, 2006), 336-41, p. 338.
4. Marianne Hirsch "Projected Memory: Holocaust Photographs in Personal and Public Fantasy", in *Acts of Memory: Cultural Recall in the Present* ed Mieke Bal, Johnathan Crewe and Leo Spitzer. (Hanover: University Press of New England, 1999), 3 - 23.
5. Bernadette Persaud. "Shastri Maharaj: History, Myth and Beyond", in *The Arts Journal: Critical Perspectives on Contemporary Literature, history, Art and Culture of Guyana and the Caribbean* (Memory and Experience: 170 Years On) 4, no. 1-2 (2008): 91-111, p. 111.
6. Patrick Colm Hogan, *Narrative Discourse: Authors and Narrators in Literature, Film and Art* (Columbus: Ohio State University Press, 2013), 65.

10: GUERRILLAS AND "BUYING HORSES"

SHARON MILLAR

I was ten years old in 1975 when V.S. Naipaul's *Guerrillas* was published. In "Buying Horses", I knew what I wanted to explore. Why does one person inflict harm upon another person? How does one portray the gradations of anger, resentment, and power that turn people violent? I was concerned with unpacking binary notions of race, violence, and the female voice in the Caribbean. "Buying Horses" is the story of a foreign girl/woman who is killed by a Trinidadian man. In my early drafts, I leaned heavily into the things I remembered as a child. I was searching to find the best medium and form to contain the story under the story.

In many ways, *Guerrillas* represents the post-colonial anxiety that marked the mid-70s in the Caribbean. One of the main characters in that novel is a foreign white man, Roche. The barren, burning, semi post-apocalyptic landscape is implicitly Trinidad. How did this sit with me some forty years later? It sat – well – strangely. And it was in this *strangeness* that I found the space and the entry point for my own story. *Guerrillas* allowed me to interrogate the landscape and the characters almost a half century after independence. What does this mean exactly? It means that I knew versions of all the characters in *Guerrillas*. I even knew versions of the dry, burning landscape. But I felt, forty years on, that I could add different voices to this narrative and come to different conclusions, portray more complex and sympathetic female characters. I knew Jane in *Guerrillas* well. I'd met numerous incarnations of her over the course of a life. It seemed that the perception of the foreign female was key to the issues at the heart of my story. Based on this, I made very specific choices and I chose to name my places in "Buying Horses". I chose to name all my female characters except the English girl who remains, simply, the English girl. We see the English girl through Damiana's and Mannie's eyes and her cultural naiveté is evident. I wanted to be clear that she was putting herself in danger by making a series of assumptions about a society she thought was simplistic.

At the end of "Buying Horses", we are, I hope, sympathetic to the English girl who loses her life through a lack of understanding. Could this story have been written like this in 1975? I don't think so. But it can be written today. Perhaps in the early days of independence we did not yet know the intangibles that would bind us.

Ultimately "Buying Horses" is a dark story. But it is also a story of hope. Narrated by a young groom who observes the unravelling of an agricultural commune in the 1970s, the story was a way for me to take control of the lens. Is the dry, barren landscape inevitable? I chose to say no. After the death of the English girl, both the characters and the landscape endure.

Perhaps in forty years, someone else will write another aspect of this story. Because that is the way in which we use stories to come to know ourselves.

"BUYING HORSES"

Some nights, when Damiana is visiting Mannie, she entertains his family by mimicking the different people who live in the commune where she works. This makes Mannie feel as if he knows them all. Some nights, Damiana pretends to be the English girl. When she is in this mood, she paces up and down the room with small mincing steps and tossing her head. I am here to do the people's work, Damiana says in the English girl's voice. I am here to help the oppressed. Fat chance of her helping anyone, says Damiana, when she can't even keep her room clean and her man fed and cleaned. Doesn't seem to bother her that she's eating my food every day, but I suppose I not looking oppressed. Maybe when you Indian, oppression is different. And whoever heard of a commune with a maid?

The English girl lives next door to the main house with her black American lover who tells anyone who will listen to him that he is God. Or at least he thought he was God before he met Mr Kalam. Mr Kalam thinks he is Malcolm X and that trumps God. When Mrs Kalam hired Damiana she offered her more money to clean the foreigners' bungalow but Damiana had refused. Mannie thinks that Damiana must sense some danger and that's why she makes fun of them. Whenever he is around the commune, the air is dense with something that seems connected to the big car that Mr Kalam drives. It sits parked out in front of the house, a big white Holden Belmont with heavily tinted windows that make it impossible to see who is inside the car. Between the heavily dark windows of his car and the dark glasses that Mr Kalam wears, Mannie wonders how the man sees anything at all. Damiana works from 7.00 am to 3.00 pm. She helps Mrs Kalam wash clothes and hang them on the line next to the guava tree and she cooks lunch for the assorted people who pass through the house.

Even though Damiana has turned down the job to clean the foreigners' house, she ends up doing it anyway, she tells Mannie it is because she is sorry for the girl but Mannie knows it's because Mr Kalam has told her to do it. The English girl lies on her bed in the heat of the afternoon. She tells Damiana that this is the hour that she cannot bear. This is the hour that makes her long for soft English rain and pigeon-breast grey skies. She actually says that. Mannie's mother Benita sometimes listens in on Damiana's conversations and she tells them that the girl's yearning is triggered by her bedroom facing west and the bed that she shares with her black American lover lies in the beam of the vicious three o'clock sun. Never lie in a bed that faces west at three in the afternoon. These are the things the locals should tell foreigners when they arrive on the island. Otherwise, these are the things that will send them mad. At Mannie's home in Sangre Chiquito, all the bedrooms face east to catch the gentle rays of the morning sun. Along the western periphery leggy immortelles filter the afternoon heat. Soon the trees will be leafy and expansive with the rain, silky with new growth. The signs of the rain come in myriad ways. Benita has taught Mannie to listen to the way birds line their songs upon layers of humidity, to listen to the way they push their love-calls into the saturated air with urgency impossible to ignore. That poor girl, is all Benita will say. The English girl has not made many friends because of the way she has come to this place. When it is her turn to peel the eddoes and grate the tannia for the evening meal, the coarse skin of these vegetables makes her skin itch.

That morning a woman had come from Port of Spain to buy a horse at Mr Lee Ling's farm and Mannie was asked to put the pretty stallion with the chestnut coat and roan tail through its paces. The woman smokes a cigarette while she looks at the horse canter on a lead line. Mannie feels sorry for the English horse, sweating in the heat, steam fanning out around him in a large plumed circle. Mr Kalam stands next to the woman, speaking in an urgent voice and occasionally touching her arm. The villagers say Kalam lived in England for a long time and Mannie wonders if that is why his skin is palely sallow even though he has black hair, kinky and wild, that lifts off his head in excited clumps. Others say his mother was a small islander and his father was a white sailor. Most people in the village know him as a red man, nothing less, nothing more than a common-or-garden red man. See how stupid foreigners could be? Dotish! They look at a man like Kalam and think he's the real deal. But they said this with a kind of pride, with little inflated chests. Imagine, a local red man gone foreign and make his mark on the white people country. Like a dog would pee on your leg. Marking territory. That had to take real stones. Benita said people like Kalam were to be watched like you would watch a two-head snake, because is only a matter of time before he eat himself up. Don't watch him in his eye, Benita tells Mannie. He will hypnotise you and pull you in. Always keep your head down when you see that red man.

Kalam is speaking with the woman now, leaning on the fence and casually stretching his arm along the fencepost, flexing like a cat, his dark glasses glinting blindly. The woman looks briefly at him before turning back to the horse. The stallion is sweating dark patches into his coat, a light foam building between his back legs. The woman from Port of Spain calls out; can you put him through the paces again? She is a tall, dark-haired woman. Her skin is olive and her thick hair is held back with a wide floral bandanna. Her lips are carefully painted with a frosty pink lipstick and she is sweating lightly in the heat. The horse is breathing heavily when Mr Lee Ling gives the signal for Mannie to put the animal out to pasture.

Mannie can tell when Mr Lee Ling is showing off by his extravagant gestures. A little man with a face like a Volkswagen Beetle, Lee Ling's nose is lost in a protuberance of cheek that matches the two globes of his buttocks above little bowlegs. He is a man who would be prone to mockery were it not for the tiny motes of savagery that float in his eyes. Next to him, Kalam leans into the woman to say something and it is not long before they have climbed into the white Holden Belmont and driven away behind the black windows.

Arima in Trinidad is not a part of the world you would expect to see a white piano travelling in the back of a large truck, tethered with black cables that stand out against the smooth finish. The piano passes some of the grooms on the stud farm as they wait to cross the road and open the wooden gates of the stables. Soon the piano is gone, the little pebbles and dust kicked up in the wake of the truck settling on their skin. The sight of the disappearing piano followed by the white car disconcerts them for a moment before the entourage disappears around a bend like a mirage.

In the pasture behind the stables, Mannie releases the stallion, unclipping the halter from the lead line. This is Mr Lee Ling's thoroughbred stud, imported from England and carrying in his blood a champion line of proven winners. The stallion has not acclimatised well and has run sulkily, winning just one spectacular derby before lapsing into tropical lassitude. Now he runs to the centre of the pasture, kicking up clods of dense mud in his wake and Mannie wonders why the woman from Port of Spain said she had come to buy a horse but, instead, has driven off in the car with Kalam. Mannie lines up everything he knows about Kalam. He had begun collecting information in the random way of casual curiosity but the happenings of this house across the highway do not follow any familiar plot, or life, or imagined tale. Truth be told, it is the mix of white and black skin, the mix of mouths with their Trini talk butting English clip and American twang that has muddied the story. It is his feeling that even though Kalam talks constantly of the fate of the black man, he does not see the grooms or any other worker. He only sees Mr Lee Ling and others who come from Port of Spain and the black men who speak with American accents and the English white men who speak with their BBC voices. He only sees the people who can give him things.

Just last week, he brought a very famous man to the farm. In England the man is a very well known singer but here in Trinidad, he is simply a pale white man with wire-rimmed glasses. Imagine, Kalam had said to Mr Lee Ling. Look who reach. Just look who reach on your farm. Don't say I don't take you places chinee man! Mr Kalam is Mr Lee Ling's friend and Mannie often drives to the house with Mr Lee Ling to deliver bags of manure. Mr Lee Ling tells Mannie that the man is trying to teach the people who live with him how to plant things and how to start a farm so they can grow their own food; as if this is not something most villages do anyway. The people who come to the house are men who don't look like the men that Mannie knows – uncles, fathers or brothers; *these* other men come from Port of Spain and they wear town clothes not garden clothes. Mostly they sit in the front gallery and smoke cigarettes, nodding to Mannie as he drags the sacks of horseshit to the back of the house. Damiana tells Mannie that the men are not farmers they are activists. They still looking for people to actually plant, she tells Mannie.

"You saw the piano pass?"

Lee Ling raises his voice slightly on the word piano when Mannie comes back from the pasture. No. Mannie looks at him as if he is mad. A piano? What piano?

"Kalam singer friend send a white piano all the way from foreign for him." Lee Ling is swaying on his bowlegs in excitement. "Go quick, they need help unloading it by Kalam, they don't want it to mash up."

Damiana must have sent a message. She would have had Mrs Kalam telephone the stable for help when the truck with the piano pulled into the small street.

He recognises the man who comes to pick him up in Mrs Kalam's small silver sedan as one of the regulars from the commune, one of the followers. The drive takes them across the highway, along the long road with a line of red flamboyant trees in bloom. The house is the third on the left. From the main road, Mannie can see Damiana gesturing with her hands and directing the truck with the piano to back into the narrow driveway. The house is part of a new housing development. It's set back from the road, a square house with windows sliced by the angular burglar bars. The gallery faces the road and there are four fibreglass porch chairs with backs that spread up and out like the tails of peacocks. Someone has planted a row of periwinkles in front of the gallery, but half of them have withered and died.

Damiana says there have been young men lounging around her kitchen all morning but now they are nowhere to be found. Between the truck driver, Damiana and Mannie, they drag the piano through the front of the house. On his way in, Mannie sees the English girl looking out of the window of the bungalow next door. The bungalow is on the next lot over but there is no fence dividing the two properties. By the time the piano is in place, the rice on the stove has burned and Damiana must rush to the kitchen and put two more pounds of rice to soak. That night she will tell Mannie how Mr Kalam came back with the lady from Port of Spain and showed her the piano, sitting at the small bench and banging the keys so that the house filled with the afternoon heat and the rising sound of hysterical notes.

After they have moved the piano, the truck driver leaves and there is no one to drop Mannie back to the farm. The keys to Mrs Kalam's small sedan have been misplaced and the Holden Belmont has disappeared again. Damiana feeds him a good lunch of pelau and cole slaw made just how he likes it, with raisins stirred into the mayonnaise but still he must walk in the hot sun to get back to the farm.

No one has told him that the English girl can drive, though when she pulls to the side of the road she does it too quickly and Mannie has to step back as the car skids in the gravel at the side of the road before coming to a halt a few paces ahead of him. It is the silver car that belongs to Mrs Kalam. He tries not to look too surprised when she reaches over to unlock the passenger door and he climbs into the front seat. Her skin is very pale, her hands long and blue-veined on the steering wheel. She is a jerky driver, riding the clutch, the car bucking when she gears down suddenly from third to first on the highway. The car heaves and shudders and for a moment he wonders if she has broken the car.

"Where are you going?" She asks him without looking at him. He understands from this question that she wants him to take her somewhere, understands that she has pulled herself off her sun-struck bed and followed him deliberately.

Lee Ling will be angry if he does not return to the farm right away and he knows that he must never say that he has climbed into the car with the English girl who thinks that she loves a man who has brought her to the end of the earth. Where do you want to go? What else is he to say?

She is dressed in a pair of brown pants with yellow circles and a sleeveless bolero jacket. On her feet she wears a battered pair of Jesus slippers and her toes are painted a pale shade of pink. When she does not answer he asks her again. Where do you want to go?

He wants to feel flattered that she has followed him but he can see she is not interested in him. He's just the maid's boyfriend, the groom who brings the manure. He tries to imagine telling the story to Damiana later. He thinks how he will mimic the English girl, but he senses that there is something at stake between them, some term that he is at yet unaware of and unable to negotiate.

He has watched the woman with the other men at the commune. He has seen the way she walks freely among them, ignorant of their lust because she believes herself safe in the shadow of her American man. He has seen her engaged in conversation with one of the men, watched her lean in to make a point with the zeal of the converted. She does not take the cues from Mrs Kamal or Damiana that men must be treated in a certain way: managed and fed; talked around and herded. Instead she walks out onto the gallery in the middling light of early evening, when the men sit around with glasses of rum or scotch or puncheon, quietly smoking long untidy joints spitting with seeds; she walks into this scene and sits amongst them as if she, too, is one of them and can talk to them in reasonable tones. It is clear to Mannie that she is unable to smell the bladed heat that pulses off these men as they smoke and drink and watch her. At the heart of it, they all know it is the schism of *foreignness* that makes her behave in this way. Mannie understands that her man will praise her for her behaviour, believing that she is teaching the men something about equality. He has seen her pinch her skin and pull it until it turns an angry red. I am ashamed of it. I want to be like you, she is saying. She is doing something that no local white woman would do and for that her foreign boyfriend will praise her, Mannie thinks, misunderstanding the unspoken paths that govern the lives of people who live here. Everyone knows that island white women are to be hated, but even they understand the rules for navigating men. Damiana has told Mannie that the English girl and the American black man, who once thought he was God, enjoy wild sex. She has overheard the men talking when she was at the back of the house killing chickens for lunch. She tells Mannie that the men talked in loud voices about what the man likes to do to the girl and how she bends over for him. Driving next to her now, Mannie is embarrassed for the girl and ashamed for her that her short, boy haircut exposes her face.

Can you take me to your mother, she asks. For the first time, she turns to look at him and the air in the car is suddenly still and silent. The radio is playing "Sunshine on My Shoulders". Do you know they are organising a private plane to go to Haiti this weekend to see a cockfight, she tells him. I'd like to see the birds fight. But there is no room for me on the plane. She talks while driving slowly and carefully. She tells him that she is quilting a bedspread and she works on it every night. Mannie wonders if she is mad.

Why do you want to see my mother, he asks, even though he knows why she has followed him out onto the main road in the silver car. The English girl must want to know her future.

Aie-yaie-YAIE! Mannie, where you going with whitey-pokey? I never take you for a man who like white meat, shouts a man from the crowd lounging on the bridge below the church. Mannie throws his hand out the window, flinging his wrist back. Hush yuh ass, panyol.

"What did they say?" The girl is concerned. Nervous. Her ears blind to the talk but not the tone.

Nothing, he tells her, but in his mind he is wondering what his mother will say when he pulls into the yard with this pale white woman. White cockroach skin.

"Does your mother have bones?"

"What kind of mad-ass question is that?" For the first time he is alarmed and looks closely at her. She keeps her eyes on the road.

"Doesn't she do that thing? Shake the bones?"

"What thing? And no, my mother does not shake bones." He knows she was referring to his mother's reputation as a seer, but he's not going to make it easy for her. Was his mother an obeah woman? He didn't think so. What she knew she knew from her mother and her mother's mother and long before that. No talk of corbeaux peeing on your head or jengay or all the other things that people say mark a woman as an obeah woman. It wasn't like that. What his mother did was different. He'd watched her, watched her collecting her herbs in the magic hour between dusk and night, careful to throw back some leaves for the spirits. The leaves suspended in bottles of liquid in a corner of their kitchen. When he'd had fever as a child, she would measure the drops into his mouth using the eyedropper from the blue bottle of Optrex that his father kept in the bathroom.

"What thing?" he asked again. Wanting her to say it.

"See into the future?"

"You can ask her when you get there."

"I've brought money."

"If she sees you, she will want you to make a donation at the church where the Capuchin monks are buried."

People said that his mother chose to live near the church but he knew it was not so. She had come to take her dead cousin's place and that's how she'd ended up close to the church. Every morning she visited the church in San Rafael and said the rosary, offering prayers for the repose of the souls of his dead half-brothers. She never said it, but he knew she confessed every time she prayed, believing her gift to be the devil's work. How does it happen, he'd asked her once. Easy, she'd said. Like a movie. Sometimes they don't even need to ask. Sometimes it's so strong, I can see it when they are walking towards me.

People came from Port of Spain and San Fernando. Rich people in big cars. They wanted to know if their wombs would quicken. Would their husbands leave them? What mark to play in Whe Whe so they could make millions. But those were not the things she foretold. The things she saw she never told them. Instead she eased out banalities. They don't want to know, she told Mannie. They think they do but they don't.

"What Capuchin monks?" the white woman asks.

"Nobody never told you that story and you living on this side so long?"

It was the type of story foreigners loved. He was surprised Damiana hadn't told it to her.

An early war between the native Indians and the Spanish, he told her. Three monks were killed.

"When was that?"

"I forget. Sometime around the end of the 1600s."

"What makes the monks so special?"

"People say when the Spanish went a year later to dig up the bodies of the monks, they were still fresh. Still bleeding. Flesh on their bones good good. Smelling like normal." Here he paused to look at her. Were you supposed to say these sort of things to foreign women? But she still kept her eyes straight ahead, listening. "They say it was a miracle. So they make them holy martyrs and move them around a few times. Talk is they going to eventually bring them here, to the San Rafael chapel. I not sure where they are now. Ask her when you see her. She will tell you."

The English girl stayed silent, driving around the corners of the road carefully and she asked no more questions.

"Turn here."

Here? Her English accent made the word sound more proper as if her here and his here were two different places.

The car drove slowly down the long winding driveway. Past the big starch mango tree and past the row of bois canot with their oversized leaves. He was pleased that the English girl was seeing where he lived, could see that he was a person with a house and a mother and father and everything was neat and tidy and pretty overhead with overhanging branches and wild lianas and wild pines sending out flowered spikes high in the trees.

By the time the English girl parked the car, Benita had come out to meet them. She was still beautiful in her fifties. She was accustomed to white people coming, but no one had telephoned and Mannie could see she was worried to see him in the car with the English girl.

Ma, this is the English girl who lives by the people Damiana working by.

The English girl said – Hello pleased to meet you. Thank you for seeing me, the words rushing out of her mouth as if she was afraid she would swallow them.

But Benita would not see her. For a moment the two women looked at each other. Benita covered her face with her hands. No, she said. No. No.

There was nothing to do but ask the English girl to get back in the car. But why? WHY? Why won't she see me?

Benita had locked the door and pulled the curtains by time the English girl was turning the car in the yard. When Mannie looked back, his mother had come out the door and was sweeping the path where the car had been with a cocoyea broom, her face down.

The English girl did not say anything for a long time. Then, when they were nearing the horse farm, she said maybe his mother didn't like white people. Maybe she didn't like foreigners. She said what a bad thing it was that people like her came all the way across the ocean to try and help people who had no rights and then these same people were so ungrateful. Mannie lit a cigarette and exhaled blue plumes out the window. When the English girl let him out opposite the farm, he slammed the car door hard as he got out and didn't look back.

That night when Damiana began to speak in the mincing tones of the English girl who had vanished all afternoon in Mrs Kalam's silver car and created panic at the commune because no one knew where she had gone, Mannie left the room and Benita asked Damiana not to do it. It was unkind. Damiana sulked for the rest of the night, sitting out in the front with a lone kerosene lamp and listening to her small transistor radio. It was only after Benita had gone to bed and he walked Damiana to her home on the main road, that he told her what had happened.

You ever saw your mother do that before?
Never.
What you think she saw?
She doesn't want to talk about it.

Early in the January of the following year, Benita told Mannie over breakfast that the snake had eaten itself. The two-headed snake would soon be no more.

It was almost a month before the grave was found under the lettuce growing tall and spindly over the mounds of manure that Mannie himself had delivered to the commune. Yes, he told the police, they kept wanting more. Said they wanted it for a compost heap and to plant. He remembers the day well because the woman from Port of Spain had come to collect her stallion and he hadn't had time to keep shovelling more manure. They had pushed the girl in and killed her. Mrs Kalam had never heard a thing. Damiana told Mannie she was sure that the girl had gone back to England. All her clothes were gone.

It's best in telling a story like this to line up all the people. To place them in their respective corners so that everyone understands what sort of story is being told. It is a story that could be told by Damiana, but how could she know all the details? She's just the maid. A young Indian girl hired to help in the house of a black power activist. Mannie perhaps could tell this story. But what could he bring to it? He is a groom on a horse farm that lies across the highway and occasionally brings manure to the house.

But the English woman had been able to tell her part of the story in the end. She had been pushed into a hole dug for composting. She'd been alive when they covered her with manure, all the men that she joined in the middling light of evening. When the foreign press had come to the tropical backwater, it had been a circus. The foreign pathologist was very good at his job because even bones will talk in the end.

Far beyond the ex-pat gaze, the lives of ordinary Trinidadians unfold in ways that foreigners find difficult to imagine. It is a curious blind spot, not unlike the sharp corners on the north coast mountain road, and no one knows what causes people to speed blindly, beyond the reach of their vision. Even though the road signs warn of danger, there are frequent collisions, the casualties mounting with alarming regularity.

On a hot day in the late eighties the bodies of the three Capuchin Monks are moved to their final resting place in the San Rafael Church. On that day Mannie, who is now middle-aged, goes with his mother to light a candle. She struggles with arthritis in her hands now and he must light her candle as well as his own. They never speak of the English girl whose bones now lie with her own people far across the ocean.

Mannie remembers though that when the lady from Port of Spain moved to England she took the stallion with her. Every time Lee Ling sees Mannie after that, he tells him the horse is living a charmed life in the motherland. Lucky bugger.

11: BEAUTY SURROUNDS THE DARKNESS: NOVELS THAT TAUGHT ME HOW TO SEE

CHAPTER 22 FROM THE NOVEL *THE WORLD NOT HERE*

KEITH JARDIM

This excerpt comes from about halfway through the work. The focus is on Syl who is involved in the drug trade and trying to recruit a young man for nefarious work. In pursuit of this, Syl visits a halfway house run by an eccentric nun. He's in a reflective mood, angry at the island, his associates, and pining for a lost love and time. Memory, and how it affects characters, especially at a certain age, is a key concern in the novel.

I wrote the novel over the last several years while I lived mainly in the Middle East. The thematic concerns of the novel span most of my life, but it is Trinidad, disguised somewhat in the novel, with its many unique problems that is of major interest to me. The descent into barbarism and insanity that rapidly laid siege to the island, especially after July 1990, disturbs me; I also addressed them in my first book, the collection of stories *Near Open Water*.

V.S. Naipaul's novels and stories, in particular *Miguel Street*, *The Mystic Masseur*, *The Suffrage of Elvira*, *A House for Mr Biswas*, *In a Free State* and *Guerrillas*, influenced my becoming the kind of writer I am. Later, in my twenties, Shiva Naipaul's novel *A Hot Country* was also a significant influence. After that, Shiva Naipaul's first two novels, *Fireflies* and *The Chip-Chip Gatherers*, and his short stories and essays in *Beyond the Dragon's Mouth*, continued to guide my development as a writer. Shiva Naipaul's register of the haplessness of the human condition is, to my mind, genius. I still believe he is one of our best writers.

The violence and injustices of the Caribbean; the failure of educational development across the whole population; the destruction of the natural environment and the politics of race and greed are what haunt the fiction of the Naipaul brothers. Today, life in our region has become much worse than at the time they were writing because of these problems. The causes are maybe numerous, but at times I wonder if part of the problem is that we've not taken our reading seriously. The Naipauls' novels and stories have been neglected by important communities in our societies. In my work, I try to hold myself responsible to what I have both experienced and read about these islands; and that means reading widely, both regionally and internationally.

Influence is neither sought nor obtained by human beings; we are born into it and made by it. As writers, we perhaps encounter a more profound adventure with influence because we have to read, to be aware of what has been done before. What a fiction writer does apart from learn his or her craft – which is a multi-decades long endeavour if he's lucky – is learn to see the truths and realities of life in all their never-ending variations, which are nowhere more apparent than in the works of the good and great writers of fiction. Influence, and the anxiety of influence, is inevitable and part of the writer's learning experience.

I believe wholeheartedly in the integrity of literature precisely because of the forces of influence that shape it and hold it to account. "The past is not dead; it's not even past," William Faulkner said. He was talking about life and literature, their influences. History. For this reason I believe in literature's magic, its power for renewal, and justice – no matter how bleak the story. I have argued in the classroom, repeatedly, that fiction is the most important, most challenging, and most noble of all the arts and should never be compromised. I have even gone further: I argue that reading and writing are the two most important things human beings can do, especially the first, for not everyone can be a writer; but everyone must have a story to be human, as Achebe said. And we all read, and must, in one way or another – most of us badly, alas, since we elect prime ministers and presidents based on the dishonest stories we believe. We carry stories around, see them, talk about them and the people involved, whether we are literary or not, whether we read books or not. No matter what one believes, what one does with one's life or does not do, one is first of all a narrative being. There is no escaping it. And for this reason most of us cannot completely escape our history, our parents, our culture, home and the violence we create and allow in the world.

But literature, whether one believes it or not, is another kind of life; it's often the more important one because literature resides in the imagination, and it's from there that we can begin, at least, to have ideas – revolutionary ones – of beauty and truth, democracy and love. That may well be what saves us, and our world – if such a thing is still possible.

All of human experience is already contained in literature, in poetry and fiction. If you want to know who you were, are, and who you will become, you must read literature: you will come to know yourself and multitudes of others who are here now, dead and long gone, and yet to be born. To be a writer worthy of the art of fiction, of literature, therefore is to join the conversation and experience of humanity.

CHAPTER 22

He drove the silver new-model Range Rover this time, the only public luxury he allowed himself, through a neighbourhood once strongly middle-class in the 1960s and 70s. The houses were hidden by walls and sturdy hedges of hibiscus and other robust plants and fruit trees – poinsettia, croton, banana, mango, sapodilla – but occasionally there were tall wrought-iron gates and he glimpsed the properties beyond: gardens nurtured and designed with near obsessive care, as if the owners had cultivated a small bit of paradise, and boxed it. The walls were solid, dark-grey structures, fungus-ridden or ivy-covered; most of them had appeared in the mid-70s, after the first oil boom. The closeness of the houses to one another had once meant neighbourly relations, aspirations to a reliable, conventional morality and class with a quiet religious base; socially responsible people whose children went either to the regional university or sought-after ones in Canada, England and America. Today the former homes looked like an array of safe houses, their very conspicuousness and similarity their camouflage. Syl was unable to determine exactly how he felt about it. His childhood had been spent not far from here; it had been one of those classic Caribbean upbringings of two fathers holding reign: one was flesh and blood, the other, and master of all, was the God of the Old Testament. The windows were sealed in many houses, air-conditioning producing another climate in hidden interiors.

About three years ago Syl had urged Andre to invest in one with him, but Andre had been uneasy: too many spies.

Syl passed along the main border street of the district as he headed east, the sea and harbour on his right for about half a mile. When he saw the huge silver funnels of the capital's main electricity station he looked left and saw the street he wanted.

At the gated driveway Syl was confronted by the security officer for "The Lord's House of Hope and Discipline run by the Good Sisters of Jesus Christ" as a black-on-white sign stated. The sign was wire-strapped at its four corners onto the gate.

"Sir, please stop. I wish to question you."

Officer Eustace Williams, the badge of the security company he was employed by and his nametag stitched onto his shirtsleeve and breast pocket respectively, raised his left arm to indicate that Syl should stop.

Palm up and flat – that classic colonial style, Syl thought. Like a man wanting to stop the world so he could be noticed. Or for certain people to get the fuck off.

Williams' right hand sought the pistol holstered on his hip. Syl sucked his teeth and stopped five feet from the gate and folded his arms, glaring at the man. His face resembled an agouti's, Syl decided, the nose prominent and narrow, upper front teeth sticking out ready to bite into something, and the chin rounded and sunk inwards, doubling. Williams' hair was thick and greying at the sides, and his face held an indistinct boyish yearning, as if he'd never quite grown up.

"Please identify yourself and your purpose here," Williams said somewhat nervously. He lowered his palm; the butt of his other hand still rested on the pistol holster.

Syl groaned quietly. Another mad man, he thought, and this one approaching middle age. We allowed them too much for too long in this cursed island, we were too long amused by them – so much so they almost running the fucking place now. How long again we go teach each other to tolerate people like him as an example of the *national* character? And is probably a cunt just like he who will kill my ass one day.

"You have ID, Mr...?"

"Syl, Sylvester Phillips," he said and gave Williams his license.

Williams' agouti eyes widened at Syl's license picture. He cocked his head, as if trying to remember something. "You look familiar, boss. You went Tranquility Secondary?"

Syl wanted to hit him, maybe kill him, to exorcise a part of the national character; a part of this island he hated. But there are too many like him, he thought. What to do? What the fuck? *One* day.

"A short time," Syl said.

"You play cricket for Junior Sec.? Nationals?"

Syl shook his head, lying.

"Sister Caston expectin' you. Funny, you don't look like a religious man."

"That's true," Syl said curtly. "I prefer it that way." He wanted to hurt him in some way, and hoped the tone would at least hurt his feelings. Though he'd never killed anyone, he had experienced the urge often enough. It had always been a sudden urge; something would just trip off in his brain, releasing raw instinct: the person in front of you was better off dead or left cowering in fear, and the sooner the better, for him, for you, and the whole shit-up island.

"What's your business?"

The agouti still sticking his head out of his hole, Syl mused. Then he grinned and said confidently, "Import export. And yours? Wait, man. Wait. I know. It looks like you practising for carnival in your security officer costume. Is a damn shame you not any more real than that."

Williams considered these remarks, his agouti lips nibbling thoughtfully. He reassessed Syl's demeanour, and chuckled. "Aha, you is a smart-man. And boldface too. How you know the good Sister Caston?"

"I don't. A Mrs Gomes send me about a young man named Maurice. Know who I'm talking about?"

Though the afternoon sun had gone past five o'clock, there was a persistent trickle of sweat down Syl's jaw. His nerves twitched, and annoyance lifted in his chest, making him warmer. He took a deep breath.

Williams nodded, returned Syl's driver's license, stepped aside and then opened the gate. Syl entered the property with long strides, noticing the fretted, wooden gables edged along the roof of the whitewashed house but not much else. He was glad to be rid of Williams. He felt watched as he went up a short flight of stairs, to where Sister Marie Caston greeted him on a wide verandah lined with potted ficus; the plants looked constrained. She was thinly moustached and hobbling, a right-hip dip of a few inches with each step. She was about eighty-five years old, alert and wiry and smelling of baby powder. A cross with a mournful, overly doll-like Christ hung above the entrance to the living room.

"Mrs Gomes send you, yes yes – I know – the gentleman willing to be of assistance. Come, come inside, have some juice – you like tamarind? Is a bit over-sweet, but that is the way Stella like it. Stella!"

A heavy dark woman appeared in a nearby doorway as if by miracle, holding a brass tray with two glasses of thick muddy-brown liquid. She was not a nun and had smooth, clear skin in a mildly sullen face. Syl accepted the drink, grateful for the jostling ice. Sister Caston took the other and had a quick sip.

"This is the gentleman Erika call me about, Stella. He come all the way from America to talk to Maurice. Imagine."

"Well…" Syl began. "Not America exac –"

"Isn't it a wonderful thing when our islanders return from abroad to assist in the development of our nation, Stella? In these times we live in – " Sister Caston raised her glass of tamarind juice to the gate, driveway, and beyond, in front of which Officer Williams stood attentive to her words – "times that all too often mark the presence of the Prince of Darkness, we have to come together as one, one people under one flag, united and purposeful in thoughts, words, and deeds."

Syl thought: Roz, girl, you would real like to hear this shit.

Stella, her eyes lowered, nodded and left.

"How is my dear Erika?" Sister Caston asked. She sat in a Morris chair and indicated he do the same.

"Very well," Syl said. "She sends her regards."

"So, Erika says you looking for a bit of local colour. Is that right?"

He smiled at the euphemism. "No, not really. I want to talk to Maurice, persuade him to return to school."

Sister Caston sat up in her chair and looked at him doubtfully. "Is Erika who ask you to do that, not so?" Then she lifted a thin arm and wagged her index finger energetically at him. "You remind me of someone, but I not sure, after all these years, if was someone I meet, hear about, or dream up."

"Long ago I lived here, as a teenager." His response was casual.

"How exactly are you going to persuade Maurice to return to school, Mr Phillips? He's barely literate. And hates books."

Syl didn't hesitate. "By giving him a steady, part-time job first, nothing fancy, not much payment, but just enough money for him to become motivated to follow through on further improvement."

"But he needs to learn to read, Mr. –"

"Of course. I will set it up so that he cannot be paid unless he has at least three lessons a week. My fiancée Roz has teacher training in English from the university."

Sister Caston's aged eyes flickered. "Hmm, that is a good thing, Mr Phillips. And you will have Maurice doing, well, what exactly?"

"To be determined. I will need time to talk to him, a week perhaps."

Sister Caston pursed her lips thoughtfully and looked out, beyond the rooftops of the neighbourhood, at the sky. Late afternoon had swept in, an immense softness of pink and mauve towering clouds: a tint of evening, of the darkness to come. The nun was subdued, appeared almost melancholy for a few moments, and then she nodded and tried to recover her earlier vivacity.

"You don't read stories? I really like a good horror story, you know, or a thriller. Something to keep me occupied at nights, as I don't sleep too well these days."

Syl considered the question. Then he said: "History." Andre always talked about that, eventually. And Fernandes had referred to it the night Syl last saw him and his proud bitch.

"I could real help you with that kind of book. My family been living here since seventeen ninety-two, so anything you need help with, don't hesitate to call. A good historical thriller is the sort of book this island needs, you don't feel? With a movie deal to follow, a big old time kind of movie, by Steven Spielberg, something on the scale of *Gone with the Wind*. You don't find?"

Syl frowned. "That could be very interesting, but I'm not here for that. I hardly find the time to read, far less write, and I wouldn't want to disturb you."

"Not at all! My whole life is about helping people in all sorts of ways. I was born to be disturbed, as the good Lord sees fit." Sister Caston spread her arms as if to embrace him. "And Mrs Gomes and I real close, so you will have plenty opportunity to see me." Her eyes were wet. "We get real close since Sister Eunice pass."

He nodded twice at her.

An extra furrow of skin appeared on her speckled forehead, and she said, "Didn't Erika tell me you also working for the UN?"

Syl almost laughed, then coughed quickly and shifted on the chair. "Oh. I'm not here officially with them. I'm supposed to be at a school full time, if they'll have me. The island is an interesting place. But I'll see where I'm needed most."

Sister Caston nodded with enthusiasm. "Well, you certainly come to the right place, and you seem such a gentleman. But be careful, this island mad no ass!" She quickly covered her mouth with her hand, eyes searching beyond the doorway, and whispered, "Excuse me."

The nun stood and went inside, calling Stella.

To be a nun, he thought, or a priest. As a child he had always wondered at the unnaturalness of it, the attire, the seclusion, the shutting off of a life on an island so devoted to its corporeal excesses. Yet Sister Caston could be enjoying the life she had; she took delight in being in the world. Syl sipped his tamarind juice, and gazed at Eustace Williams, who was about thirty yards away, staring into the branches of a mango tree and cooing at a dove.

The desire to be part of an adventure had intrigued Syl at an early age. Sports, and later owning and supervising a gym, had satisfied him for a while. Then the financial security he needed had tempered the urge for adventure, bringing on a rhythm of unremarkable months and years. The owning of another gym, and then another, and he'd been managing three by the end; and it was honest, dull work, occasional dalliances with lonely or adventurous women only temporarily alleviating the boredom and the inevitable contemplation of mortality. He wanted excitement, something new, another career. He began to liaise with the local UN education office and invested in a ketch, large enough to attract the more careful in his present business, but small enough to be ignored by all categories of its powerful and often repugnant elite.

He sipped the tamarind juice. The tart, sweet liquid brought a memory of Roz and Neesha in bed one hazy, hot afternoon. He'd entered the guest cottage set apart from Andre's house and was sucking a piece of tamarind the gardener had given him. Neesha was propped up on her back against a clump of pillows, her reading glasses on the tip of her nose, long dark hair mussed, her gaze directed between her legs. With a long leg down the middle of Roz's back, she was urging her on, Roz's head between her legs. The music player was on, Bob Dylan's "Lay Lady, Lay..." and he'd entered quietly in shadow, his heart burning at the sight. And he'd stayed there, unseen, the strip of tamarind in his mouth.

That, and the ketch, had been Neesha's idea. The woman had worked and played with unchecked ambition and mamaguyed them all.

Sister Caston returned to her chair and gave him a slap on the knee. "Got to loosen up round here, my boy! Can't be too serious about life!"

Syl, a bit uneasy, glanced at the mournfully hanging Christ above the entrance to the living room, and thought: Indeed not, Sister.

"Stella!"

The miraculous Stella reappeared, a little flustered. This time she spoke. "Maurice say he playing ping-pong."

"Thank you, Stella," Sister Caston said, dismissing the maid with a wave of her hand.

The nun briefly considered this bit of news, and grimaced. She got up from her chair again. "Please follow me, Mr Phillips. Only two things that boy listens to – the good Lord and his belly."

They went through the house, high ceilinged and "built in the late Victorian period", Sister Caston informed him with shy pride, to a yard lower than the main floor. A dull-white wall with faded moss stains enclosed a rectangular area roughly sixty feet square. Trees from surrounding properties hung over parts of the wall. A mango tree stood in the yard's centre, and under it two young men were playing table tennis. Syl and the nun halted at the top of four steps.

"Maurice!" Sister Caston shouted. "The gentleman Mrs Gomes send to see you is here."

Maurice ignored the nun, but he stopped playing the game. His partner, a rough-looking East Indian, sauntered off, mumbling something to Maurice. He left along a narrow alley on the side of the house. Then Sister Caston said, tapping her watch, "Dinner at 6:30 sharp, Maurice. And there's dessert. If you behave."

She smiled at Syl, winked, said something about doing the good Lord's work, and re-entered the house.

He went down the stairs, greeting Maurice with a casual good afternoon, and extended a hand. Maurice stood near the ping-pong table, his face tight, arms folded. He wore tattered jeans, lace-less sneakers and a sleeveless jersey. He was about twenty-five, slim and bronzed, with a prominent scar across his left bicep.

"Who send you?"

"Mrs Gomes," Syl said. "Well, not too true."

Maurice said, "Why you people so meddlesome, eh? Why you must come here and pretend like you want to help us? Why you really here?"

Maurice tilted his head up slightly, focused on something in the distance; looked at the ground again. He wouldn't respond when Syl asked him about his background, his family, jobs he'd had in the past three years, how he'd made money. He told him he could help, and Maurice said: "Give me money, then." He looked hopeful, his eyes going soft, flirting. Syl said no.

"Go back to whatever hole you come out from. And take the nun bitch."

He began walking away slowly, following the same route his friend had taken earlier along the side of the house.

"You want a good work?" Syl asked.

Maurice stopped, looked back halfway. "What you offer?" He faced Syl and his eyes went soft again, this time with a sad interest asserting itself on his face.

"Enough."

"No less than ten thousand, all in large notes. Don't talk here. And I doing nothing mad."

"I'll give you twelve, and a phone with plenty credit. Meet me tomorrow at this time by the Ministry of Education – or, by the Oval is better. I will pass for you, a silver Range Rover. And one last thing: keep your Indian friend out."

Maurice gave Syl a hard stare and nodded at him. "Tell Sister I say you could have my cake and ice-cream." And he began to walk briskly along the route on which his friend had left.

Syl stayed there awhile, looking around at the yard.

The grass was still green under the mango tree, but he imagined the sun hitting the tree relentlessly day after day until it drooped, as it had begun to do. The tree beginning to die, dying slowly, and then, once more, surging to life again when the rains came, he'd often seen it on St. Palm. But not only trees and plants responded with life to rain. It was what I did, he thought, getting into this business. *I wanted to live, and feel it.*

One afternoon, when he was eighteen and returning home from school during a thunderstorm, he ran down the driveway of the house Neesha was living in with the man she'd fled her home for. She was nineteen then and had been there two years. The neighbourhood was a quiet place of sudden, twisting lush hills on the slope of a mountain in the island's north; and houses were far enough apart that each harboured its own relative seclusion. After lingering in the empty, double-car garage, Syl went up the back steps to the main lawn and gardens. At the top of the steps there was a narrow, grey seven-foot wall extending from the house for six feet. Behind the wall was a little square, compact garden. The dining room window looked right onto it, young palms splaying their leaves against the window and making net-like patterns on the dining-room table on sunny mornings. Elephant-ear plants clustered among orchids blooming on potted, decomposing branches. Anthuriums bloomed orange and red-flamed spathes, and jasmine vines lolled bunches of their small blue-purple petals alongside a winding pebbly path – "made for dancing douens", Neesha had once said. A section of the house's roof partly covered the garden, and there was a large spout reaching down from the roof. When it rained, the water gushed down onto a rather ungainly-looking but solid, chest-high structure of quartz boulders glittering with crystals.

After the lightning and thunder of that afternoon the rain continued, furious, the wind lashing the water against his face and back, legs and arms as he ran up the steps, knowing Neesha's man was off the island. Shivering, he picked the door lock and entered the dining room. He trod carefully on the tiled floor to the bathroom for a towel. In the spare bedroom he stripped to his underwear and dried himself and returned to the dining room, and there, about to get a snack from the kitchen, he saw Neesha naked in the little garden, one hand directing the water spout over her head, the other resting on the quartz. Occasionally she positioned the spout to gush directly onto the quartz boulders, their uneven shapes scattering the water in every direction; and then she walked around the quartz structure, turning, the water hitting her everywhere. She lifted her arms at one point, as if celebrating, her nude figure ghosting in the pale green vegetation and rain. The half enclosed garden prevented the wind from whipping the flowers and plants into a mess, but gusts entered now and again, lifting her always long, always black hair, dancing the elephant-ear plants, the anthuriums frantic and painting their flames in the grey-green, framing the nude woman in the garden of wind and rain.

Syl saw the sky had turned ultramarine, and the leaves of the mango tree were quite dark. The back steps of Sister Caston's halfway house had become a pale grey. He sighed, waiting for the first star.

How young they had been.

"Mr Syl?"

He started and turned. Stella was on the back porch, leaning against a wooden post. She appeared to be hesitating above the wobbly-looking concrete steps that descended into the yard. A dim yellow light shone from the centre of the ceiling, its glow casting the servant into a vague apparition. Yet he noticed she had changed her nurse-like uniform of earlier and wore jeans, sandals and a loose cream-beige blouse; a red handbag was slung over her right shoulder.

"You want a lift somewhere?" he asked.

"Sister say, if you don't mind…"

"No problem."

"Another hour for curfew. I not going far."

Syl wondered if there was anything useful she might know. As he walked toward the porch, he imagined the night gathering into fullness and heard an easy breeze stirring the leaves of the mango tree behind him. A smell of damp, vegetal earth came to him: someone was watering a garden on the other side of the wall. He tried to forget Neesha and think about what he could ask Stella, who, like Maurice, like everybody he had ever known on the island, probably wanted something that could only bring sorrow.

12: PRELUDE TO A READING OF AN EXCERPT FROM *HERE*

RAYMOND RAMCHARITAR

I chose to read this section of the poem (11-23) because we're in Chaguanas, the seat of Hinduism in the country, as it were, and that's where the excerpt is set. There are many references to Hinduism in the poem. Actually more than references; Hinduism suffuses the excerpt. Chaguanas is also the seat of the Naipaul clan.

This excerpt comprises two parts of a long poem of five sections. The poem ("Here") is itself one of five long poems or cantos, which constitute an autobiographical narrative. Naturally, you can't say "autobiographical poem" without calling to mind Walcott's *Another Life* and Brathwaite's *Arrivants*. One is intensely personal, seeing history through its eyes; the other plunges itself into history and weaves itself into its fabric or tapestry. But there's also another contributor here: the fictional poet John Shade's autobiographical poem, *Pale Fire*, which taught me a great deal about the low-key ironic tone. That's important.

This bit of "Here" sets the stage for my personal history. It describes my pre-history, if you like. Where I came from, who lived there, how they came to be there. The village is Chaguanas, the characters are people I remember – everything is true, though not always factual. Multiple stories are fused, characters reshaped and so on. But, apropos of John Shade's poem, you'll note that it begins elsewhere, in New York, with a reference to a poem by Frederick Seidel ("The Sickness"), in the Metropolitan Museum of Art. (The book then moves to North America and Europe, and beyond; a stone skipping over water. It's as effective a form for autobiography as any other.)

I suppose you could say this illustrates a cornerstone of my artistic and academic work: my origins, our origins, are not single, isolated strands of history in a mosaic or tapestry. A more apt analogy is a particle collider in which individual atoms and other exotic particles are hurled by forces out of their control into space, and collide, fuse, or annihilate each other.

The other four long poems in the book describe a bus trip to Holland from London, my marriage, a sojourn in Toronto; it ends with a mini-epic, which is an homage to my gods. The forms and styles of the different sections vary – the excerpt is rhymed, metred and in quatrains. All the sections are metred and most rhyme. One is in heroic couplets, another in blank verse, another in terza rima, one in a mix of forms. Part of this is conceit, part practicality.

As for practicality: you have a massive arsenal/repertoire at your disposal as a poet, yet most poets choose a club. I try out everything I can get my head around. Clearly, distressingly, the surprisingly large number of Trinidadian poets now being published disagree. They proudly handicap themselves in an astonishing variety of ways. They lock themselves into ethnic, gender and political cages. They lack imaginative reach and agility, and have no knowledge of history, current events, pop culture, art, even movies and television. And virtually without exception, the work is unbelievably bad, showing clumsiness with words – unfamiliarity with the possibilities of weight, lightness, magic, fantasy and gravitas.

Hence another reason for my affection for formal structures: there's too much bad poetry out there, and my objective is not to add to it, but stand apart from it – well apart. A strict formal approach (rhymed, metred and allusive) is rare in poetry today. My choice to be formal is a statement of a personal credo of what I believe to be the essential components of poetry: discipline, learning, attention to technique, and a thorough knowledge of what preceded you.

But back to this poem. To repeat, I read it because it starts in Chaguanas, but moves to Port of Spain, into the "Creole world". In a sense this is doing what national art is supposed to do, that is, place the various constituents of a nation together in an artificial but seemingly organic way. The contrast seems shocking – Chaguanas is a pagan-rural landscape, a riot of colour, nature, ugly imitation Miami structures, temples, mosques, shacks, and a recent addition: claustrophobia, which comes from mushrooming housing developments, businesses, and cars, cars, cars, all contained in a space originally designed to be an agricultural village, and which has not been redesigned. Port of Spain, the urban-Christian landscape is less claustrophobic, if as replete with its own horrors – the Beetham and Laventille, east Port of Spain. But it also has its miniscule designated spaces for art and humanity. I mean the Savannah, the Little Carib Theatre, the art galleries, the wine bars; all this stuck in between the absurd architectural pretensions dedicated to commerce, law and government.

That sliver of humanity and art in Port of Spain is decisive. It's not there in Chaguanas. I went to Presentation College and we were not taught literature. We did English Language. We were never exposed to art, in any form. Most of the boys I went to Presentation with have paid a heavy price for this. Those boys are now very rich professionals but cannot read, do not read and don't understand why this is a bad thing. In a wider frame, as discussed in the poem, Chaguanas is rural Hindu India outside of India –

a peasant menagerie. The peasants have become doctors, lawyers and men and women of commerce, but while they've learned the technical skills associated with those professions, without artistic and cultural knowledge, they haven't really evolved as people, as "a people" if you will. There is no logic or order to their existence. It's negative chaos, contained and constrained by geography and politics. Not a positive, creative chaos from which comes something of use.

This difference between Chaguanas and Port of Spain (the lack of even a trace of the artistic urge in the former) is new; after all, the elder Naipaul, who created and nurtured his sons' ambitions, is from Chaguanas. But the disappearance has an easy explanation; what I call "the great hollowing out" – the mass emigration of almost a third of the population between 1960 and 1990, which continues today. There is a mystifying, deliberate avoidance of this fact in assessments of the present. Many of the best, brightest, and most intellectually capable simply left. Many who could barely read and write left and are today professors at good universities in the US, UK, and Canada. The people they left here swelled to fill the material space, but not the mental space.

This lack of a mental world was one of the gifts we gave ourselves at independence; one of the pieces of dastardly colonialism we chucked. I believe this mental world is known in the *Bhagavad Gita* as the *sattvas*, which exists along with the two other *gunas* (categories of the senses); the *rajas*, devotion to passion and material things of the world, and *tamas*, dullness, indolence and ignorance. The Naipauls represent *sattvas*, and their memory is nonexistent here.

But if he doesn't exist here in Chaguanas, V.S. Naipaul is known in the Creole world and the wider world, even if that knowing in Trinidad is stained with resentment and mindless rage. In Port of Spain, Naipaul is disliked for his novels, his travel writing, and his journalism which showed Trinidad for what it was and would become at the moment of independence. Words like "unpatriotic" and "racist" are often used. Naturally, the basis of the resentment is ethnic, as Lloyd Best, C.L.R. James, Derek Walcott and, not least, Eric Williams, said the same and worse to no obloquy, and even to great praise. So while I'm happy to read this poem here today, I have no illusions about what I'm doing. Will this poem make any difference? No, it won't.

II

A dream: a poem that sounds like a warning –
Seidel's "The Sickness", which ends on Eighty-Sixth
Street, near the Park, one ordinary morning:
an early soubrette, a fuming bus: a fixed

Routine. In this dream, there's nothing to do for hours
'til the Met opens – what draws me there is always
the same: the Egypt exhibit, the Sphinx that glowers
knowingly, Pharaoh, Anubis, the Hebrew slaves

Who etched the scallops in each gryphon's wing –
The spectacle of God's chosen people at slaughter –
courtesy Cecil B. DeMille, presenting
Charlton Heston in a skirt, while Pharaoh's daughter,

Anne Baxter, and her maids, fretted in Technicolour.
I begin there, in New York, or there, in Egypt.
Anywhere, you might say, but *here*, in duller
light, and an obscurer story, where the whip

Played the starring role, and often still does.
So I'd better get to it: there are still fields
that remember the mud between the forlorn toes
that threaded furrows, behind the iron wheels

Of oxcarts pregnant with cane-stalks, and whispered
Bhojpuri curses beneath acidic breath,
or love poems – whatever came through the blistered
betel-stained lips stank of violence, threat.

Then evenings, on dirt floors swept with palm fronds,
the oiled joints of tawny bodies squatting outside
the smoke-blackened tin-roofed barracks, murmuring songs,
low and primal, smooth rum, bhang, the slide

From history into the samadhi state,
gazing at the saffron-faced horizon
where black-limbed havan smoke hung frozen, in wait
for the haughty Aryan gods to realise an

Offering had been made, then coaxing them
with tears and music, but they never came,
and the whispered strophes dissolved into pablum.
The blue-skinned gods were stunned by shame

That ten million fierce-moustached kshatriyas armed
with the Vedas, fed by the headwaters from Shiva's
topknot, could be effortlessly damned
by a hundred thousand chinless, blue-eyed reavers,

And they pretended not to see the havans
that flowered from the lonely Caroni Plains
in fragrant ghee, or hear the plaintive bhajans
that wavered like the flickers of wood-torch flames.

The slender, manicured nails slowly grazed
the indigo chins, as they lounged in Indra's demesne
and wordlessly the mercuric eyes blazed
assent, like jewels in velvet: *sudras weren't men*.

And left them to diabetes, uxoricide,
and a thick-fingered crushing boredom, whose cure
was ganja, rum, the Manas, a child bride.
They took a century and a half to find the door

Out of those fields, and god knows how much more
to forget them.
    So much for history.
You could still see the cane fields from our
back porch as late as the 80s. By then the mystery

Of the rough-edged past had become a silky fetish,
and you saw the younger coolie doctors in koortahs
and heard the tinny music, and felt the rush
of memory incarnating Hema and Mumtaz

As Sita and Parvati, invoked and worshipped
every Wednesday in the Hylite drive-inn,
when they let coolies in by the carload, and slipped
them fliers for yagnas and satsanghs – the hives in

Which their droning could meet, mingle and multiply,
like the accordion folds that wheezed the mournful
melodies that softened the strophes from the dry
epics – as penance for the indulgence in scornful

Lowbrow peasant leelas, where Amitabh
and the crooning, fair-skinned Bollywood simulacra
were molecules, dancing to dissolve the drab
barrack compound, so coolies could re-make

A gold-leafed pastoral, with devas in brass,
and bestiaries of Aryan-animal hybrids.
The gods became works of art in the age of mass
reproduction – an orgy of eyes and limbs on all sides,

Oozing the pink-skinned beauty peasants crave;
the sapient sadhu became a hedonist
decked in organza and tulle, as he traced the grave
ash on each forehead, the sacred thread on each wrist;

And they brought the robed charlatans from Bharat
to babble the Sanskrit words, as they fed Agni
the ransom, and petition for a new concordat
For a New World. The gods blinked and weighed the sagging

Clouds, heavy with gold bibelots the peasants
offered, like a low-born lover offers stars,
then laughed a little; the coolies were like infants.
Heaven had changed after an age of wars

And only fragments of their magic remained:
the prayers, offerings, and flags were mere ornaments
now. They'd grown bored, the epics had become mundane
and kingdoms of stone and magic dwindled like incense.

But the robed charlatans, the sacred thread
and the offerings to Agni, now properly proffered,
had to be honoured. They stirred, sighed and bled
their ichor into the ether, and prepared to suffer

A final, absurd round of incarnations
to walk the improbable spaces of crumbling Maya,
near her navel, in those far-flung stations
where their lost children sat, drunk and crying.

But in the profane cane fields, the peasant body
could not practice austerities, was too enmeshed
in the syrupy world; avatars became godly
satyrs whose immanence succumbed to flesh.

I remember Hanuman, the monkey god,
in the body of a red-eyed government clerk
who carried a flask in his back pocket. He would
caress the bottle's curves and complain about work,

His children, his wife, Ravana's ugly sister
as his breath roared, his furious heart heaved
with rage, then laughter, then tears, as he choked, then kissed
the bottle's neck, as he dreamed of how to deceive her

Into taking the children and leaving forever,
Giggling, splitting the human face apart
at moments, as the liquor burned to sever
the monkey's laughter from his stubborn heart.

Every day, I passed by Ram who beat
the gold-skinned Sita bloody, but she stayed,
and Lakshman who staggered down the main street
sometimes at night, singing, unafraid,

Of the marigold faces of trembling peasant girls
whose fathers, enflamed at night by spirituous fires,
consumed the innocence spun in the whorls
of petal soft cheeks, and crushed them into Apsaras.

The older women understood the words
and shook their silver-streaked heads; some cried a little
and would never say why. These instants were the surds
etched on the veils of a karmic joke, the riddle

We lived in – a fragrant island of neon, afloat
on black water, a Republic of smoke
ruled by a white-masked god with a black-skin coat
where slant-rhymed heroic couplets deposed the sloka.

III

Vishnu thinned hair and lips to become a Samajist
and uncle. He drove me to school in his Hillman Minx,
unravelling the mysteries in every twist
of the road to Carli Bay, as the sea blinked

Through the gauzy tassels trailing the shafts
of the cane arrows erupting from springy leaf
calyxes, and I bounced on his horse-laughs
as he spoke fondly of Odysseus, the thief

Who relieved Polyphemus of his eye;
Arthur, who inveigled Excalibur from stone;
Apollo, whose Cadillac chariot blazed the sky;
and rose-lipped beauties biding in every crone.

In the village school where he was Raj and prelate,
the sunburnt vassals, with dim eyes and callused palms,
offered their clear-eyed children to a lighter fate
through the salvation of his sheltering arms.

I don't know if the children ever grew up,
or if around the innocent, adoring eyes
were lambskin masks that hid a cold, corrupt
desire that used the books and prayers to disguise

Its intent: to lacerate the smooth green
of the fields, to strangle the moody, insatiable sea
that haunted them and swallowed every dream
that lived in the word they traced in the sand: *free*.

Free from the tireless cartwheels of rebirth,
free from its red-ink laws and karmic bonds
the weary ships drew tighter around the girth
of the old world, and their quicksand desponds

Known in other worlds as *boredom*. The cure
was faith in a single death and final rebirth
whereupon the souls who'd been certified pure
would claw triumphantly out of the dirt.

It was enchanting: the thought of vast sound-stages
on the Caroni plains, the thousand-limbed
forests as extras, with Rakshas and white-haired sages
to tend the ancient spools that wound the film

Of life after life, and gods for every moment –
to spin those maelstrom lives to a single gyre
of one story, all the pain to a single lament,
was, for those crushed by the wheel of life, inspired.

"Don't believe the nonsense about prayer and fasting,"
he said, one day, in a moment of anger. "You know,
in India, a brahman saw a beggar passing.
The man asked for food, but dharma did not allow.

The brahman saw the same man the following day,
dead, and thought, "He is gone back to be reborn".
But suddenly he realised, 'I say
what I've been taught. It is useless to mourn

The dead. They return to a station their
Karma dictates. But suppose there is no spirit?
What if all we can hope to achieve is living here?
What if the Law of Karma is Brahmanic shit?'"

He laughed as he said it, a little cruelly.
Early in his life, he'd shown promise
and was taken from it, away from the unruly
rage of bejewelled gods, and the razor-tongued bliss

Of rum gave way to the red-faced impatience
of Irish priests, whose prickly brogue knit fear
as they forced the coolies to their knees for stations
of the Cross, as prelude to the tortures of Shakespeare

And Homer. The grimness of the priests had gone
by like visions Christ contrived in the desert,
by the time he unravelled the *Odyssey* along
the Byzantine Carli Bay Road. I saw their worth

Only much later. He took an age to die,
holding on to life because he knew
the void awaited, his soul would not fly
to Samsara, but evaporate like the dew

On the stolid canes, and his children would amount
to nothing. Even his dreams could provide no harbour
as he watched them flower, then fade and fall into gaunt
middle age, and the lurid cult of Sai Baba.

I remember him since I, too, sidestepped the mud.
By then, pink priests had been replaced by dark
votaries in white habits, converts who would
console the new Republic, where the black clerk

Had straightened his back and become the Black Master
whose sins could only be heard by a Black Confessor.
The College of Our Lady of Disaster
was history's white-faced diamond, its impresa

On the fallow fields, set in dogmatic concrete.
The Virgin took the best of the peasants' litters
and infected them with the virus of conceit
to set them, like brown Adams, above the creatures

Of the field, who galumphed across the earth and made
its machines run, who spirited rum, and killed
their wives. We would be siddhis for which they prayed –
the crystals that had grown in the humid, stilled

Suspension of lonely plains, emptied of oxcarts
and the swish of cutlasses cleaving the spindly shanks
of cane, and of loose-limbed bodies that moved like larks
moved through love poems. In truth, we were blanks

In khaki trousers and white shirts, blinking
at the precision of the quadrangle, the strict
order of the lawns, and curious sprinkling
of boys in stark black skins, being slowly mixed

Into our flock by stony Shepherds whose virtue
was that they, too, had sat in the steel and ply
chairs, and watched old masters bring new
light to old mystery in the dark chalkboard eye

Whose retina etched it all: the Black Power
fists in the 70s, the black scuts in the shaved
heads, as the coolie renaissance began, and flowered.
The Shepherds and dark monks remained enslaved

By Our Lady of Inertia, by whose grace
Newtonian mechanics and the calculus
prevailed, and left the frozen marble face
unlined by time, like our prosaic prospectus –

The mantissa of Indenture – who could achieve
Nirvana as doctors, lawyers, scientists.
But when *our* time had come to be deceived
an era folded as our Holy Father Narcissus

Died. The physics changed with the atmosphere.
The Shepherds retreated into broken spines
of old texts, whose dogma withered in the new air;
their stories faltered, and Fordist assembly lines

Stuttered. Clermont, the giant whose biceps split
his sleeves, began to wear open-toed sandals
and mixed basic math with relativity;
he told us stories of youth, girls, and scandals

Always averted by leaden morals: *hold off, wait* –
the catechist's cure for our youth – *atrophy*.
And we saw the malaise in its advanced state
in Satra, the Jain who taught geography

And tried to sell us school supplies. "You know,"
said Singham, the science man, "you fellers are lucky
to be here." As obvious as gravity, as if no
more needed saying, no effort to unlock

The theorems of Black Nationalism, or Boy George
dressing like a girl, or how Michael Jackson
conquered the moon, or the cowboy frenzy that surged
through the old empire, launching attacks on

The value of art. The college became the Church
of the Machine, and we its acolytes,
groomed to look down from glass windows, perched
atop new factories, manned by troglodytes,

Our brothers. Bureaucrats did not need the arts –
what use were the sly seraphs of literature
in factories to calibrate missile parts?
Softness was too much light for a creature

Bred for the earth's dark places. Orthodoxy,
decreed in the New CXC syllabus,
erased the traces of Wells, Orwell, Huxley
and replaced them with Montesinos and las Casas.

And thus released from the hair shirts of tradition
we careened into the waiting idle hands
of the world outside, the Creole conurbation
whose vice, and music, and laughter, were Caliban's –

The anti-hero, born in another epic
I would learn later: The father of the Other
race, who were not accounted for in the mystic
texts, and whom history, they said, had tried to smother

In the crib. We were taught his picaresque story –
one with no heroes, morals, or cities of gold
but catalogues of grief and former glory
he made, which were stolen by the world.

13: MUDDLING THE MIDDLE: CYNICAL REPRESENTATIONS OF ETHNIC RELATIONS IN V.S. AND SHIVA NAIPAUL

KEVIN FRANK

> Diversity needs the presence of peoples, no longer as objects to be swallowed up, but with the intention of creating a new relationship. Sameness requires fixed Being, Diversity establishes Becoming. Just as Sameness began with expansionist plunder in the West, Diversity came to light through the political and armed resistance of peoples. As Sameness rises *within* the fascination with the individual, Diversity is spread *through* the dynamism of communities. As the Other is a source of temptation of Sameness, Wholeness is the demand of Diversity. You cannot become Trinidadian or Quebecois, if you are not; but it is from now on true that if Trinidad and Quebec did not exist as accepted components of Diversity, something would be missing from the body of world culture.
> — Édouard Glissant, *Caribbean Discourse*

What I offer here is part of a larger project focused on how Caribbean writers deal with "race" and ethnic relations in the context of creolisation. In this work I am less concerned with Caribbean authors' ethnic or racial affiliations than I am interested in discovering which of our writers show us a way forward, both in the sense of what we may become and what may be most becoming of us, as we, Caribbean people, continue on our quest for transformation from fragmentation to wholeness. (Just for the record at this point, I find Trinidad's Earl Lovelace and Guyana's Harischandra Khemraj, who regrettably has only produced one novel, to be at the forefront of showing us a progressive path.) The nature of creolisation as an essence of Trinidadian and Tobagonian and, more broadly, Caribbean culture, despite the legacy of both open and more subtle resistance to that process, makes it a fertile patch of ground for evaluating the Naipauls' – Seepersad and his sons – contributions to the Caribbean literary tradition, our cultural formation, and our ongoing pursuit of ontological transfiguration.

While it may not be obvious to a tourist, the casual observer if you will, it should be transparent to those with a more discerning eye, with a Carib eye (to borrow a phrase from Edgar Mittelholzer), that in many parts of the

Caribbean, racial beliefs underlie suspicions, resentments, fears and loathings (including, in some instances, self-loathing) that fester just beneath the surface, waiting for the right conditions to erupt. This is especially true in Trinidad and Tobago and Guyana, where elections have historically been the times when the right conditions are concocted. Shiva Naipaul could well be referring to these two societies in particular when, in *Journey to Nowhere*, he speaks of "lethal resentments and no less lethal visions frothing to the surface everywhere in the English-speaking Caribbean".[1] We saw again the face of *apanjaat* or "vote for your own kind", which means voting in accordance with your racial or ethnic affiliation, leading up to the May 2015 elections in Guyana, and you would have seen it again in Trinidad and Tobago's elections some months later, in September of the same year.

The outcomes of these elections are beside the point. That is politics, the business of gaining and holding governmental and hegemonic power, and the first job of the politician is to be elected. Some may feel that some politicians seem to think that their *only* job is to be elected. But, again, that is politics.

What about our writers? Shouldn't our writers be above such politics? How do the Naipauls (father and sons) write about creolisation and about racial and ethnic relations? When V.S. Naipaul writes the foreword to his father's *The Adventures of Gurudeva and Other Stories*, he mentions a crucial ideal in his father's approach to writing, picked up from Gault MacGowan, editor of the *Trinidad Guardian* and supporter of Seepersad Naipaul's writing. This ideal is quite meaningful in examining what all three Naipauls offer the Caribbean literary tradition with respect to the problem of "race", through their representations of both intra-ethnic and inter-ethnic relations:

> In 1951, my father wrote to me: 'And as to a writer being hated or liked – I think it's the other way to what you think: a man is doing his work well when people begin *liking* him. I have never forgotten what Gault MacGowan told me years ago: 'Write sympathetically'; and this, I suppose, in no way prevents us from writing truthfully, even brightly.[2]

In the line, "I think it's the other way to what you think", we have an insight into V.S. Naipaul's view which, on the evidence over his career, could be summed up as follows: "A writer is doing his work well when people dislike, perhaps even despise him." He continues,

> It was through his journalism on MacGowan's *Guardian* that my father arrived at that vision of the countryside and its people which he later transferred to his stories. And the stories have *something of the integrity of the journalism*. [...] There is reformist passion; but even when there is shock [...] there is nothing of the protest – common in early colonial writing – that implies an outside audience; the barbs are all turned inwards. This is part of the distinctiveness of the stories. I stress it because this way of looking, from being my father's, became mine. [my emphasis][3]

Here, Sir Vidia suggests that there is a link between his work and his father's, connected, among other things, to journalistic integrity, to truth that does not preclude sympathy. Of course, here he is writing as a literary critic of his father's work, and the appeal to journalistic virtue is somewhat odd, especially as it pertains to fiction, even if informed by his father's journalism. Moreover, as he puts it, the "journalism" under MacGowan's stewardship at the *Guardian* was one with a "taste for drama"[4] that unsettled some: "Voodoo in backyards, obeah, prisoners escaping from Devil's Island, vampire bats."[5] This seems more the material of journalistic sensationalism than journalistic probity. Still, there is something strikingly disingenuous about V.S. Naipaul aligning himself with a literary heritage, such as his father's, not concerned particularly with an outside audience, especially given that some of his greater successes have come from his travel writing, works which cannot reasonably be said to have been written with the native or local as the primary, intended audience.

Additionally, in "The Dark Visions of V.S. Naipaul," first published in *Newsweek* (1981) and later in the collection, *Conversations with V.S. Naipaul*, Charles Michener begins by referring epigraphically to Edward Said's review of *Among the Believers* in *New Statesman* (1981). Said assesses,

> Naipaul the writer now flows directly into Naipaul the social phenomenon, the celebrated sensibility on tour... [He] carries with him a kind of half-stated but finally unexamined reverence for the colonial order. [There is] a deep emptiness in Naipaul the writer for which Naipaul the social phenomenon is making others pay... All this to promote an attitude of distant concern and moral superiority in the reader."[6]

There is something quite revealing in the idea of "making others pay" that makes it meaningful in examining Naipaul's claim of inheriting his father's sympathy as a writer. The latter seems irreconcilable with the former. Establishing the setting and further inscribing the thematic frame of reference for his conversation with Naipaul, Michener writes, "Some critics charged Naipaul himself with cruelty after he began to travel and produce his wounding, wounded reports on the West Indies and India. West Indian intellectuals attacked him for narrowness and arrogance after *The Middle Passage* appeared in 1962".[7] Michener rightly describes this work as one of Naipaul's castigating books, and he adds that it is "precocious about racial assertion: 'Negro racialism... has profound intellectual promptings... in the realisation that the Negro problem lies not simply in the attitude of other to the Negro, but in the Negro's attitude to himself'".[8] Gordon Rohlehr perhaps puts it best when he observes that, among the many things with which V.S. Naipaul "has not come to terms [is] ... the Negro-Creole world in Trinidad".[9] As we will see, the same could be said of his younger brother.

In "The Adventures of Gurudeva", the story that lends its title to the entire collection, Seepersad Naipaul's ethnic outlook seems best represented in Schoolmaster Sohun's views regarding creolisation, assimilation, and authenticity. Cautioning Gurudeva in his fight against Pundit Biswas, in his insistence upon his version of orthodox Hinduism, Sohun declares,

> In a country such as the West Indies, Western culture and habits are the passport to progress. You people want to build a little India of your own in Trinidad. You are trying to dance top in mud. It cannot be done. The difficulty lies in the fact that you are too much of a majority to assimilate, too much of a minority to dominate. On every hand you are pressed by Western influence. You cannot be entirely Oriental, nor entirely Occidental; you can no more be entirely Western than you can be entirely Eastern; neither a hundred per cent European nor a hundred per cent Indian. You will be distinctly West Indian."[10]

At this moment, what appears as only an intra-ethnic and related religious problem has tremendous implications for inclusive, holistic Trinbagonian and, more broadly, Caribbean identity formation. The schoolmaster makes the case for embracing creolisation and locating one's authenticity in the reality of that fully mixed heritage. However, there is an equally great significance in his speech. He rightly identifies the majority/minority complex hindering the assimilation process and underlying the quest for political domination that plays out in various ways and at various times, but especially – and not without aspects of the carnivalesque – during election times, when the struggle for ascendancy is further energised by "race"-baiting.

In a later edition of his seminal work, *The West Indian Novel and its Background*, Kenneth Ramchand explains his addition of a chapter on Earl Lovelace's *The Dragon Can't Dance*:

> This essay on Lovelace's novel of 1979 is included in this new edition as a new chapter, and inserted after the discussion of *A House for Mr. Biswas* because it takes the argument forward from *Biswas* into a discussion of Indian-African relations and towards an exploration of the place of cultures other than European and African in the making of the creole culture of Trinidad and Tobago. These are crucial issues.[11]

These are pivotal matters, and they are as pressing today as they were at the time Ramchand wrote those words, if not more so. What Ramchand means by taking the argument forward from *Biswas* is that in *A House for Mr Biswas*, "Naipaul shows his Indians confronting, not the Africans themselves but the city where the Africans are in the majority".[11]

It is in the confrontation with the Africans, that is with "blackness" – that inescapable presence in the creole continuum – that there is a marked, albeit understandable difference between Seepersad and both of his sons. Naipaul, the father, writes before the "Black Power" movements that appear to disturb his sons. This "blackness" problem pertinent to creolisation in the Caribbean and its literary tradition is at the heart of Selwyn Cudjoe's critique of R. M. Lacovia's reading of V.S. Naipaul: "While Caribbean culture is African-based, it is suffused with many other elements (East Indian, Indian, Chinese). Therefore, it is irrational to set up guidelines based on a static concept".[13] Of course, Cudjoe unwittingly risks replicating the very problem he is addressing in his privileging of Africa at the foundation of the culture when he unquestioningly declares Caribbean culture African-based, even while granting there are other elements. This is in itself a stagnant formulation and it is both ironic and contradictory given Cudjoe's good intent, for suffusion would mean all the elements are spread throughout the culture, including at the base of the culture.

A telling interview pertinent to examining V.S. Naipaul's inheritance of the sympathetic writing hand is his response to Bharati Mukherjee's and Robert Boyers' question concerning *The Middle Passage*. They asked: "But it was said, when it appeared, that you were approaching the country with preconceived conclusions – that you went to confirm expectations rather than to explore what was before you".[14] Naipaul responds,

> Yes, there were complaints. In the 1960's people were shouting for certain political movements in those places I visited, so when I stepped in to say that this is stupid, that this is just routine, nothing more than public affairs, those who were shouting did not approve. [...] And you know, I think that the books of real writers, even *when they are reporter's books*, must be judged on their ability to stand up. [my emphasis; here is that journalism link][15]

Regarding a book's ability to stand up, one question is, stand up for what, or for whom? I am being somewhat tongue-in-cheek. Nevertheless, it is one thing to insist upon the test of time as a measure of literary merit; it is entirely another to evaluate standing up for higher principles, such as objective, holistic truth instead of narrow, jaded, personal truth as objective moral judgment.

This dilemma is a particular point of contention as Naipaul continues his retort to the accusation of seeing with a predetermined eye:

> If *The Middle Passage* is found untrue today, 18 years later, then I will debate what seems untrue... I refused to go in with preconceived notions ... Don't tell me... that I shouldn't have said what I say about the illiterate black man shouting for racial redemption and found to get nowhere. Will you say they have gotten somewhere? ... I say they've taken several large steps back to the bush. And it's surprised me. I never thought that after 300 years of the new world an African people could return to the bush.[16]

Mukherjee decries, "What is amazing to me is the confidence with which you can say that the objective truth is they have returned to the bush."[17] Naipaul explains,

I'm being very provocative, but I'm also speaking with a lot of bitterness. And much unhappiness. Because it is not pleasant to see the place where you were born destroyed, and that is the bottom of it. There are no institutions, nothing to refer to any longer. You cannot refer to any idea of law, or honesty about public money or the rights of all men, because racialist politics in a way rejects all these values.[18]

Of course, a partial truth exists in Naipaul's complaint: racialist politics do undermine the rights of all men, and he is provocative, unhappy and bitter, which he apparently was at the time of writing *The Middle Passage*. This is precisely why he could not help but go in with preconceived notions, and why he could not do otherwise than to see and write unsympathetically and cynically, meaning in the interest of his own group.

There are many rich moments in *The Middle Passage* where V.S. Naipaul's acrimonious, self-interested, and group-interested political views are on display. But one that stands out prominently and serves the purpose is his summation of the problems with "race" in Trinidad. Despite the appearance of an all-round condemnation of racialism in the work, ultimately, Naipaul represents Indian racialism as benign, in stark contrast to baleful African racialism. "Though now one racialism seems to be reacting on the other," he surmises, "each has different roots".[19] The point is in the contrast as he carries on: "Indian politicians have created Indian racialism out of harmless egoism", whereas the Negroes' racialism is the result of prejudices "inherited from the white man." Moreover, seen as "the sentimental camaraderie of skin which provides the cheap thrill of being 'African'", the connotation regarding Negro racialism is that it is pernicious. That idea is driven home in the violent threat of Negroes demonstrating upon Lumumba's death, who "were singing hymns, which contrasted with the violence of their banners and placards".[20] A related problem is that Naipaul's partial truth suggests that the peril of racialist politics is one-directional, emanating solely from African people in the new world – "the black man shouting for racial redemption." It is a cynical position, through which he can distance himself and his ethnic group from the pitfalls of "race" that permeate his society and all in it. It is a self-serving, captious position through which he can claim a moral superiority and align himself with the supposed moral superiority of his main readers, the outside audience, while confirming their expectations.

"Black Power" similarly discomposes the imagination of Sir Vidia's younger brother, Shiva Naipaul, resulting in misanthropic compositions on those he sees as the Other. A good case in point is Shiva's journalistic jaunt, *Journey to Nowhere* (first published as *Black and White*). He clearly projects himself as a writer in the journalistic tradition when he declares, "Journalists, I was aware, were not generally welcome in Guyana",[21] which brings us to the consideration of his objectivity and whether he measures up to his father Seepersad's ideal of writing sympathetically, which is connected to the notion of fairness or impartiality in pursuit of truth. However, the way in which Shiva depicts racial conflict raises questions about his objectivity and suggests that his sympathy is decidedly one-sided:

> Fourteen years earlier when I had left Trinidad for England, British Guiana had been caught in the toils of yet another bout of racial warfare between blacks and Indians. The Mighty Sparrow (Trinidad's top calypso singer) was singing: 'I don't care if the whole of B.G. burn down/ I don't care if the whole of Bookers burn down...' But Guyana's troubles had started long before that. I was eight years old in 1953 when, in fear of a Communist takeover by the People's Progressive Party led by Cheddi Jagan, the Constitution was suspended and British troops landed. From then on, the place became indelibly associated with unsavory tumult and drama.[22]

What is left unsaid here, the dangling connotation, is that the unsavoury tumult is the direct and sole result of "the excesses of an unrestrained and cynical black supremacy",[23] led by Forbes Burnham. This view is confirmed when he tells of his conversations with the PPP (Cheddi Jagan happened to be away, so Janet Jagan stands in as the party's representative). He concludes, "A child could understand that the PNC was a black-supremacist party of the worst kind, a projection into public life of savage instincts and gangster ideology. But not, it appeared, the PPP".[24] On the one hand, he condemns the PPP for being naïve in not seeing the PNC as he sees it. On the other hand, that childish association with naïveté connotes the PPP as innocent of such racial-supremacist ideology and savage instincts. The message is in the double entendre of "But not, it appeared, the PPP."

Shiva Naipaul's representations of ethnic relations in Trinidad are also *parti pris*. For instance, speaking of the disdain for agriculture that developed among both Indo- and Afro-Trinidadians, he describes the problem in a manner consistent with his fear stemming from the "Black Power" movements: "These attitudes were reinforced after the coming of Independence when the government put in power by urban-minded, 'coolie'-despising blacks, ignored the Indian-dominated countryside, a process brought to completion by the onset of oil-fed prosperity in the late sixties".[25] Statements like this insinuate that Trinidad is unambiguously partisan, with cliquish, "Black Power", Afro-Trinidadians detesting Indo-Trinidadians, and not the reverse. Indeed, later in the same essay, Shiva implies such feelings and actions would have been beyond him and, by extension, those like him: "The clannish, hierarchical Hindu past known to the older members of my family... had all but dissolved by my day, been split up into its various, often warring, fragments, each of which rigorously pursued its own interests".[26] In other words, disintegration of clannishness, discontinuity with the past, and the warring fragments implies the impossibility of a common cause and the improbability of any corollary that approximates the threatening Black Nationalism, such as East-Indian tribalism.

Much like his brother Vidia's portrayals noted above, Hinduness and East Indianness seem unblemished by anything resembling political motive: "For a while yet, our 'Hinduness', our awareness of ourselves as members of an exclusive and important clan, Brahminical princes among the Hindu community, came to life once a year or so when we all gathered for some days in my uncle's house".[27] He concludes, "India, as represented by its ties of caste and clan and shared memory, lasted less than sixty years in Trinidad." However, his anodyne account of East-Indian nationalism and antipathy is discordant with that of Joseph P. Farrell's who, borrowing from Daniel J. Crowley's work, posits that East-Indian nationalism in Trinidad was a direct response to their creolisation: "This high degree of assimilation and loss of ancestral culture has alarmed some of the East Indian elite and had led to a greatly increased emphasis on separate Hindu and Moslem schools, where Hindustani is taught, the Indian anthem sung, and various others attempts made to stimulate Indian nationalism".[28]

The apex or, better, abyss of Shiva Naipaul's "Black Power" anxiety, which impairs his objectivity and reveals his ethnocentricity comes, arguably, when he writes about Rastafarianism. Note, for example, the apocalyptic vision (somewhat reminiscent of the fears expressed in Yeats' "The Second Coming") as he opines, "Between the visit of Haile Selassie and the funeral of Bob Marley a great deal had happened; a great deal had come to fruition in Jamaica. Most portentously, the Rastaman had crawled out of the shadows of nightmare and been crowned a king: a phoenix risen from the ashes of the Black Power era".[29] Here, "shadows" and "nightmare" and "ashes" paint a clear picture of what, from Shiva's perspective, "Black Power" augured and augurs, as already malignant. It spawns the ominous Rasta. This kind of rhetorical play for the benefit of his largely non-Caribbean readership is further evident when he proclaims, "In 1970, to the far south of the Caribbean Sea, Trinidad, that most innocent land of the calypso and the humming bird, was recovering from the recent shock of a mutiny by its fledgling army, some of whose officers had been inspired by Black Power ideology."[30] Of course, no honest Trinidadian, regardless of "race" or ethnicity, would be under any illusion about their island nation being a land of innocence, particularly in association with what is at times a most ribald local musical tradition, the calypso. But like his brother, Shiva Naipaul's primary audience is outside, and is likely to miss the evidence here of someone "playing mas", if you will, through rhetorical craft. Locals or those otherwise in the know would see it for what it is, a pappy show, nonsensical, but not inconsequential.

Like his elder brother, Shiva Naipaul's pappy show is the design of a writer estranged from his homeland: "The assumptions of affinity I took away with me in 1964 have ceased to be tenable".[31] It is the construct of a litterateur alienated from those he views as Other – if there ever were any attachments in the first place: "The evolutions and convolutions of 'black consciousness' (I am, when all is said and done, of Indian ancestry) have nothing, as such, to do with me. I recoil from the degraded ideologies that would reclassify me as 'black.'"[32] Coming from a society suffused in creolisation that recoils from anything "black" is precisely why Shiva, like his brother Vidia, is unable to write objectively about racial or ethnic relations. Indeed, they have both sided with the outsider, their outside audience, as is indicated by Shiva's summation of his externalisation: "A new marginality has been thrust upon people like myself by the assorted wog-doms that have come into being during the last twenty-five years – those penitential states of mind that are equated with 'liberation'. Marginality is sad. But, in my case, it is a sadness beyond my control."[33] "Wog" is the key to understanding Shiva's declaration of his allegiance here, with the British, his former colonisers: the pejorative term is, after all, mainly British for a dark-skinned foreigner.

Derek Walcott approaches V.S. Naipaul delicately regarding his racial representations in a 1965 interview, originally published in Trinidad's *Sunday Guardian*: "Do you think that having lived in Trinidad, in a multi-racial society, has helped you to achieve a more balanced perception?".[34] Naipaul's response seems surprisingly noncommittal: "I really don't know…" However, seen through the lens of his cynical perceptions, his answer is not surprising. The cynical eye informing Naipaul's representations of race in *The Middle Passage* is remarkably similar to that of his brother Shiva in *Journey to Nowhere* and *Beyond the Dragon's Mouth*. Both of Seepersad's sons turn to cynicism in their psychosocial analyses of racial problems. For example, Shiva introduces the racial dynamic at the core of his thesis by referencing Surinam's Indian exodus, a result of pre-Independence fear of "Black Power":

> If Guyana, their immediate neighbor, loosed into the world by the British in 1966, was anything to go by, the Hindustanis, the Chinese and the Javanese – these last an exotic reminder of the Dutch colonies in the East Indies – had every reason to be worried and fearful about the implications of Independence.[35]

The elder brother is more subtle and paints with a broader brush, appearing to label all of Trinidad cynical: "For if such a society breeds cynicism, it also breeds tolerance, not the tolerance between castes and creeds and so on – which does not exist in Trinidad anyway".[36] The most important point is the link between cynicism and lack of tolerance. The connection is reinforced as he turns to people's "selfishness" in "the race struggle"/"the Negro-Indian rivalry."[37] Both brothers wish to appear above racial prejudice. However, the synergy of their self-interest and their racial belligerence/race baiting undermines that desire. Subjective and pessimistic, Vidia and Shiva favour one side in the Indo- and Afro-Caribbean racial antagonism. The fact is, no racial ideology is innocent or benign. In writing more for an outside audience, neither brother inherits the father's ideal of the writer as journalist, writing truthfully, which does not preclude writing sympathetically.

Endnotes

1. Shiva Naipaul, *Journey to Nowhere: A New World Tragedy* (New York: Simon & Schuster, 1980), 15.
2. V.S. Naipaul, foreword to *The Adventures of Gurudeva and Other Stories* (London: Andre Deutsch, 1976), 14-15.
3. V.S. Naipaul, foreword to *The Adventures of Gurudeva*, 15.
4. V.S. Naipaul, foreword to *The Adventures of Gurudeva*, 14.
5. V.S. Naipaul, foreword to *The Adventures of Gurudeva*, 14.
6. Charles Michener, "The Dark Visions of V.S. Naipaul", in *Conversations with V.S. Naipaul*, ed. Feroza Jussawalla, (Jackson: University Press of Mississippi, 1997), 63-74, p. 63.
7. Michener, 69.
8. Michener, 69.
9. Gordon Rohlehr, "The Ironic Approach: The Novels of VS. Naipaul", in *Critical Perspectives on V.S. Naipaul*, ed. Robert D. Hammer (New York: Three Continents Press, 1977), 178-193, p. 178.
10. Seepersad Naipaul, *The Adventures of Gurudeva*, 92.
11. Kenneth Ramchand, *The West Indian Novel and Its Background*, 2nd ed. (Kingston: Ian Randle Publishers, 2004), 172.
12. Ramchand, 174.
13. Selwyn R. Cudjoe, *Resistance and Caribbean Literature* (Athens: Ohio University Press, 1980), 71.
14. Robert Boyers and Bharati Mukherjee, "A Conversation with V.S. Naipaul", in *Conversations with V.S. Naipaul*, ed. Feroza Jussawalla, (Jackson: University Press of Mississippi, 1997), 75-92, p. 82-3.
15. V.S. Naipaul, quoted in Boyers and Mukherjee, 83.
16. V.S. Naipaul, quoted in Boyers and Mukherjee, 83.
17. Boyers and Mukherjee, 83.
18. V.S. Naipaul, quoted in Boyers and Mukherjee, 83.
19. V.S. Naipaul, *The Middle Passage*, 2nd ed. (New York: Vintage Books, 2002), 81.
20. V.S. Naipaul, *The Middle Passage*, 82.
21. Shiva Naipaul, *Journey to Nowhere*, 23.
22. Shiva Naipaul, *Journey to Nowhere*, 20.
23. Shiva Naipaul, *Journey to Nowhere*, 15.
24. Shiva Naipaul, *Journey to Nowhere*, 94.

25. Shiva Naipaul, *Beyond the Dragon's Mouth* (New York: Viking, 1985), 18.
26. Shiva Naipaul, *Beyond the Dragon's Mouth*, 25.
27. Shiva Naipaul, *Beyond the Dragon's Mouth*, 26.
28. Joseph P. Farrell, "Education and Pluralism in Selected Caribbean Societies", *Comparative Education Review 11*, no. 2 (1967): 160-181, p. 177.
29. Shiva Naipaul, *Beyond the Dragon's Mouth*, 378.
30. Shiva Naipaul, *Beyond the Dragon's Mouth*, 378.
31. Shiva Naipaul, *Beyond the Dragon's Mouth*, 394.
32. Shiva Naipaul, *Beyond the Dragon's Mouth*, 394.
33. Shiva Naipaul, *Beyond the Dragon's Mouth*, 394.
34. Derek Walcott, "Interview with V.S. Naipaul", in *Conversations with V.S. Naipaul*, ed. Feroza Jussawalla, (Jackson: University Press of Mississippi, 1997), 5-9, p. 7.
35. Shiva Naipaul, *Journey to Nowhere*, 14-15.
36. V.S. Naipaul, *The Middle Passage*, 73-74.
37. V.S. Naipaul, *The Middle Passage*, 75.

14: "MY SENSE OF DISTANCE AND TIME WAS SHAKEN": GLOBALISATION BEFORE ITS TIME IN THE WORK OF V.S. NAIPAUL

JIM HANNAN

Although V.S. Naipaul's career straddles the shift from Commonwealth literature to postcolonialism, neither of these terms adequately accounts for the intensive relationship to local places and regions that recurs in Naipaul's work. Naipaul is capable of deploying, and dismissing, the local colour prized in Commonwealth literature, but also of moving from anecdotal observation to the kind of sweeping, universalising statements disavowed by postcolonial theory.[1] Those aspects of Naipaul's work that seem to cause alarm in readers and critics alike cannot be accounted for by such features of postcolonial theory as "a condition of nativist longing in post-independence national groupings", or "an oppositional form of 'reading practice'",[2] or "the celebration of Third World agency".[3] Naipaul, that is, follows neither what one literary critic calls the "appreciative internationalism" of Commonwealth literature nor the "more activist anti-imperialism" of postcolonial studies.[4]

But what can seem to be a contrarian streak in Naipaul's work has been identified differently by Naipaul himself in his 2001 Nobel Lecture, in which he says that his way of writing has been "intuitive".[5] Rather than explain his body of work according to a systematic logic, Naipaul instead sees unity in his varied subjects: "the land [of Trinidad]; the aborigines; the New World; the colony; the history; India; the Muslim world; Africa; and then England".[6] Although Naipaul titles his Nobel Lecture "Two Worlds", this list of subjects suggests a broader, more complex, approach to the world and his representations of it. Writing in 1974, Kenneth Ramchand captures to some degree Naipaul's more intuitive rather than systematic approach. Noting Naipaul's concern in the early 1960s that West Indian writers, in Naipaul's words, "reflected and flattered the prejudices of their race or colour groups", Ramchand observes that *A House for Mr Biswas* "refutes Naipaul's own view… for it shows how possible it is to write with great particularity about a specific group in West Indian society without writing for that group, and without writing so exclusively about the group that the West Indian-ness of their experience is denied."[7]

Ramchand's observation points towards a key facet of almost all of Naipaul's work: it is global in the broadest, and also most productive, sense of the term. Deeply motivated by the will to represent the varieties of local experience, Naipaul's work is also persistently suspicious of the types of affiliation that locality often demands. The political theorist James Rosenau identifies one way of thinking about globalisation with the phrase "distant proximities". Rosenau writes that this phrase expresses "the idea that what seems remote in the present era also seems close-at-hand, thereby compelling [people] to cope continuously with the challenge of distant proximities", of, that is, "the intertwining of... the global and local, the public and the private, the coherent and incoherent".[8] The phrase distant proximities can be used to describe a tendency in Naipaul's work to reverse the familiar mantra enjoining people to think globally and act locally. Naipaul, that is, thinks intensively about locality as a way to understand the processes of global action. Think locally, act globally.

In this chapter, I will turn to some of Naipaul's early writing on India as a way to approach how he thinks through the local in order to form those distant proximities that Rosenau identifies as a feature of globalisation. In a few essays that Naipaul wrote during the early 1960s, and in *An Area of Darkness*, his first book on India, published in 1964, Naipaul repeatedly remarks upon behaviour he observes in India that contradicts modernism's division of the world according to different stages of historical development. Naipaul's remarks demonstrate the pervasive influence of modernity upon his view of India, which he represents as a land and people that exhibit vivid differences between traces of a fantastical, mythic, but ultimately superstitious and uncouth antiquity and a dreary, unhopeful present. As he portrays them, however, people in India continually fail to distinguish the modern from the residual and archaic. "The contractor's wife, so anxious to demonstrate her Westernness, regularly consulted her astrologer and made daily trips to the temple to ensure... her good fortune. The schoolteacher, who complained... about the indiscipline and crudity of Indians, proceeded... to change his clothes in public."[9] In Naipaul's account, Indians don't appear to notice the contradiction between professed modernity and continuing archaism. Naipaul, however, as a writer-observer versed in the ways of modernity, continuously remarks upon these jarring dichotomies.[10] Always detecting what he takes to be the conflicting traces and signs of the ancient and the modern, Naipaul represents India, and what he perceives to be its dysfunction, according to his own modernity.[11]

Naipaul has famously represented himself as a man without a place to belong. In *The Enigma of Arrival* he writes that "I had thought that because of my insecure past – peasant India, colonial Trinidad... the colonial smallness that didn't consort with the grandeur of my ambition, my uprooting of myself for a writing career, my coming to England with so very little... I had been given an especially... raw sense of an unaccommodating world."[12] He delineates in *An Area of Darkness* how this condition reflects a schism between India and Trinidad. India, in the form of language, religious rituals, ideas about food and cleanliness, permeates his Trinidadian childhood, but, given the intervention of distance and time, he decrees that "the India... which was the background to my childhood was an area of imagination. It was not the real country."[13] Naipaul will make this point about India in Trinidad thirty-five years later in his Nobel Lecture: "Half of us... were *pretending*... that we had brought a kind of India with us" to Trinidad [my emphasis].[14] Indeed, upon first arriving in India, Naipaul realises that his physical resemblance to other Indians doesn't differentiate him as an Indian from Trinidad from the people around him. "For the first time in my life I was one of the crowd... It was like being denied part of my reality... I had been made by Trinidad and England; recognition of my difference was necessary to me".[15] But this comment is paradoxical: precisely because in India Naipaul has lost the semblance of difference, has become the same, he feels himself as a Trinidadian yet further different from Indians. Sameness becomes the ground for difference.

Naipaul's comment on the difference that does and does not exist between Trinidad and India is a version of the distant proximities that Rosenau asserts characterise the global condition. In *An Area of Darkness,* Naipaul recounts an experience that unsettles him precisely because it forms an unexpected proximity between what he had thought were widely separated worlds. During his first trip to India, Naipaul visits the village from which his maternal grandfather left India decades earlier for Trinidad. His account in *An Area of Darkness* suggests that this visit radically upsets his careful division of the world between the archaic and the modern and, most importantly for Naipaul's own experience, between India and Trinidad. Long before Naipaul's visit to India, his grandfather had sent money from Trinidad back to India to erect shrines in his natal Indian village. Naipaul writes that during his visit to his grandfather's village in India, the villagers showed "me my grandfather's name carved on the shrines. They unlocked the grilled doors and showed me the images... My mind leapt years, my sense of distance and time was shaken: before me were the very replicas of the images in the prayer-room of my grandfather's house" in Trinidad.[16] The images Naipaul sees in India are only replicas of those he grew up knowing in Trinidad, and as such they suggest a type of mediation consonant with the distance between India and Trinidad that Naipaul takes for granted. To the young Naipaul in colonial Trinidad, India was, as he says in *An Area of Darkness*, "a country out in the void beyond the dot of Trinidad; and from it our journey had been final".[17] Naipaul has believed throughout his first visit to India both in the finality of his ancestors' journey from India and in the irreducible division between what he calls in his Nobel Lecture the "remnants" of India in colonial Trinidad and the experience of India that he undergoes on this first trip to the country.[18] He thus finds himself shocked when these replicas impose his life in Trinidad upon his journey to this Indian village. "Again and again", he writes of this return to his grandfather's village, "I had that sense of dissolving time, that alarming but exhilarating sense of wonder at my physical self".[19] Naipaul expresses wonder, that is, that his body could suddenly be susceptible to a "distorted" sense of time and space when otherwise throughout his year of travel in India he refuses to allow this feeling of distortion, this feeling of "exaltation", into his rationalist appraisal of India's past and present.[20]

This brief passage from *An Area of Darkness* illustrates the problem that concerns me in this paper. In these few pages Naipaul unexpectedly describes the displacement and simultaneity that we can associate not with modernity, but with the decentring and deterritorialising effects of contemporary globalisation. He describes a break in his own and modernity's interest in the distinctions that produce temporal and spatial difference. In doing so he gives us, well before the historical turn towards postmodern globalisation is evident, an image of what will become the increasingly compact and compressed organisation of the world that typifies globalisation. A sentence in Naipaul's Nobel Lecture is particularly striking in this context. Referring to that trip forty years after it took place, Naipaul says, "I went to India, my ancestral land, for a year; it was a journey which broke my life in two".[21] One sign of this world broken in two is the jarring sensation of those distant proximities theorised by Rosenau as a sign of globalisation. In India, and recollecting that moment forty years later, Naipaul moves from the immediacy of locality into the global.

Naipaul, so often in his travel writing exquisitely attentive to his own sensibility, even when this means pointing out, as he does in *An Area of Darkness,* that he "yields" to "rage", "contempt", "failure", and "hysteria", indicates the alien nature of this nascent global sensibility by emphasising its "alarming [and] exhilarating" qualities.[22] Determined even at this early stage in his career to declare his metaphorical "homelessness",[23] Naipaul throughout *An Area of Darkness* underscores his own alienation from India.[24] "Indians could walk among these relics with ease; the romance had always been partly theirs and now they had inherited it fully. I was not English or Indian; I was denied the victories of both".[25] But the visit to his grandfather's village removes the barrier that Naipaul has erected between his own life as a Trinidadian colonial subject and the frustratingly fantastic land of India. This moment anticipates a form of the global condition, in which localities imagined to be discrete and particular become inextricably linked in a manner that destabilises time and place and that produces new relations that lessen distance and create proximity in its stead. In Naipaul's work, such global thinking does not lead to the multicultural position that identity and cultures are fluid. Naipaul, the cultural Hindu in Trinidad,[26] the ambitious West Indian in England, the New World man in ancient India, does not anticipate a programme of postmodern cultural hybridity, but instead expresses here the formal composition of globalisation as a new approach to time and space, as the erasure of the sense of difference and distance to which Naipaul's modernity otherwise commits him. For Naipaul in India in the early 1960s, this moment does not last – "exaltation died. I became again an impatient traveller"[27] – but the brief appearance of this temporal-spatial form indicates the potential emergence of a new, cultural globalisation as well as the potential to consider Naipaul a writer of global, rather than, say, national or regional literature.[28]

In virtually all U.S. editions of his books, Naipaul's biographical blurb states that he has followed no profession other than writing. As a writer from mid-twentieth-century Trinidad, then, he faced a substantial problem because, as he states in an essay from the late 1950s, in Trinidad "it is felt that writing is its own reward" and therefore requires no financial compensation.[29] This comment, though in part a gibe made at the expense of colonial Trinidad, also demonstrates how explicitly Naipaul maintained a pragmatically professional, rather than an idealistic approach to the process of making literature.[30] Defending Naipaul against charges that he "betrayed the West Indies" by remaining in England, Bruce King offers a factual, rather than ideological, explanation for such a decision. "Naipaul, Selvon and others… had little choice. Trinidad is not Australia. It has no well paying magazines and newspapers, no Arts Council funding writers, no large educational market in which writers… can find a steady income when their works become set texts for examinations."[31] But, as the young Naipaul puts it, to "live in England and depend on an English audience" while writing "about Trinidad, and more particularly the Indian community there," is not entirely satisfactory.[32] The work he produces at that time risks being marginalised, treated as exotic by a readership still defined according to the divide between the periphery and the metropolis. Put succinctly by Naipaul, "the very originality of the material makes the work suspect" with the English reader.[33] And this originality puts the young Naipaul in an awkward position precisely because "I write for England", even though the English reader might be "fed up with Trinidad and Trinidad dialect".[34]

Naipaul illuminates here a contradiction for the writer who remained located between the defining poles of the colonial relationship. Even if, as in his earliest books, Naipaul writes about or from the perspective of

Trinidad, he still writes for a readership that, he worries, can easily regard such work as merely local, merely particular, and not sufficiently integrated into the expectations of those metropolitan readers who do not like or have grown tired of dialect and details about distant places and people that they can dismiss as local colour. And yet to submit to the standardising demands of commercial publishing threatens the corner of the market to which Naipaul can, at that time, lay claim. In the face of this dilemma, the young Naipaul remarks, "the only way out is to cease being a regional writer... I would like nothing better".[35] Naipaul will make an attempt, during his year in India, to write, in *Mr Stone and the Knights Companion,* the English novel that will signal the end of his regionalism. But with such a novel Naipaul remains enmeshed in the limitations of colonialism, having merely substituted one side of the colonial binary for the other. The critic Fawzia Mustafa suggests that in writing *Mr Stone*, "Naipaul appears to be testing his contention that all literatures are regional, and imbued with their own private languages, in this case an essentialist 'Englishness'".[36] But to make this case already suggests that Naipaul has broken out of the centre / periphery division and claimed as his own legitimate region the subject of English society.[37] Such a claim problematises the category of regionalism as such. To what region would Naipaul, quite capable of writing a thoroughly English novel (and writing it in India, no less), a thoroughly West Indian novel, and much else besides, belong? Of what use, that is, is regionalism if a writer such as Naipaul can claim more than one as his own?

Naipaul will more importantly break with the claims of regionalism by ceasing to write exclusively about the Caribbean or England and turning his attention to various locations around the world. Before making this break with the duality of colonialism, his ambivalence over the problem of place, his reluctance, given his own emphatic individualism, to be put in place, is evident. Again writing in the late 1950s, Naipaul says, "I have... achieved the Buddhist ideal of non-attachment. I am never disturbed by national or international issues. I do not sign petitions. I do not vote. I do not march. And I never cease to feel that this lack of interest is all wrong. I want to be involved".[38] While it is difficult, in the face of these comments professing detachment, to ignore Naipaul's often contentious remarks on Africa, India, the Caribbean, or Islam, I suggest that these early ruminations by Naipaul expressing discomfort about his location as a writer anticipate the sense of simultaneity now associated with globalisation. To put this differently, we certainly could see how Naipaul's supposed "non-attachment" cynically mutates into what the historian William Dalrymple, referring to Naipaul's remarks that the destruction of the Babri Masjid in Ayodhya was a "great moment" for the "soul" of India,[39] calls Naipaul's erroneous and misleading reading of history as a way to justify sectarian conflict.[23] We could also, however, see his construction of the unlocated, or unlocatable, writer, as a precursor to what Michael Hardt and Antonio Negri identify as the pre-eminent form of power in the global condition, that is, a world market that "counter[s]... any division between the inside and outside" because "the entire globe is its domain".[24] Naipaul's heightened awareness of his own location as a writer within a literary market that will eventually give way to a new sensation of distance and time, seems to be an appropriate form of ambivalence for Hardt and Negri's global domain.

In his Nobel Lecture, Naipaul lists the subjects that he has intuitively come to write about – "the land [of Trinidad]; the New World; India; the Muslim world; Africa; and England". This suggests that if Naipaul is always highly attentive to locality, he is attentive with what he calls in the lecture a "special point of view". This, arising from an ancestry "far from authority", enables him to envision what might be thought of as "space beyond place".[42] "Space beyond place" is a term used by some writers on globalisation to postulate a move away from local structures, such as nation-states or regional identity. For the sociologists Darren O'Byrne and Alexander Hensby, space beyond place is "a level above" the local which "cuts across and impacts it", even as the globe itself is not imagined as a single, homogenising place.[43]

I will conclude by noting that Naipaul indicates that a global perspective is far from a settled perspective. In his 1987 novel *The Enigma of Arrival* Naipaul remarks that he had extensively researched, in England, the history of Trinidad for his 1969 book *The Loss of El Dorado,* or, as he puts it in *Enigma,* he had been "reading the documents of my island in London".[44] After working so intensively in the archives, Naipaul states that, "I wanted to see the island where I had been living in a new way in my imagination for the last two years, the island I had restored, as it were, to the globe and for which now I felt a deep romance. [Upon my return to Trinidad] I found an island full of racial tensions and close to revolution. So, as soon as I had arrived at a new idea about the place, it had ceased to be mine".[45] For Naipaul, this failed romance of possession, of origins, of location, is best conducted from a distance. This distance, however, allows him to imagine, if only textually, an intimacy that facilitates the distant proximities prevalent in the global condition.

Endnotes

1. This disavowal can be seen in postcolonialism's connection to poststructuralism's rejection of master narratives and essentialism. Naipaul doesn't share this rejection and instead reproduces certain master narratives (regarding race, Hinduism, Islam, etc.) that depend upon essentialism.
2. Stephen Slemon, quoted in Ashcroft et al., *Key Concepts in Post-Colonial Studies,* 188.

3. See Vivek Chibber on this dimension of subaltern studies in *Postcolonial Theory and the Specter of Capital*, 9.
4. Graham Huggan, quoted in John C. Hawley, "The Colonizing Impulse of Postcolonial Theory", 785.
5. V.S. Naipaul, "Two Worlds", in *Literary Occasions,* 183. Hereafter cited in the text as "Two Worlds".
6. V.S. Naipaul, "Two Worlds", 190.
7. Kenneth Ramchand, "The West Indies", in *Literatures of the World in English*, ed. Bruce King, 205, 206.
8. James Rosenau, *Distant Proximities*, 3.
9. V.S. Naipaul, "In the Middle of the Journey" (1962) in *The Writer and the World,* 6-7.
10. To consider visits to an astrologer, or changing clothes in public, archaic is to impose a temporal regime upon others that they might not share. Dipesh Chakrabarty comments upon the use of a related term, contemporary, and its suggestion that only certain versions of the present and future will prevail. "The word 'contemporary,' whenever used to convey a sense of historical time, is never a disinterested word. Its historicist... use is always political. Some... are always more contemporary than others... [T]he futures these others are building for themselves... will soon be swamped and overwhelmed" by another present, another future. (Dipesh Chakrabarty, "Marx After Marxism", in positions 2, no. 2 (1994): 446-63.)
11. Writing in a completely different context from Naipaul, and with insights gleaned from poststructuralist and postcolonial theory, Dipesh Chakrabarty also discusses how temporality works from the perspective of an Indian intellectual. "For most Hindus, if not for most Indians, gods, spirits, and the so-called supernatural have a certain 'reality'... [T]o talk about the violent jolt that the imagination has to suffer in order to be transported from a temporality co-habited by gods and living beings to one from which the gods are banished is not to express an incurable nostalgia for a long-lost world. Even for the members of the Indian upper classes, this experience of travelling across temporalities can in no way be described as merely historical" ("Marx After Marxism", 58, 61). Whereas for Naipaul these different temporalities appear to be incongruous, the sign of an incomplete conversion to modernity, Chakrabarty points to these multi-temporalities to see if it makes sense to "attempt to inscribe horizons of radical otherness into the visions of Marx's critique of capital" (58), a critique that demands attention because "the story of becoming an 'Indian' academic-intellectual and having to... deal... with thoughts that never fail to remind you of their European origins, does not make sense without there being a concomitant narrative locating the emergence of such an intellectual class in the history of capitalist/European imperialism" (56-57).
12. V.S. Naipaul, *The Enigma of Arrival* (N.Y: Vintage Books, 1988) 92.
13. V.S. Naipaul, *An Area of Darkness* (London: Penguin Books, 1964) 41.
14. V.S. Naipaul, "Two Worlds", 187.
15. V.S. Naipaul, *An Area of Darkness*, 43.

16. V.S. Naipaul, *An Area of Darkness*, 254.
17. V.S. Naipaul, *An Area of Darkness*, 27.
18. V.S. Naipaul, "Two Worlds", 187.
19. V.S. Naipaul, *An Area of Darkness*, 258.
20. V.S. Naipaul, *An Area of Darkness*, 257.
21. V.S. Naipaul, "Two Worlds", 193.
22. V.S. Naipaul, *An Area of Darkness*, 230.
23. V.S. Naipaul, *An Area of Darkness*, 266.
24. Many have observed Naipaul's deracination. Recently Anjali Gera has pointed out that not only is Naipaul "fashionably" "nomadic", but that he "chose to occupy this uncertain zone before" it became a "paradigmatic condition of humankind in the postmodern world" (Anjali Gera, "Strange Moves: Girmitya as Cosmopolitan", in *V.S. Naipaul: An Anthology of Recent Criticism*, ed. Purabi Panwar (Delhi: Pencraft, 2003), 26-42, p. 26.). Noting that actual homelessness is an undesirable condition, Gera, with evident dissatisfaction, concludes that Naipaul rejects Trinidad and India as two possible homes and settles on England and the status of a writer in exile (Geera, 27). Few of Naipaul's critics view his work dispassionately; to quote from many of them would be to run the risk of parody. Gera, for example, remarks that in his Nobel Lecture Naipaul exhibits "amnesia" about the influence of the Caribbean on his childhood. But in that address Naipaul speaks about the obliteration by colonial history of the meaning of the name of his birthplace in Trinidad; about growing up in his grandmother's reclusive Hindu household; and about his general ignorance of India while a child. Gera may object to the way Naipaul portrays his childhood in Trinidad, but when she states that his Nobel Lecture overlooks that part of his life she makes what at best is a dubious claim. Naipaul's advocates also make untenable claims on his behalf. Bruce King, for example, refers to "a highly vocal group of critics who detested Naipaul for what they perceived as his political views" (Bruce King, *V.S. Naipaul*, 2nd ed. (Basingstoke: Palgrave Macmillan, 2003), 1.). When King dismisses those critics who object to Naipaul's political vision because, as King believes, they have "commitments" (King, *V.S. Naipaul*, 178), he trivialises often serious objections to Naipaul's work. King remarks that "what upsets [Edward] Said and his followers is Naipaul reporting what he has seen and experienced rather than explaining the world in the way they want others to see it" (King, *V.S. Naipaul*, 196). It is difficult to understand how King could conclude that in such works as *The Middle Passage, An Area of Darkness, In a Free State, Guerrillas* or *A Bend in the River*, Naipaul simply records the world as it is rather than brings to bear his own biases, predilections, insights and intelligence. King repeatedly claims, but does not demonstrate, that Naipaul has sympathy for black Americans and Africans and views colonialism, not the colonised, as the problem. What then of a passage such as this, where Naipaul pronounces on the fate of "island blacks": "They will forever consume; they will never create. They are without material resources; they will never develop the higher skills. Identity depends... on achievement; and achievement here cannot but

be small" (V.S. Naipaul, "Power?", in *The Overcrowded Barracoon*, (London: Andre Deutsch, 1972), 250.). This does not seem to be an objective description of a given situation. Naipaul invents a way of representing the region. He does not simply tell it like it is.
25. V.S. Naipaul, *An Area of Darkness*, 98.
26. Bruce King observes that "although Naipaul is a rationalist he has a Brahmin's devotion to study, scholarship... vocation; there is a Brahminian consciousness of cleanliness, purity, food and the various duties expected of a well-regulated life" (*V.S. Naipaul*, 15).
27. V.S. Naipaul, *An Area of Darkness*, 258.
28. I have found one other, much later, example of a similar temporal and spatial simultaneity in Naipaul's work. Willie Chandran, the narrator of *Half a Life* (2001), visits the governor's house in a country that closely resembles Mozambique. Chandran, originally from India, learns that the very old furniture in the very old house came from "Goa in Portuguese India [...] So unexpectedly I found myself very close to home. I had been trying to take myself back two hundred and fifty years to the building of the governor's house, trying to find some footing in that unimaginable stretch of time... I had been thinking like that, and then instead of Africa there had come India and Goa... It was like being given a new glimpse of our own history. Two hundred and fifty years: in certain parts of London that time would have been within reach, and romantic to re-create; in India, too... but here... so far from everything, so far from history, it was terrible" (V.S. Naipaul, *Half a Life* (London: Picador, 2001), 201.). Unlike the visceral reaction in *An Area of Darkness* that attests to the power of Naipaul's globalising experience, here Naipaul distils Chandran's perception through a trope of Africa as empty and thus denies the unsettling power of the spatial-temporal simultaneity.
29. V.S. Naipaul, "London," in *The Overcrowded Barracoon*, 9. Hereafter cited in the text as "London".
30. Naipaul's *Letters Between a Father and Son*, which publishes his correspondence primarily with his father and older sister during his first years in England, documents Naipaul's early decision to make a career as a writer, and the difficult financial burdens this decision placed upon him and his family.
31. King, *V.S. Naipaul*, 196. By joining Naipaul and Selvon here, King fails to account for an important difference in the reception of these two authors. Often critics of Naipaul object not to his decision to write from the former colonial metropolis – as indeed Selvon, Lamming, Mittelholzer, and so many other Caribbean writers from the boom period did – but to his bias against the colonial world and its supposed incapacity to modernise.
32. V.S. Naipaul, "London", 9.
33. V.S. Naipaul, "London", 11.
34. Even as an accomplished writer, Naipaul insists on recognising that writing occurs in a commercial setting. "Books are not created just in the mind. Books are physical objects. To write them, you need a certain kind of sensibility... To get your name on the spine of the created physical object,

you need a vast apparatus outside yourself. You need publishers, editors, designers, printers, binders; booksellers, critics, newspapers, and magazines and television where the critics can say what they think of the book; and, of course, buyers and readers. I want to stress this mundane side of things, because it is easy to take it for granted; it is easy to think of writing only in its personal, romantic aspect" (V.S. Naipaul, "Our Universal Civilization" in *The Writer and the World* (London: Picador, 2002), 506.). Naipaul makes these remarks while discussing his movement from the periphery of Trinidad to the centre of England; only England, he maintains, and not the Caribbean, or the Islamic world, or China, Japan, Eastern Europe, the Soviet Union, "black Africa", or "even" India, would have made the "literary vocation" as Naipaul understands it possible (V.S. Naipaul, *The Writer and the World*, 506-507). Thus, what seems potentially like a liberal, even progressive, statement – because, by stressing these "mundane" materialist contributions to the business of books, Naipaul demystifies the role of the culture producer and acknowledges the necessity of other forms of creativity and labour – must be positioned within Naipaul's cynical and stereotyped construction of the non-European world.

35. V.S. Naipaul, "London", 14.
36. Fawzia Mustafa, *V.S. Naipaul* (Cambridge: Cambridge University Press, 1995) 91.
37. For an example of Naipaul's continuing Eurocentrism, see "Our Universal Civilization" (in *The Writer and the World*), where he condemns the fundamentalism of Islam ("it was an article of the Arab faith that everything [that occurred] before the faith was wrong"), and notes dismissively an abiding interest among Muslims in the products, but not the process, of modernity [508, 514-515]). Naipaul praises the way "civilization" in Europe (and presumably in the United States, where he delivers the address and which can therefore be included in the possessive adjective of the title) has shed its imperialising, racist past and now makes an "extraordinary attempt… to accommodate the rest of the world, and all the currents of that world's thought" (516).
38. V.S. Naipaul, "London", 16.
39. V.S. Naipaul quoted in Patrick French, "How India Moved on from Ayodhya", *BBC*, 6 December 2012, accessed 24 October 2015.
40. William Dalrymple, "Trapped in the Ruins", *The Guardian*, 19 March 2004, accessed 24 October 2015. For a vigorous refutation of Dalrymple's argument, see Farrukh Dhondy, "Sufism Is as Important to India as Flower Power is to America." *Tehelka*. N.d. Web access 24 October 2015.
41. Michael Hardt and Antonio Negri, *Empire* (Cambridge: Harvard University Press, 2001), 190.
42. V.S. Naipaul, "Two Worlds", 194.
43. Darren O'Byrne and Alexander Hensby, *Theorizing Global Studies* (New York: Palgrave Macmillan, 2011), 151.
44. V.S. Naipaul, *The Enigma of Arrival* (N.Y: Vintage Books, 1988), 157.
45. V.S. Naipaul, *The Enigma of Arrival*, 156-8.

15: FROM TONKA BEANS TO MAGIC SEEDS: V.S. NAIPAUL'S LATE CAREER FICTION OF SELF-RETROSPECT

HYWEL DIX

This paper makes an interpretation of V.S. Naipaul's last novel, *Magic Seeds* (2004). The essay is a work in progress, part of a larger project I have been carrying out about late career fictions more generally. One of the things I asked myself quite early in the research was: when we consider the life and work of a particular writer, how often do we come to the conclusion that that author's masterpiece – his or her career-defining work – also happened to be one of his or her last pieces of work? It seems to me that we are quite accustomed to thinking about artists and writers through recourse to a retrospectively created series of stages or phases, so that it is perfectly possible to talk about T. S. Eliot's major poetical works or the late plays of Shakespeare.[1] But rarely if ever does the idea of the major work coincide with the final stage of the career. On the contrary, the very idea of a major phase implies a subsequent later phase that is somehow less significant or more minor and therefore somehow less innovative or less important than those works produced during the writer's so-called major phase.

This problem is particularly acute when considering contemporary literature: we are given to think of the idea of the contemporary as something existing rather than something coming to an end, so that the idea of the late career stage of certain contemporary writers has barely been operative at all.[2] One of the results of this has been a peculiar distancing or historical displacing of the contemporary, whereby significant contemporary writers are primarily associated with work that they produced years, or even decades earlier, rather than with their own current work.

Frustrated with this realisation, I started to try and develop a way of thinking about what is specific to late career fictions. This took me to Edward Said's own final book, *On Late Style: Music and Literature against the Grain*, in which Said identifies the characteristics associated with late career productions as stylistically resistant to their audience, awkward, and unaccommodated. He suggests that if late-career artistic work were to be seen as merely a serene taking of leave, the capacity of art to intervene in social and political conflicts would be negated, and the work produced would be incorporated into the social order rather than entering a critical dialogue with it. By refusing such incorporation the power of late style is a negative power: the negation of conformity, or "what happens if art does not abdicate its rights in favour of reality".[3]

Despite the identification of the characteristics of late-career work, however, there is in *On Late Style* a lack of conceptual definition of "lateness" and how to situate it within the trajectory of an overall career. Said tells us what late work feels like, but not what it is. Indeed, though the characteristics recur, Said associates the term *late* with at least five different meanings. Dissatisfied with that, I started to research different theoretical ideas about the different stages that make up a literary career. In the process, I came across a book by Mark Savickas about career construction theory – which initially didn't interest me at all. A book about the training of practising career counsellors didn't seem to have any relevance to a project of literary research. As I read it, however, I began to see that career construction theory had considerable potential application as a new theory of authorship that is worth elucidating here before going on to talk about V.S. Naipaul's late novel, *Magic Seeds*.

Career Construction Theory: A Brief Overview

Because career construction theory is mainly purveyed by practising counsellors, their initial point of contact with clients is often an experience of trauma or some similar negative experience or problem. As the counsellor Kobus Maree puts it: "We assume that clients' stories start only when things go wrong. How else!"[4] However, this is not necessarily the case in an authorial career. On the contrary, the particular difficulty associated with late career fictions can be expressed not as failure or difficulty, but as a problematic of success. More specifically, it is the question of how to go on authoring new works after considerable critical and/or commercial success has already been achieved. Once this stage of a career has been reached, the very name of the writer in question serves as a kind of hallmark or indicator of assumed intrinsic worth, so that the author's name alone serves as a signature for the "prolongation" of the career.[5] So much to the good. But this career stage once reached also lays down certain expectations for what the next work by that author should be like, at both the thematic and the formal level. Those expectations threaten to limit the capacity or otherwise for authorial renewal and newly invigorated kinds of creativity. How could V.S. Naipaul revisit the themes of his career-defining *A House for Mr Biswas* in a subsequent work and avoid the charge of having written a merely inferior version of it? Career construction theory offers a partial and provisional resolution to this dilemma because the central preoccupation of career counselling is to account for an individual's non-self-identity with other versions of that self by creating a narrative continuity between the different career stages that comprise a single overall career.

In *Career Counseling* (2011), Savickas explains that an important stimulus for the development of his practice was generated by the uncertain employment conditions created by rapidly changing economic patterns, especially in post-industrial societies. Career theories emphasising stability and continuity were inappropriate to what he calls the "postmodern economy" of the late twentieth and early twenty-first centuries, in which frequent change and flexibility had become a regular part of the pattern of working life.[6] By contrast, a theoretical approach to career trajectories that explores different ways of managing the distinct stages in a continually unfolding and evolving career in a fluid and dynamic way were more applicable to the needs and circumstances of an increasing number of people turning to career counselling. This is the first context in which career construction theory should be understood.

The second key insight of career construction theory, unlike both vocational guidance and career education, is to depart from an objectively-orientated stress on what any stage in a given career can help its subject to achieve and to see the career stage itself as being the subject of an ongoing, dynamic process of redefinition and critical reflection. As a result, and unlike those other areas of guidance practice, career construction theory introduces the new elements of dialogism and narrative. Or as Savickas puts it, "[c]areer counselling, from the project perspective of individual design, views clients as authors who may be characterised by autobiographical stories and who may be helped to reflect on life themes with which to construct their careers."[7]

Throughout *Career Counseling,* and indeed in the work of a number of other career construction practitioners such as Kobus Maree, Larry Cochran and Peter McIlveen, the concept of individual clients authoring – or in some cases co-authoring alongside the counsellor – a new chapter in the narrative of their own professional development has the status of an extended and controlling metaphor. The preponderant emphasis on the narration of life themes is one of the main departures made by career construction theory from other, more traditional ways of defining career stages: "Practitioners apply career construction theory when they perform career counselling to (a) construct career through small stories, (b) deconstruct and reconstruct the small stories into a large story, and (c) co-construct the next episode in the story."[8]

The high status in career construction theory of metaphors of telling stories, writing and authorship suggests a potentially fertile but hitherto unexplored area of connection between career counselling and contemporary literary study. This is because theorists like Savickas not only employ the concept of authorship as a metaphor in their work but also draw on many of the key insights of literary theory for helping their clients reimagine themselves in new roles. This paper redeploys the insights of career construction in the literary domain and hence renders what is metaphoric in the cases of other careers literal in cases of authorial careers: authorship itself. More specifically, Savickas's metaphor of episodes – or as Peter McIlveen has it, career chapters[9] – are a useful way of conceptualising the different stages that comprise an overall career and hence of considering what is specific to the late stage. In doing so, it is also possible to retain Savickas's emphasis on dialogism as an unfolding sense of self and critical self-reflection. This is because career construction theory employs a "narrative method"[10] whereby the author recreates himself as such with each new career chapter (that is, with each new work), so that what is effectively narrated is the trajectory of a career overall. The notion of dialogue between the work associated with one career stage and that produced during an earlier stage can be developed to explore the notion of self-reflection as a specific kind of metafiction peculiar to literary work produced during the latter stages of an author's career.

This necessarily brief discussion of Career Construction Theory as a new way of thinking about authorship implies that there are three main reasons why career construction theory can fruitfully be used to analyse works produced by authors at that late stage. First, the theoretical model provides a paradigm for identifying the different stages that compose an overall career. Second, the repeated emphasis on storytelling and re-narration inherent in career construction theory implies an important convergence between authorship as a literary practice and authorship as a constructivist theory. And third, career construction theory offers a potential – and provisional – resolution to the problematic of late career authorship identified above – namely, the problem of a given author's non self-identity in different works over time. It will be argued here that career construction theory offers to resolve this problem dialectically by proposing a continuum of subject positions, whereby different expressions of an authorial self as such become manifest at different points within the overall trajectory of the authorial career.

V.S. Naipaul's Retrospective Stage

An example of this non-self-identity of the author with his own work over time is what has happened in the career of V.S. Naipaul. Naipaul's 1961 novel, *A House for Mr Biswas*, was initially outside the literary canon, coming as it did from the geographic and cultural margins of late imperial Britain. It has however been subsequently incorporated into a more distinctive "canon" of postcolonial works. The "retrospective status"[11] that it enjoys means that it is more likely to feature on a school or university syllabus, to be borrowed from a library, or to be picked up by an interested general reader than many other works of postcolonial writing – including Naipaul's own later work. For this reason, Naipaul's more recent work must consciously bear the weight of the success of an earlier work trapped in an extended present: Naipaul remained our contemporary up until his death in 2018, but 1961 is not contemporaneous with us.[12]

A House for Mr Biswas portrayed in epic form many of the large themes in anti-colonial history: the conflict between private property and common ownership; tensions between individual and social constructions of the self; and culturally variable ways of constructing the family unit. These things are expressed through the symbolism of the house that Biswas dreams of buying. By telling readers in the prologue that Biswas is fated both to have bought his own house by the time of his death and to have almost lost it through extended mortgaging, Naipaul sets the novel up as a self-fulfilling prophecy in which the outcome of Biswas's economic struggles is less important than the aspiration they represent. Those struggles are represented through the depiction of Biswas's attempt to escape his wife's wealthy and powerful family, which is in turn a fictional portrayal of Naipaul's father's attempts to achieve autonomy from his own parents-in-law, the Capildeos. This means that the novel is not so much about anti-colonial history in the abstract as about Biswas (and Naipaul senior's) effort to secure the objects of their aspiration in the concrete. This sense of a tangible material ambition is conveyed in the novel through Naipaul's portrayal of the Shorthills Estate, where one of Biswas's early unsuccessful attempts to build a house takes place:

> In the grounds of the estate house there was a cricket field and a swimming pool; the drive was lined with orange trees and gri-gri palms with slender white trunks, red berries and dark green leaves. The land itself was a wonder. The saman trees had lianas so strong and supple that one could swing on them. All day the immortelle trees dropped their red and yellow bird-shaped flowers through which one could whistle like a bird. Cocoa trees grew in the shade of the immortelles, coffee in the shade of the cocoa, and the hills were covered with tonka bean.[13]

This highly impressionistic rendering of the house and grounds creates a sense of natural plenitude which symbolises the material aspirations that Naipaul associates with Biswas. Yet it does so by insisting on discernible, physical realities rather than through recourse to abstract symbolism or allegory. Throughout the novel there is a proliferation of factual textual detail associated with each of the different places where

Biswas lives. The Tulsi children are "compelled to gather tonka beans, to pick oranges and avocado pears to be sent to Port of Spain."[14] The seedlings "were planted along the drive and hedged around with bamboo stakes."[15] The flora, the fauna, the materials used in the construction of each building, the age of the people and their occupations, the size of the land, the ingredients of meals, even the fabric used to make every garment that is worn: time and again this provision of verifiable information militates against too abstract and symbolic an interpretation of Biswas's epic struggle and turns the reader back towards the literal. Thus although it is possible to make an interpretative leap from Biswas's life to the major themes of anti-colonial history, those themes are downplayed in the novel itself, where they are instead embedded in a series of relationships expressing something smaller, more localised and perhaps more personal to Naipaul than those world-historical conflicts. Like Seepersad Naipaul, Biswas encounters as lived experience a process which, were the novel constructed in more abstract theoretical terms, might have been depicted as the dilemma between the desire for private space and the impulse for social and communal attachment in the decolonising world. As it is, Naipaul seems to vindicate personal aspiration over social solidarity and Biswas finds solace from his conflicts in the highly individualistic practice of silent reading: "In the grotesques of Dickens everything he feared and suffered from was ridiculed and diminished, so that his own anger, his own contempt became unnecessary, and he was given strength to bear with the most difficult part of his day."[16]

Dickens is Biswas's hero not only because of the mockery of class relationships and the implicit subversion of authority that we find in Dickensian fiction, but also because like many of Dickens' protagonists Biswas is a character filled with anxieties about his place in the world. This symbolic affinity between Biswas and those characters generates in turn a wider stylistic affinity between Naipaul and Dickens, so that *A House for Mr Biswas* is written with a mood and idiom that, despite Naipaul's commitment to a Trinidadian vernacular, feels Dickensian in tone. This enables Naipaul to pay tribute to one valued precursor in the art of prose fiction, even while Naipaul's career as a writer represented an important fulfilment of the frustrated vision of another writer precursor – his own father, Seepersad. The superseding of his father's abortive writing career by his own underlines Naipaul's interest in the material conditions in which authorship occurs and helps explain his choice of career for Biswas: like his father, and himself, a would-be writer. Indeed, that distinction between protagonist and author would narrow during the course of Naipaul's subsequent career as he would turn more explicitly to the use of protagonists who are also authors, elevating his work to a metafictional realm that is only present in embryonic form in this early work.

The development of a metafictive practice in Naipaul's work after *A House for Mr Biswas,* can be seen in such novels as *The Mimic Men* (1967), *The Enigma of Arrival* (1987), *A Way in the World* (1994) and *Half a Life* (2001). It is a development that culminated in his final novel *Magic Seeds* (2004), which revisits the themes of *A House for Mr Biswas* in a highly self-conscious way. Its writer protagonist, Willie, is criticised by his sister Sarojini for not having achieved anything revolutionary in his life. He goes back to India to join a group of guerrilla rebels in Kandapalli, where a blunder results in his joining the "wrong" group and being imprisoned, from which he is only released because of his contribution to Indian culture as a writer. Back in London, he stays with the lawyer, Roger, whom he had known thirty years earlier, and works for an architecture magazine while Roger tries to get involved in the booming property market with the tycoon Peter.

A House for Mr Biswas uses the symbolism of the house to convey the themes of anti-colonial history in a local and tangible way. For Biswas, the dream of a house is concrete and literal, a genuine material ambition. Stylistically, however, this portrayal contrasts sharply with the much more abstract and allegorical representation of houses in *Magic Seeds*, where for Willie and Roger the English property market is described in highly metaphorical terms: it is the "London property beanstalk" that has grown up on the ironic "magic seeds" of the title:

> Roger said, 'The little Marble Arch house was the seedcorn. I've been climbing up that property beanstalk all the time, and it's got me here. It is true of at least half the people on the street, though we might pretend otherwise.[17]

Roger has already started to climb the property beanstalk, moving from the "little" house in Marble Arch to the much more impressive one house in St John's Wood where he receives Willie. But despite the importance of these properties in the overall narrative trajectory of *Magic Seeds*, the clarity of sensory perception that Naipaul associated with each house in *Biswas* is no longer here: the real seedlings and nuts on the Shorthills Estate are now rendered purely abstract. That is to say, *Magic Seeds* returns to the same themes as the earlier novel using a comparable symbol of the house, but now in a more metaphorical and less concrete way. This is conveyed through the portrayal of the author-protagonist Willie, who, like his creator Naipaul, is returning after decades away to cast a self-conscious and critical eye on the world he rediscovers:

> Cricklewood: twenty-eight years ago it was a mysterious pace for Willie, somewhere far to the north of Marble Arch, where in his imagination people lived regulated and full and secure lives...
> London here, as created by the builders and developers of sixty or seventy years before, a kind of toyland, cosy and confined: this is the house where Jack and his wife will live and love and have their litter,

this is the shop where Jack's wife will shop, this is the public house at the corner where Jack and his friends and his wife's friends will sometimes get drunk.[18]

Naipaul's unrelentingly savage representation of suburban life at the end of the twentieth century is a world away from the naïve dreams of home ownership he had earlier portrayed in *Biswas*. There, the idea of the house was an end in itself, whereas here it has become associated with a culture of economic greed and competitive individualism to the detriment of any notion of common good. *Magic Seeds* is therefore an example of the unforgiving stylistic harshness and uncompromising world view that Edward Said – an important critic of Naipaul's work – associates with late-career works of art and literature more generally. Even the allusion to fairy tale renders Naipaul's critique all the more trenchant, implying as it does the existence of a myriad suburban Jacks trying to scale the property Beanstalk, all the while losing sight of any wider political or cultural aspiration. Peter's house does not make him happy: his wife has a lover whose house is bigger and more valuable. The same is true of Roger, who in turn is driven to an affair with a younger woman, Marian. Their affair is articulated mainly through the transition between her council estate upbringing and the private flat he buys her, and which makes him desperate rather than happy or fulfilled:

> We are talking about city properties. They are not easy to value. It is always possible to be a couple of million out. We are also in a time of rising property values. Something bought for ten million today might in three years sell for fifteen, and no one will raise an eyebrow. That is why this property caper could pass for a long time unnoticed. It passed unnoticed for twelve years. But then somebody noticed and people began to make trouble.[19]

The important theme of house prices that mattered to Mr Biswas at the mainly local level and that symbolised hope for betterment has been redeployed in this portrayal of a world where private property is understood as an aspect of personal character and hence of greed and selfishness. This brings with it cultural malaise and political quiescence in place of the aspiration for change conveyed in the earlier novel. There is deep irony in Roger's words about people making trouble for him and Peter, as this passage comes at a stage in the novel when they have been guilty of fraudulently manipulating the prices of houses they are selling. Roger tells Willie: "All my life I have prepared for this moment. I am ready to run down the beanstalk and take an axe to the root."[21] But this cannot be seen as representing a desire to effect revolutionary change; it represents rather the defensive reaction of those who have been caught flouting the rules.

Where *A House for Mr Biswas* was able to suggest a brief moment of optimism in its capacity to imagine change, *Magic Seeds* has no real resolution. The plot does not end so much as stop, as if the capacity to imagine alternatives to the system of competitive economic expansion has disappeared. This perhaps is why Naipaul places the Indian writer Willie in the kind of London he portrays. Having failed to achieve a meaningful contribution to postcolonial political struggles, all Willie can do is try to climb the magic beanstalk. There is little sense that he will be able to overthrow the tycoon Peter who is the giant at the top. In other words, the fictive author Willie uses as a symbol of failed hope the same metaphor of the housing market that Naipaul had earlier used to symbolise aspiration. It seems that Naipaul's last author-protagonist is left looking back over a long career that coincides with the whole stretch of postcolonial history and asking himself what real contribution he has made to that history. Since Naipaul underwent the same process of looking back and summing up while writing what would prove to be his final novel, Willie thus represents a fictional avatar of Naipaul himself.

A conventional approach to the different stages comprising Naipaul's career would tell us that this late work is embittered, ugly, uncreative and evidence of a decline in mastery of the literary arts on the part of the author-creator.[21] This is both how *Magic Seeds* has been received, and also how late career works by authors of prose fiction more generally have often been discussed. Using the insights of career construction theory, however, enables a different approach, making it possible to consider the novel in what Wayne Booth describes as the way it "invites" us to read it.[22] When read this way, it need not be seen merely as a less creative expression of a narrative theme that the author has already used up, but as a critical return to that theme during work produced in a new career stage. This is how *Magic Seeds* asks to be read: as a work produced late in a career and in the conscious presence of the earlier work from which it is therefore necessarily stylistically different and by the standards of which it therefore cannot be judged.

The use of author as protagonist is not particular to Naipaul's latest work. On the contrary and as we have seen, many of his protagonists throughout his career were writers. Indeed, Naipaul can be seen as a highly metafictive writer throughout his work, bearing the particular kind of critical self-consciousness that postcolonial writers often brought to their work as they internally questioned the validity of creating that work at all. On the other hand, we can say of the relationship of *A House for Mr Biswas* (1961) to *Magic Seeds* (2004) that an element of critical conjunction exists in the latter that would have been impossible in the former. Naipaul and his fictive protagonist writer are consciously returning to and revisiting the themes of his earlier work, so that a new element of retrospective authorial representation breaks through. The fictive writer Willie is an autobiographical figure, a fictional author writing themes that Naipaul himself had already written about and therefore also the fictional author of Naipaul's real work. Over the course of half a century, V.S. Naipaul has been absorbed retrospectively into a literary canon from which he was an outsider during the late stages of colonial history. This retrospective recognition of his early work has had the effect that his last works remain eclipsed by it. To remain innovative he then had to achieve in fiction a symbolic return to the themes of that earlier work: *Magic Seeds* can be seen as a work of fictional self-retrospect.

Conclusions

To think about the relationship between *Magic Seeds* and *A House for Mr Biswas* using the insights of career construction theory leads me to a provisional answer to one of the questions that I started out with. That is, how to define lateness in the context of a literary career. Late, it seems to me, is a relational rather than a purely temporal concept, and is defined as *coming after* (an already achieved novel, play, piece of work, life stage or career phase) rather than *moving towards* (death, retirement, historical and/or epochal change). In other words, although *Magic Seeds* was written during Naipaul's old age, its lateness is not an effect of biological age.[23] Rather, it is a temporally belated relative of *A House for Mr Biswas* because it enters into a creative and critical dialogue with it. This way of figuring lateness liberates the concept itself from mere biological age so that (although this is not the case with *Magic Seeds*) it would be possible to consider a particular work as belated even if produced in its author's thirties – provided it comes after an even earlier achievement that lays down a set of expectations for what should follow. For this reason, I suggest that the term *late* is better replaced by the idea of the *retrospective*, precisely to avoid conflating the late with simplistic questions of numerical age that are not relevant.

This substitution of the surface idea of "late" with a more complex idea of the *retrospective* is not specific to Naipaul's own career and provides a potential new category for discussion, that of fictions of self-retrospect. It is a category that makes it possible to consider late career works in the relational – as opposed to biological – sense described above. Or to put it another way, thinking about fictions of self-retrospect in the way they ask to be read is a way of thinking about them not defined by some kind of deficiency or lack relative to works produced earlier in the authorial career, but as a specific kind of work and achievement that can only be produced during that career stage. What is specific to fictions of self-retrospect, in other words, is not that they are less creative or less original than the works produced during the earlier career stages. Rather it is first, their capacity to make extreme demands on the reader precisely because they are created in forms, media or genres that are uncompromisingly difficult to appreciate and stylistically resistant to their reader. And second, it is that they often exist in a metatextual dimension commensurate with a high level of critical self-reflection and authorial self-renewal. That is, they put the presence of the author back into the work in a way that is both critically probing of the world and self-questioning of the individual writer's own accomplishments.

Extrapolating from these points leads to three conclusions, which can be seen as the key arguments of this paper: First, that the kinds of work produced by an author during the retrospective stage are necessarily different from the earlier and mid career works (for which he or she might be better known). Second, that for this reason, the kinds of criteria we apply when judging the quality of such works should be different from those that we apply to the early-mid career works precisely because our consideration of the later has to take into account the prior existence of the earlier. Third, that work produced during the retrospective period in an author's career is often profoundly metafictive. It reveals authors returning to the themes and forms they had used in the work for which they are best known and self-consciously attempting to write about them again, as if for the first time.

Endnotes

1. For a theoretical critique of historical constructions of late career writing see Gordon McMullan, *Shakespeare and the Idea of Late Writing* (Cambridge: Cambridge University Press, 2006).
2. The question of how to define the theoretically impossible notion of contemporaneity is the subject of Giorgio Agamben's essay "What is the Contemporary"? See his *'What is an Apparatus?' and Other Essays* trans. David Kishik and Stefan Pedatella (Stanford, CA: Stanford University Press, 2009), 39-54.
3. Edward Said, *On Late Style: Music and Literature Against the Grain* (New York: Vintage, 2009), 9.
4. Kobus (writing as Jacobus) Maree, *Counselling for Career Construction: Connecting Life Themes to Construct Life Portraits: Turning Pain into Hope* (Rotterdam: Sense, 2013), 63.
5. Edward Said, *Beginnings: Intention and Method* (London: Basic Books, 1975), 257.
6. Mark Savickas, *Career Counseling* (Washington, D.C.: American Psychological Association, 2011), 4
7. Savickas, 8.
8. Savickas, 5.
9. Peter McIlveen, "Life Themes in Career Counselling", in *Career Counseling and Constructivism: Elaboration of Constructs* ed. Mary McMahon and Mark Watson (New York: Nova Science, 2010), 78-79.

10. Larry Cochran, *Career Counseling: A Narrative Approach* (Thousand Oaks, CA: Sage, 1997), 5-7.
11. Jenny Hockey and Allison James, "Back to Our Futures: Imaging Second Childhood", in *Images of Aging: Cultural Representations of Later Life*, ed. Mike Featherstone and Andrew Wernick (London: Routledge, 1995), p. 146.
12. A further theoretical investigation into the idea of the vanishing contemporary in art is provided by Jean-Luc Nancy, "Art Today", *Journal of Visual Culture* 9, no. 1 (2010), 91-99.
13. V.S. Naipaul, *A House for Mr Biswas* (London: André Deutsch, 1961), 414.
14. Naipaul, *Biswas*, 428.
15. Naipaul, *Biswas*, 428.
16. Naipaul, *Biswas*, 394.
17. V.S. Naipaul, *Magic Seeds* (London: Picador, 2004), 183.
18. Naipaul, *Magic Seeds*, 223.
19. Naipaul, *Magic Seeds*, 226.
20. Naipaul, *Magic Seeds*, 242.
21. Claire Chambers and Susan Watkins have shown that this conventional decline narrative ironically contributes to the mechanics of literary canonisation (and hence also of marginalisation and exclusion of what is not canonised) since "to embody the qualities of late style you have to be, or once have been, a genius." See Chambers and Watkins, "Writing Now", in *The History of British Women's Writing, 1970–Present: Volume Ten* ed. Mary Eagleton and Emma Parker (Basingstoke: Palgrave Macmillan, 2015), 254.
22. Wayne C. Booth, *The Company We Keep: An Ethics of Fiction* (Berkeley, CA: University of California Press, 1988), 107.
23. In a critique of the typical "decline" narrative that associates ageing with loss of creativity once an imagined high point has been passed, Peter Laslett has argued that "[n]o passage from one to the other need occur, for an individual with these characteristics [of creativity] is doing his or her own thing from maturity until the final end. Artists, the consummate artists, are the best examples." See Laslett, *A Fresh Map of Life: The Emergence of the Third Age* (London: Weidenfeld and Nicolson, 1996), 5.

16: CONSTRUCTIONS OF MASCULINITY IN VIDIA NAIPAUL'S *A HOUSE FOR MR BISWAS* AND SHIVA NAIPAUL'S *FIREFLIES*

ELIZABETH JACKSON

This essay examines the tensions arising from the multiple and sometimes paradoxical constructions of masculinity encountered and performed by the male protagonists in Vidia Naipaul's 1961 novel *A House for Mr Biswas* and Shiva Naipaul's 1970 novel *Fireflies*. Notions of masculinity are not fixed or uniform, but are always being negotiated and contested. As Steph Ceraso and Patricia Connolly point out:

> An exploration of masculinity within a single culture is complex enough, yet the effect is infinitely multiplied once creolisation... [and] colonialism... are taken into consideration and examined through Naipaul's male protagonists... Their masculinity is frequently destabilised through competing cultural representations of manhood.[1]

Writing about masculinity in the Caribbean, Linden Lewis has observed that the way in which it is constructed and practised is always "mediated by modalities of race, ethnicity, age, class, sexual orientation and religion, and by the way in which these social forces coalesce within a given cultural context".[2] Although gender as a social relationship sometimes predominates, it does not stand outside other social relations. As Patricia Mohammed reminds us:

> Our race or ethnic group... and the class we typify within a particular culture constantly inform and mediate our social experiences and influence how we express our masculinity and femininity, as well as the expectations of others of our masculinity and femininity.[3]

Examining the historical development of Indo-Trinidadian gender ideologies, she points out that because the Indian female was in shorter supply during indentureship, "she had greater opportunity to select a male partner or to desert him if he did not fulfil her... needs".[4] Indo-Trinidadian women therefore gained a degree of independence and freedom during indentureship which threatened the internal patriarchal order of the group. This trend was partially reversed during the post-indentureship period when many Indo-Trinidadian men began promoting a return to traditional patriarchal values and practices within their community. This attempt to reclaim a traditional sense of Indian masculinity was also an endeavour to define themselves in opposition to other ethnic groups. Inventing a shared notion of the culture of India was one part of forming a collective East Indian identity in Trinidad, and one of its central ideologies was the idealisation of the patriarchal family. Indeed, the insistence on maintaining patriarchal power within the household was also a response to the pressures of colonialism and creolisation, both of which were experienced as profoundly disempowering by many Indian males.

On a more general level, Linden Lewis has argued persuasively that:

> What is of central importance to the concept of masculinity... remains the exercise of power and the issue of control. Masculinity is predicated on the presumption of power, whether real or imagined. Though not all men exercise power, all nevertheless view it as an entitlement. Masculinity therefore is often associated with access to and control over resources, privileges and status.[5]

Consequently, "the construction of masculinity reproduces patterns and relations of domination and subordination",[6] and "though women are usually the victims of patriarchal power, subordinate or marginalised men are also negatively affected by patriarchal rule".[7] Keith Nurse agrees, arguing that "most masculinities are complicit in patriarchy or tied together through the oppression of women", and that "the marginalisation of subordinate masculinities is an essential component in the reproduction of the myth of male power".[8] Finally, it is worth noting that "though patriarchy is a powerful force organising society's social relations, it is not absolute. Women and subordinated or marginalised men do not simply accept patriarchal rule without resistance."[9]

Bearing all of this in mind, in analysing Vidia Naipaul's *A House for Mr Biswas*, I want to begin by challenging the interpretations of literary scholars who have emphasised the so-called "emasculation" of Mohun Biswas in the Tulsi household. Ceraso and Connolly, for instance, have argued that "in the private sphere, Mohun's public display of respectable masculinity is destabilised by matriarchal rule. Home is a place primarily controlled by Shama and the female-dominated Tulsis."[10] Gordon Rohlehr is even more direct, contending that "Tulsidom depends for its very existence on the psychic emasculation of the men and on the maintenance of their sense of inferiority".[11] These interpretations are evidently based on the assumption (shared by the character Mohun Biswas himself) that because he is male, he ought to be automatically entitled to power and status within his wife's family household. This assumption in turn illustrates Linden Lewis's observation that:

Recipients of privilege, irrespective of whether such privilege is based on gender or race or class, so fully internalise its benefits that they often regard it as normative or view it as something they have somehow earned. They seldom interrogate the basis of their privilege, or how it is made possible at the expense of others.[12]

Furthermore, the application of the term "emasculated" to a man who is disempowered reveals an uncritical acceptance of the normative association between masculinity and power – and by implication, femininity and weakness.

My contention is that although Mohun Biswas himself is disempowered within the Tulsi household, it is not a female-dominated family. True, the women are certainly numerous in the Tulsi household, but all are engaged in supporting a patriarchal system. Even the family matriarch has a surrogate patriarchal role, holding her figurehead position temporarily between the death of her husband and the coming-of-age of her son who will take over the leadership of the family as soon as possible, despite being younger than all of his sisters. We see precisely the same situation in Shiva Naipaul's novel *Fireflies*: a young man who marries into a large, prestigious family in which the women are far more numerous but far less powerful than the men. In both novels an elderly and decrepit widow serves as a temporary figurehead who quickly relinquishes her leadership role to a son who is younger than her many daughters.

Both Vidia Naipaul's Tulsi family and Shiva Naipaul's Khoja family are marked by reverence for an ancestral family patriarch. In *Fireflies* we are told that:

> The elder Mr Khoja had emigrated from India as an indentured labourer. He was an indistinct, almost mythical figure, about whom very little was known for certain, though the Khojas tried to pretend otherwise. As depicted to his descendants, he bordered on saintliness. He had been kind, thrifty, virile and ambitious, a paradigm of secular virtues.[13]

In *A House for Mr Biswas* the masculine nature of family identity is so complete that females are often erased from the discourse. For instance, when the young Mohun is questioned by the Tulsis about his own family origins, it is tacitly assumed by the characters – and indeed by the narrator – that his family consists of males only: his father, his uncle, his grandfather, and so on.

It is instructive to compare the representations of masculinity in *A House for Mr Biswas* with those of *Fireflies*, not least because these two novels dramatise remarkably similar family dynamics from different angles. In contrast to Vidia's resolute focus on masculine experience and masculine perspectives, Shiva's novel *Fireflies* portrays a similar family from the perspective of a marginalised female character who gradually becomes central in the narrative. So in *Fireflies* the competing constructions of masculinity are thrown into sharp and critical focus through the eyes of Vimla – usually referred to in the narrative as Baby or Mrs Lutchman.

Comparing the narrative perspective and narrative voice in the two novels we notice a striking difference from the very beginning. From the prologue to the end of *A House for Mr Biswas*, the third-person narrator focuses exclusively on the perspective of Mohun Biswas in a way that calls on the reader to sympathise with him:

> And during these months of illness and despair he was struck again and again by the wonder of being in his own house, the audacity of it.[14]
>
> How terrible it would have been... to have died among the Tulsis, amid the squalor of that large, disintegrating and indifferent family; to have left Shama and the children among them, in one room; worse, to have lived without even attempting to lay claim to one's portion of the earth; to have lived and died as one had been born, unnecessary and unaccommodated.[15]

In the first chapter we also notice that this narrator is scornful toward males – but never females – who passively accept the conditions of their lives. He speaks of Mohun Biswas's grandfather:

> Futile with asthma, [he] propped himself up on his string bed and said, as he always did on unhappy occasions, "Fate. There is nothing we can do about it."
> No one paid him any attention. Fate had brought him from India to the sugar-estate, aged him quickly and left him to die in a crumbling mud hut in the swamplands; yet he spoke of Fate often and affectionately, as though, merely by surviving, he had been particularly favoured.[16]

Finally, the masculinist language throughout *A House for Mr Biswas* implies that only *male* experience is significant and worthy of notice. For instance, in the statement "birth was unimportant; a man's caste should be determined only by his actions",[17] the word "man" clearly does not mean "man or woman"; on the contrary, it applies to males only, erasing females from its vision of the human condition.

All of this is in stark contrast to the perspective and voice of the third-person narrator in Shiva Naipaul's novel *Fireflies*, who focuses on the experiences of Vimla Lutchman. From the very beginning, we get the narrator's detached, matter-of-fact perspective of her and her situation:

> For Baby, the marriage was a bad one, but it never entered her head that she might complain or refuse to marry Ram. As a girl, she was automatically of less importance; as an indirect descendant (the elder Mrs Khoja was her great-aunt), she hardly mattered. Fortunately, in her eyes what others might have considered an injustice, she considered a law of life.[18]

The narrator goes on to describe the disastrous early years of the marriage, in which Vimla serves as nothing more and nothing less than a servant to her husband Ram:

> Their lives were separate, crossing only at the points of elementary physical duties: the preparation of food, the washing and ironing of his clothes, the questions that sought necessary information ("You coming home for dinner tonight, Ram?"), and, occasionally, a hurried, formal lovemaking.[19]

Ram is away from the house for extended periods, visiting rum-shops and prostitutes with his friends. After the birth of their first child, Ram begins a pattern of beating Vimla, with the approval and encouragement of his neighbour Naresh:

> "That's the way, Ram. Blows and babies. That's the way to keep them in order. You should have give she about four baby by now. She wouldn't have had no time to make trouble then. But it never too late to learn." [20]

Like many people struggling with their vices, Ram "went through cycles of violence and calm, drunkenness and abstinence, brutality and concern".[21]

However, far from being a 400-page endorsement of negative stereotypes about Caribbean men, the novel *Fireflies* presents constructions of masculinity in a much more interesting and nuanced way. Significantly, Ram Lutchman re-invents his entire persona when he takes a job at the Ministry of Education and the family move to a small but respectable house near the Queen's Park Savannah in Port of Spain. Although he does not become a paragon of virtue overnight, the narrator tells us that "Mr Lutchman took his job seriously. He drank far less than he used to and only visited prostitutes occasionally."[22] His arguments with Vimla no longer culminated in wife-beating, and although he was still distant from her at first, the narrative traces a gradual thawing of their relationship over the years, particularly after the end of his extramarital affair with a white woman named Doreen. By the time of Ram Lutchman's sudden early death from a heart attack, he and Vimla are developing a warm relationship, and he is showing signs of becoming a likeable character. But this is only the midpoint of the novel, and afterwards it is Vimla's story, including her observations of other men and their diverse constructions of masculinity.

In *A House for Mr Biswas*, we do not see the same dramatic development of the male protagonist as we do in *Fireflies*, partly because Mohun Biswas is presented as a more consistently admirable character than Ram Lutchman. Although Mohun Biswas is far from idealised, he works hard, rarely drinks, never philanders, and hits his wife only once during the course of the narrative. This is years into their marriage, and the reaction of husband and wife to this unexpected incident is telling:

> Another serious quarrel... went over the same limited ground until, unable to control his rage, he hit her.
>   They were both astonished. She was silenced in the middle of a sentence; for some time afterwards the unfinished sentence remained in his mind,

as though it had just been spoken. She was stronger than he. Her silence and her refusal to retaliate made his humiliation complete. She dressed Anand and went to Arwacas.[23]

It is notable in both novels that despite the lack of education and relative lack of power of the main female characters (Shama Biswas and Vimla Lutchman), both are portrayed as stronger, wiser, and in most ways simply better than their husbands. However, while Mohun Biswas's weakness is presented as a product of his *situation* (his disempowerment within the Tulsi household and within colonial society), Ram Lutchman's weakness is clearly shown to be a product of his *personality*. True, his personality is multifaceted and constantly evolving, but its worst aspects are encouraged and justified by toxic gender ideologies. Examples are abundant throughout the narrative of *Fireflies*. We have already seen that Ram's friend Naresh advocates the assertion of masculinity through drunkenness, infidelity, domination of women, and domestic violence. "That's the way to treat them," he says. "A few more beatings like that and she go know she place."[24] At some level, Ram sees his own shortcomings but wants to wallow in self-pity, blind to everyone's suffering but his own. For instance, to his male friends at his father's funeral, he expresses tenderness toward his young son but never toward his wife: "You know, I haven't been as good a father as I should have been to this boy. Too much worries does affect a man, not so?"[25] And the only way his friends know how to comfort him is by handing him a glass of rum. So in this particular construction of masculinity, men are allowed to be "bad" because they suffer, and the remedy from other men seems to be alcohol, which leads to further bad behaviour. Later in Mr Ramgoolan's shop we see an example of the ideological belief in the masculine need for relaxation with alcohol. He hides his rum from his wife, explaining that, "She hate to see me drinking. But a man must have something to relax with is what I always say."[26]

Even in the absence of alcohol, Ram is given to comically absurd self-assertion. For instance, when he is sacked for crashing a bus, he talks about breaking the windows at the bus company. His response to his wife's warning not to do it is, "You keep out of this, woman. None of this is your business",[27] as if it is none of her business that her husband (on whom she and her child are completely dependent) is out of work and threatening vandalism. In this crisis, when Vimla proposes to open a vegetable stall on the roadside to help support the family, Ram is aghast. The point is made very clearly that he is more concerned about himself and his image in the eyes of other men than he is about the wellbeing of his wife and child: "'Hey,' my friends go say. 'I see your wife selling provision these days out on the Eastern Main Road.' How do you think I go look in their eyes, eh? Eh?"[28] Ram's selfishness and hypocrisy continue but take on different forms after he has re-invented himself as a respectable man who works at the Ministry of Education. After Doreen more or less openly propositions him, he goes home and takes some time to come up with justifications in his own mind for having a mistress. The best idea he can come up with is remarkably trivial: "He looked at his wife and was irritated by her increasing fatness."[29] After the affair has run its course, the narrative traces the gradual improvement in Ram's relationship with his wife, as part of the growth in his wider capacity to empathise with others. This growth is cut short by his early and sudden death from a heart attack, like the fatal heart attack of the author at the age of forty.

Subsequently, throughout the second half of the novel, diverse constructions of masculinity are critically presented by the third-person narrator, often through the perspective of Vimla Lutchman. Chief among these is the critical portrayal of the family patriarch, Govind Khoja, which constitutes a remarkably comprehensive interrogation of the ways in which hegemonic masculinity is constructed and reinforced. Everyone around him colludes in making Govind Khoja feel superior. "From childhood", we are told, "he had been accustomed to receive the respect and adulation of his [six] sisters."[30] As an adult, his status is propped up by his wife, who works hard to create an aura of deference around him. She guards him from casual visitors and constantly reminds everyone (including relatives) of how busy and important he is. Govind enjoys the deference accorded to him at the annual cattha party at his house but stays aloof from the crowd of relatives, occasionally visiting them in a condescending manner:

> After he had had his separately cooked dinner, Mr Khoja made his descent to the lower regions… He threaded his way through the maze of faces, many of which he did not know, amiably contemptuous of everyone. Now and again he would raise his hand in mild salute to someone he wished to grace, but these vague intimations of friendliness only had the effect of leaving the recipient ill at ease.[31]

To be fair, Govind Khoja as family patriarch does have duties as well as privileges. "He performed his duties punctiliously," we are told, "and was invariably present at the birth, marriage or death of any member of the clan."[32] We see him at his best when he intervenes to bring Vimla's son Bhaskar home after a nervous breakdown while studying in India. Only his mother and Govind Khoja are there to greet Bhaskar upon his return, and the narrator tells us that this is when "Mr Khoja… was at his kindest and most sympathetic, fussing around Mrs Lutchman. He was one of those people who, if they flower at all, do so only in the face of tragedy".[33] At a funeral, he is evidently responsible for absolutely everything, right down to the arrangement of the funeral wreaths. This is the way in which a hierarchical society functions. Decision-making is concentrated in very few hands, so it is a skill which is never developed among most of the population.

Not content with his absolute power and godlike status within the family, Govind Khoja also entertains political ambitions, and this brings out his weaknesses, in particular his need for constant reassurance of his own status. We are told directly that he needed "constantly to be surrounded by tangible reminders of his learning, his goodness, his importance. [In his library] he studied the furniture, the books, the carpet. They were all suitably heavy and imposing."[34] This illustrates Linden Lewis's observation of men's tendency to define themselves "in terms that objectify their masculinity – that is, cars, boats, houses, dogs, guns may become extensions of one's masculinity".[35] Disappointingly, Govind's sense of his own importance is shaken when he looks at his wife: "How fat she was!"[36] However, if his family is a source of embarrassment to him, they are also an important source of his self-esteem as he fights his disastrous election campaign. This is nowhere more evident than during a visit when Vimla and Govind's wife Sumintra sit there flattering him for ages, talking about how he is sure to win the election:

> He enjoyed hearing himself discussed in this way. It was from the sum total of impressions such as these (that is, the reflection of himself in the opinions of other adoring people) that he was able to piece together an idea of what he was or, more accurately, what he imagined himself to be. They formed the basis of his self-esteem and, therefore, needed constantly to be replenished; more so than ever in these latter days.[37]

Although a character like Govind Khoja is the target of much narrative irony in *Fireflies*, his insecurity is not unfounded because power relationships (particularly between men) are never fixed or static. On the contrary, they are remarkably dynamic: always open to challenge and often in a state of flux. Govind himself gradually loses authority within the Khoja family after his election defeat, and particularly after the death of his mother when her will becomes the subject of intense family feuding. Similarly, in *A House for Mr Biswas* Mrs Tulsi's brother-in-law Seth initially functions as her powerful henchman, but he gradually falls from favour as the young son Owad comes of age and takes over the leadership of the Tulsi family. In contrast to the Khoja family, which is depicted as fractured and rudderless after the demise of Govind, the Tulsi family in *A House for Mr Biswas* remains firmly patriarchal precisely because of the authority granted to Owad by his family, particularly his elder sisters:

> [A week after his return from England] Owad was still followed by admiring eyes, it was still an honour to be spoken to by him, and everything he said was to be repeated... Regularly in the evening there were gatherings in the drawingrooms or, when Owad was tired, in his bedroom. Mr Biswas attended as often as he could.[38]

> The sisters now sought audience with him singly or in small groups... Every scandal was gone over, every petty dispute, every resentment. And Owad listened.[39]

Neither *Fireflies* nor *A House for Mr Biswas* portrays patriarchy as a system of domination imposed by men on women. On the contrary, both novels emphasise the ways in which the power of hegemonic males is constructed and supported by men and women, as well as the anxious competition between males for status and dominance. Indeed, there is always a hierarchy among the males of the Tulsi household in *A House for Mr Biswas*:

> Mr Biswas was pained to see Govind [one of the brothers-in-law] in the presence of Seth. His handsome face became weak in every way. His eyes became small and bright and restless; he stammered and swallowed and gave nervous little laughs.[40]

> In Seth's presence Mr Biswas felt diminished. Everything about Seth was overpowering: his calm manner, his smooth grey hair, his ivory holder, his hard swollen forearms.[41]

Beyond this, all males in the Tulsi family are privileged simply by virtue of being male. Education, scholarship applications, and even swimming expeditions are reserved exclusively for the two young sons:

> Despite their age they were admitted into the councils of Seth and Mrs Tulsi and their views were often quoted with respect by sisters and brothers-in-law. To assist their scholarship, the best of the food was automatically set aside for them and they were given special brain-feeding meals, of fish in particular.[42]

Thus we see the ways in which these two boys, from a young age, are being groomed for power, not only within the household but also within the wider society through education and opportunities abroad. However, even the lower status males in the household are automatically entitled to the benefits of female servitude. Mohun Biswas, during his brief engagement to Shama, feels slighted because "as yet he had no wife to single him out for attention, to do the little services he saw Shama's sisters doing for their husbands: the ready ladle, the queries, the formal concern".[43]

If all of this is familiar criticism of traditional patriarchal conventions, a more interesting aspect, perhaps, is the awareness shown in both novels of the performative nature of masculine roles. In *A House for Mr Biswas* this is seen most clearly in the young Mohun's performance as a Brahmin male:

> Mr Biswas had never questioned the deference shown him when he had gone to Tara's to be fed as a Brahmin and on his rounds with Pundit Jairam. But he had never taken it seriously; he had thought of it as one of the rules of the game that was only occasionally played.[44]

In *Fireflies* Ram Lutchman very consciously cultivates different behaviours, different speech patterns, and even different personae for the various roles in his life. For instance, when Doreen first approached him in the office, "he did not answer immediately, but continued to scribble in the margins, frowning as he wrote. He had taken great pains cultivating this special office manner".[45] He tries to imitate her vocabulary, "impressed with its elegance",[46] but meanwhile his speech at home remains much the same, reflecting his non-elite upbringing and limited education.

Perhaps the most striking example of masculinity as performance is enacted by Ram and Vimla's son Romesh, who grows up to construct a persona for himself based on gangsters in Hollywood films. Seeing this, Vimla remarks that "you seeing too much film and taking it for real life".[47] Romesh's increasingly daring exploits, accompanied by much cinematic posturing, culminate when he turns up at Govind Khoja's house, drunk and looking for trouble. He "smiled his Hollywood smile",[48] "laughed loudly and unnaturally", and then kept calling Govind "smart guy" while threatening him and vandalising his home.[49] At Romesh's trial, "his Hollywood gangster smirk never left his face".[50] Here we see Romesh from his mother's point of view: "As she looked at him standing there, handsome and cinematically arrogant, his hair neatly parted and smarmed down, his hands thrust into his trousers pockets, she had constantly to remind herself that this youth was indeed her son".[51] Crucially, Romesh's performance is carefully calculated to impress his gang of male acolytes:

> On the very last bench, the members of Romesh's gang of drinking companions had ranged themselves, all of them chewing gum and studying their hero with a slightly fearful admiration. Many of Romesh's more cinematic remarks had been uttered simply for their benefit and they had shown their appreciation by applause and hooting.[52]

This is in keeping with Linden Lewis's argument that "ultimately, men seek the approval of other men in the performance of their masculinity", though of course "masculinity also has much to do with men's relationships with women".[53] One of the most striking examples of this is a phenomenon more recently dubbed the trophy wife or trophy girlfriend, which we also see in *Fireflies*. Here the young Renouka becomes intimate with a "commercial traveller" who is never named but described as someone so completely imbued with the spirit of his profession that he speaks in the language of advertisements[54] – another identity constructed from capitalist production. His relationship with Renouka is portrayed as nothing more and nothing less than a way of enhancing his status in the eyes of his male companions:

> The commercial traveller was not primarily interested in Renouka's alleged fortune. What he savoured was the fact that she was an Indian girl ("and no ordinary BATEE either") and a relation, however minor, of a large and important family. He had stormed a barrier he always believed to be impregnable and his friends treated him as they would an adventurer who had explored hitherto unknown lands.[55]

He boasts about his sexual exploits with her, and "his friends were awe-struck at the ascendancy he [allegedly] commanded over this girl…

The commercial traveller had never been so happy."[56] When she finally severs ties with this young man, his main concern is "What would he tell his friends?"[57]

Significantly, each of these novels ends with a small victory for a male character. Mr Biswas dies, if not happy, at least satisfied that he finally inhabits his own house, however flawed its construction. *Fireflies* ends with Vimla's son Bhaskar departing for England with his young bride, Sonya – a girl who is considered "damaged goods" because she has already had a child out of wedlock. However, Bhaskar is a damaged young man himself, having suffered from failure, disappointment and depression. The narrative ends on a cautiously hopeful note about their future together. A warm and honest relationship has been built up between the two of them, suggesting that they can offer comfort and support to each other in the face of a demanding and often hostile world. However, no such comfort is envisioned for his mother Vimla Lutchman. Widowed, reduced to poverty, dependent on the charity of relatives, abandoned by both of her sons, neither of whom has turned out as she would have wished, she is shown to pay a heavy price for the various performances of masculinity in her family.

Endnotes

1. Steph Ceraso and Patricia Connolly, "The Destabilization of Masculinity in *A House for Mr Biswas* and *The Mimic Men*", in *Mosaic* 42, no. 3 (2009): 109-26, p. 111.
2. Linden Lewis, "Caribbean Masculinity: Unpacking the Narrative", in *The Culture of Gender and Sexuality in the Caribbean*, ed. Linden Lewis (Gainesville: University Press of Florida, 2003), 94-125, p. 108.
3. Patricia Mohammed, "Unmasking Masculinity and Deconstructing Patriarchy: Problems and Possibilities within Feminist Epistemology", in *Interrogating Caribbean Masculinities: Theoretical and Empirical Analyses*, ed. Rhoda Reddock (Kingston: University of the West Indies Press, 2004), 38-67, p. 39.
4. Mohammed, 60.
5. Lewis, 97.
6. Lewis, 98.
7. Lewis, 102.
8. Keith Nurse, "Masculinities in Transition: Gender and the Global Problematique", in *Interrogating Caribbean Masculinities: Theoretical and Empirical Analyses*, ed. Rhoda Reddock (Kingston: University of the West Indies Press, 2004), 3-37, p. 13.
9. Lewis, 102.
10. Ceraso and Connolly, 116.
11. Gordon Rohlehr, "The Ironic Approach", in *The Islands in Between*, ed. Louis James (Oxford: Oxford University Press, 1968), 135-168, p. 168.

12. Lewis, 94.
13. Shiva Naipaul, *Fireflies* (London: Andre Deutsch, 1970), 11.
14. V.S. Naipaul, *A House for Mr Biswas* (London: Penguin, 1992), 8.
15. *A House for Mr Biswas*, 13-14.
16. *A House for Mr Biswas*, 15.
17. *A House for Mr Biswas*, 116.
18. Shiva Naipaul, *Fireflies*, 7.
19. *Fireflies*, 15.
20. *Fireflies*, 16.
21. *Fireflies*, 17.
22. *Fireflies*, 37.
23. V.S. Naipaul, *A House for Mr Biswas*, 92-3.
24. *Fireflies*, 24.
25. *Fireflies*, 27.
26. *Fireflies*, 107-8.
27. *Fireflies*, 18.
28. *Fireflies*, 20.
29. *Fireflies*, 51.
30. *Fireflies*, 21.
31. *Fireflies*, 74.
32. *Fireflies*, 22.
33. *Fireflies*, 338.
34. *Fireflies*, 62.
35. *Fireflies*, 97.
36. *Fireflies*, 64.
37. *Fireflies*, 274.
38. V.S. Naipaul, *A House for Mr Biswas*, 540.
39. *A House for Mr Biswas*, 547.
40. *A House for Mr Biswas*, 106.
41. *A House for Mr Biswas*, 108,
42. *A House for Mr Biswas*, 104.
43. *A House for Mr Biswas*, 96.
44. *A House for Mr Biswas*, 70.
45. Shiva Naipaul, *Fireflies*, 41.
46. *Fireflies*, 41.
47. *Fireflies*, 299.
48. *Fireflies*, 311.
49. *Fireflies*, 313.
50. *Fireflies*, 316.
51. *Fireflies*, 316.
52. *Fireflies*, 318-19.
53. Lewis, "Caribbean Masculinity", 95.
54. *Fireflies*, 261.
55. *Fireflies*, 263.
56. *Fireflies*, 263.

17: NAIPAULIAN MOTHERS AND MOTHERLANDS

PAULA MORGAN

Naipaulian mothers exist on a continuum. On one end of the spectrum are impoverished, maudlin and relatively ineffectual mothers, who are to varying degrees, subsumed into stifling, extended families which in turn are controlled by other mothers – powerful, self-assured, wealthy matriarchs who are astute overseers of sprawling family networks which they govern strategically, consolidating power and authority through judicious use of "feminine wiles". Alongside these powerful mothering women, who are ostensibly functioning within patriarchal extended families, are selected male strongmen who act as their extended hands, and a veritable army of impotent and emotionally needy males. This paper probes correlations between male impotence, paradoxical evocations of mothers, and the alien and alienating family locations of male protagonists. It argues that at the root of Naipaulian angst are psychic legacies of broken historical origins, gaping deficiencies in mothering and early ejection from nurturing womb spaces. I argue that these produce an enduring sense of unhomeliness and displacement from motherlands for many of V.S. Naipaul's male characters.

There are in V.S. Naipaul's fiction recurrent motifs of the impact of hostile landscapes, alienation and nonbelonging to motherlands. This finds its fullest representation in the story "Tell Me Who to Kill":

> My brother. I remember a day like this, but with heat. The sky set black night and day, the rain always coming, beating on the galvanize roof, the ground turn to mud below the house, in the yard the water frothing yellow with mud, the pará-grass in the field at the back bending down with wet, everything damp and sticky, bare skin itching.
> [...]
> It is a bare room and the bare cedar boards have nothing on them except nails and some clothes and a calendar. [...] And my pretty brother is trembling with the ague, lying on the floor on a floursack spread on a sugarsack, with another floursack for counterpane. You can see the sickness on his little face.[...] It is how I think of my brother, small and sick, suffering for me and so pretty. I feel I could kill anyone who make him suffer. I don't care about myself. I have no life.[1]

This recurrent shaming scenario is a haunting Naipaulian evocation of Bhabha's unhomely moment when as a result of the discombobulating effect of enforced "social accommodation", displaced "cultural location" or "historical migration", the world impinges on the home and the "private and the public become part of each other forcing upon us a vision that is as divided as it is disorientating".[2] The evocation from "Tell Me Who to Kill", selected because of its power to convey the atmospheric tincture of the working out of suppressed personal and communal histories, is carefully set in the present and present continuous time. It expresses a haunting reality which can never be relegated to the past. It is invasive, flooding the psyche through every door of perception: a split psyche – a fragile, beautiful younger brother who represents the unnamed narrator's unspoilt self, brimming over with lost potential; a nascent subject bereft of a place of nurturance, belonging, comfort and succour; an inimical, threatening natural environment – sweltering heat, blackened sky, incessant rain drumming on the galvanized roof; a sparse, inhospitable poverty; a scarred built environment; an intimate shelter flawed; a vulnerable, diseased body, subject to marauding mosquitoes, itching skin and ague; the nauseating smell of smoke and food; an inadequate sense of security and belonging, as represented by an impotent father; an overwhelming sense of looming harm and threat to life – in short a state of abjection. This anguished split man / child – the experiencing physically dis-eased self and the observing psychically dis-eased suffering self – epitomises Naipaul's unnecessary and unaccommodated adult males, adrift in hostile landscapes, who inhabit his biographies, personal narratives, travelogues and fictions, whose most intimate shelters – their fragile, human bodies – are woefully inadequate and imperfect as protective shells.

   Why then have I selected this haunting vignette as the point of departure for a discussion of mothers and motherlands? A central issue, as reflected in the title "Tell Me Who to Kill", is that of blame. Who is the enemy? Who is to bear responsibility for tragic lives laid waste? The answer resides in a complex of historical forces which cannot be unravelled in order to determine who is to be punished for its outcome. Naipaul raises this question in *"The Overcrowded Barracoon"*: "Who is the enemy? The enemy is the past".[3] Significantly, though, in the short story titled "The Enemy" in *A Flag on the Island*, the youthful narrator, whose father dies of fright during a storm and who struggles for individuation in relation to his strong willed mother, identifies another enemy – the mother.

> I had always consider this woman my mother as the enemy. She was sure to misunderstand anything I did, and the time came when I thought she not only misunderstood me but quite definitely disapproved of me, I was an only child, but for her I was one too many.[4]

   Naipaul raises numerous issues in relation to mothering and motherlands: the benefits and terrors of the extended family network which may democratically ensure shelter, food and a modicum of care for all; but may also foster the furtive exchange of intimacy, sex and love between those linked by blood and marriage within residential arrangements with minimal privacy and unclear structures of belonging. It may also promote hierarchies and shifting power dynamics in domestic and intimate relations which keep the system running smoothly – for all those members who have a place in the order, but destroys those who are out of place. In this structure there is the interface of the iron will and feminine wiles necessary to manage and maintain complex domestic arrangements; a delicate balance between wives emasculating and affirming the fragile male egos of their husbands, which as mothering women they negotiate with delicacy and skill. V.S., like the younger brother Shiva, also portrays the performative nature of spectacular physical and psychic violence against children in a terrorist system intended to generate mass fear among the beaten and to confer prestige to the beater. And this is not an exhaustive listing.

The discussion that follows zeroes in on portrayals of ambivalent mothering, which finds fullest expression in the representation of Hanuman House and its army of mothers as the locus of imprisonment as well as nurture; erasure of individuality as well as shelter and protection; and as a womb and creative birthplace for its writerly son. In *A House for Mr Biswas*, the quintessential matriarch, Mrs Tulsi, surrounded by her multiplicity of daughters, stands guard over a cultural anomaly, masquerading as a guardian of tradition. Whereas in the new world many taboos had been shed in the general population, those relating to the basic cyclic events – birth, death and marriage – still obtained. But in the interest of expediency, the Tulsi system tampers even with these. Mrs Tulsi enforces her will by a subtle combination of feminine wiles and iron control and the system moves smoothly with her as the focal point of the household. She can be read as an embodiment of the great mother archetype, balanced by Seth, who is an allegorical representation of male power. The system is largely an economic one in which the many daughters provide the labour for running the house; their husbands provide the labour for the estate and commercial ventures. Marriage becomes a "cat in bag affair" as V.S. Naipaul memorably puts it, to remove the disgrace of having unmarried daughters while providing generations of future workers and managers of the system; and generally enhancing the prestige of the household. The husbands are reduced to quintessential Brahmin dulahas whose existence enhances Tulsi social privilege.

Mr Biswas, in pitting his puny strength against this Tulsi rule, is thus asserting his individuality against an oppressive, dehumanising system. His struggle is double pronged. He is on the one hand fighting against archaic cultural mores, and, at the same time, he is revealing and combating rampant cultural decay. He constantly uncovers the hidden motivation, the psychological blackmail by which the organisation operates: "Which foot you rub? [...] You should be glad they allow you to touch a foot. You know, it does beat me why all you sisters so anxious to look after the old hen. She did look after you?"[5] he taunts his wife Shama.

In *A House for Mr Biswas,* the Tulsi household thus represents the decay of a transported culture which appears falsely comforting to the displaced individual, most of whom are adrift in a state of anomie. The novel shows, however, that this is comfort bought at an excessively high price; the loss of self. In V.S. Naipaul's representation, the structures of the house and, particularly, its vast reservoirs of maternal power are shown as not truly supportive of the individual. Instead they threaten to annihilate the person in the interest of the collectivity and in service of a code dedicated to the accumulation of goods and capital. In many ways, the psychic location and the role of mothers is yet more complex than this. In a recurrent scene in Naipaul's narratives, which features a traumatic storm, the fictionalised father in "The Enemy" dies of fright and in *A House for Mr Biswas* he suffers a nervous breakdown. In the period leading to his mental collapse Biswas dreams about the mothering woman:

> He was on a hill, a bare brown-green hill. A woman was at the foot of the hill. She was crying and coming to him for help. He felt her pain but he didn't want to be seen. What help could he give and the women – Shama, Anand, Savi, his mother – kept coming up the hill. He heard her sobs and wanted to cry to her to go away.[6]

All of his frustrations, inadequacies and impotence are focused around ambivalent images of mothering. He has a sharp awareness of male fragility, the physically weak as well as those he perceives as weak-willed, including his weak and hysterical son, Anand, who is demanding material and psychic support Biswas is unable to provide. But when his family arrives, the pregnant Shama embodies multifaceted dimensions of his anxiety: both threat and comfort. She is woman, self-assured, immersed in the act of childbearing and rearing, living out her life in set patterns, fussing and clucking over her children, fanning and sweating in her frilled embroidered ornamented clothing. She is another version of the matriarch of Hanuman house who by her complete acquiescence with that life-denying system is emasculating him and negating his individuality. When she rests her heavy, dark, hand upon him she becomes like the witch of the fairy tale "Hansel and Gretel", who touches only to ascertain if the body is ready to be eaten: "No, I not fat enough yet. You got to put me back and feed me some more. Here why don't you just feel my finger?"[7] At this point, she is bearing his fourth child, the fourth millstone to hang around his neck, destined to become more the product of the Hanuman House organism than the child of Mohun Biswas.

With his full recognition of the factors loaded against him in the Tulsi colossus: Seth and the corrugated iron box; Hari and the black box; the decaying cultural and religious mores; and Shama the engulfing woman, Mr Biswas decides to stay in his room and die. Seen in this light, the kick to Shama's belly when she approaches him during this crisis is appropriately aimed. He hoists himself into the window to escape her and the stick with which he arms himself becomes suggestive of the phallus rendered impotent by the power of women. Discarding the stick, which proves to be useless as a weapon of defence, he kicks her swollen belly to halt her progress. This is the depth to which Biswas descends in his struggle to sever the umbilical cord which ties him to Hanuman House. It seems symbolically appropriate that the mental collapse of which his attack on Shama is a sign leads to his return to Hanuman house like a child wrapped in his adversary Govind's arms. Laid to rest in the house:

> He welcomed the warmth and reassurance of the room. Every wall was solid; the sound of the rain was deadened; the ceiling of two and a half inch pitch pine concealed corrugated iron and asphalt; the jalousied window sat in the deep embrasure was unrattled by wind and rain.[8]

In classic Freudian terms, the deep embrasure protected by a jalousied window suggests the opening leading to the womb. The perpetually dark silent shelter is opposed in every way to his unfinished house with yawning windows which had burst open to admit the black void. Enclosed in "this wordless room, this nothingness", Mr Biswas returns to foetal phase, where since before time began he had enjoyed the security and protection of the maternal womb, free of all responsibilities and fears. He "had surrendered and this surrender had brought peace".[9]

It is symbolic that Shama, lying in confinement in the neighbouring pink room, is brought to bed with the child whose slumber in the maternal womb had presumably been disturbed by Mohan's vicious kick. The parallel confinement of the couple suggests Shama's labour will also give birth to her husband. "He remained in the Blue Room, feeling secure to be only a part of Hanuman House, an organism that possessed a life, strength and power to comfort which was quite separate from the individuals who composed it".[10] His basic strength of character nonetheless saves him from total engulfment. He eventually relinquishes his anxiety, shakes off his death wish and emerges from the Blue Room to resume his search for individuality and his position in the emergent chaotic multicultural babel of Port of Spain.

My final concern is questioning the extent to which the mothering dispensed by Hanuman House, with its interface of ancient traditions and cultural accommodation – Hinduism as well as admixture of alternative spiritual traditions – has birthed the Naipauls as architects of the postcolonial house of fiction. Rahim in her perceptive essay "The Shadow of Hanuman" suggests that "the paradoxical play of traits embodied by the monkey god is actually not uncharacteristic since in the Hindu pantheon he belongs to the class of ambivalent deities as the eleventh avatar of Rudra/

Shiva, the destroyer. Although the benevolent traits of the deity are popularly recognised in orthodox Hinduism, it is his tricky, duplicitous trait that Naipaul chooses to negotiate in the text's mytho-religious reworking of the Rama and Sita story of exile and home coming".[11] In the real life setting of V.S. Naipaul's upbringing, particularly when the family moved to Nepaul Street, his father, Seepersad's own reading and writing may have lent comfort and sustenance to offset anonymity and erasure within the Capildeo family structure and he would have thus embodied the persistent quest for the stuff of fiction in order to claim the right to function as a valid perceiving subject and being in the world. The other choice, as V.S. Naipaul's fiction suggests, is to be a faceless, anonymous, voiceless cog in the Tulsi machinery. Such a choice is the stuff that generates the material of fiction. The stance of trickster comic artist and disrupter of received order, in short the monkey of the Hanuman House system, is the inspiration which brings V.S. Naipaul into voice and expression. In the foreword to Seepersad Naipaul's *The Adventures of Gurudeva and Other Stories*, which the son published in honour of his father's memory, Naipaul terms the tale "They Called Him Mohun" the only piece of autobiography his father permitted himself. The birthing of the mature writer in Naipaul the younger is built squarely on the literary heritage and the actual life of his father.[12] Moreover this fictional construct was built based on the father's advice. In 1952, Seepersad writes a letter to Vidia:

> As soon as you can, get working on a novel. Write of things as they are happening now, be realistic, humorous, when this comes in pat, but don't make it deliberately so. If you are at a loss for a theme, take me for it. Begin: "He sat before the little table writing down the animal counterparts of all his wife's family. He was very analytical about it. He wanted to be correct; he went to work like a scientist. He wrote, 'The She-Fox', then 'The Scorpion'; at the end of five minutes he produced a list which reads as follows:...". All this is just a jest, but you can really do it.[13]

In compliance with this spirit of revolt in Hanuman House, Naipaul records his emergence into creative voice in "Prologue to an Autobiography". In the rooms reserved for freelancers in the BBC's offices in London he adopts the posture of a monkey when he produces the first sentence of the first work he writes, the memorable lines with which *Miguel Street* begins. In the process, he embraces the ethos of trickery, duplicity, shadowing, disruption, tomfoolery, pretending, and posturing which is inherent to Hanuman the monkey god and to the survival modalities of Mr Biswas within to the structure and daily operations of Hanuman House. This includes the ability to navigate the divergence between its grand whitewashed external face and its ramshackle internal structure; and most significantly to find his way through its army of mothering women.

In Naipaul's early novels the mothering women demonstrate a resourcefulness, sure-footedness and flexibility which generations of men strive for but never achieve to the same extent. These are women rooted in ancient rhythms and biological functions and shielded from the anomie and harshest social demands of the emerging multicultural nation state. For the women belonging to a wealthy extended family network and operating as a collectivity imparts a further strength and certainty. By the time acculturation becomes unavoidable, the women discover within themselves a capacity to adapt. The males, however, inherit an insecure sense of self. They are the product of generations of weak and impoverished men, at times with malicious and violent fathers, who have only negative male role models. Literature echoes life as life shapes literature. Naipaul's recent biography delineates his own brand of disloyalty and cruelty and an impulse to treat women who have given him their love and loyalty as the enemy. Bound like the ancient mariner to wander through human societies as though they were desolate landscapes, mapping their deficiencies and turning a satirical eyes on their foibles, he is nevertheless constrained to acknowledge his debt to the mothering organism of Hanuman House and his life long obsession with the worlds within and without its corrugated iron gates.

Endnotes

1. V.S. Naipaul, "Tell Me Who to Kill", in *In a Free State* (London: Andre Deutsch, 1971), 63-108, p. 66-67. The discussion here of "Tell Me Who to Kill" is adapted from a fuller treatment in Paula Morgan, *Banal Violence and Trauma in Caribbean Discourse* (Mona: UWI Press, 2014).
2. Homi K. Bhabha, *The Location of Culture* (London: Routledge, 1994), 9.
3. V.S. Naipaul, *The Overcrowded Barracoon and Other Articles* (London: Andre Deutsch, 1972), 271.
4. V.S. Naipaul, *The Overcrowded Barracoon and Other Articles*, 62.
5. V.S. Naipaul, *A House for Mr Biswas* (London: Andre Deutsch, 1961), 115.
6. *A House for Mr Biswas*, 245.
7. *A House for Mr Biswas*, 247.
8. *A House for Mr Biswas*, 266.
9. *A House for Mr Biswas*, 269.
10. *A House for Mr Biswas*, 272.
11. Jennifer Rahim, "The Shadow of Hanuman: V.S. Naipaul and the 'Unhomely' House of Fiction", in *Created in the West Indies: Caribbean Perspectives on V.S. Naipaul*, eds. Jennifer Rahim and Barbara Lalla (Kingston: Ian Randle Publishers, 2011), 165-182, p. 195.
12. John Thieme, *The Web of Tradition: Uses of Allusion in V.S. Naipaul's Fiction* (Hertford: Dangaroo Press/Hansib Publications, 1987), 58.
13. V.S. Naipaul, foreword to *The Adventures of Gurudeva and Other Stories* (London: Andre Deutsch, 1976), 17.

18: KARMA AND THE NAIPAUL BROTHERS

FARIZA MOHAMMED

Brinsley Samaroo argues in his essay, "The Indian Connection" that "The Westindian East Indians will be neither Westindian nor East Indian until they first of all come to terms with themselves."[1] Coming to terms with oneself is a huge undertaking in all circumstances and under conditions of diasporic dislocation, it is particularly so, since it may involve not just the loss of the tangible but also of the intangible which includes cultural concepts and patterns of thought and behaviour. An examination of one such concept, the concept of karma, as represented in V.S. Naipaul's *A House for Mr Biswas,* and Shiva Naipaul's *Fireflies* is undertaken to demonstrate the point.

In order to delve into the philosophical concept of karma in the selected novels, it is necessary to have a working understanding of the term[2]. As Gananath Obeyesekere reminds us in *Imagining Karma*, the concept is by no means confined to Eastern cultures and is as readily apparent in the Buddhist as it is in Amerindian and Greek cultures. Sarah Shaw on the other hand examines the concept in terms of two South Asian traditions, Buddhism and Jainism, and explains:

> ...for Jains, karma was conceived of as a material substance that adhered to the soul and weighed it down, obscuring its natural omniscience and bliss and keeping it from attaining moksa. All actions bound karma, even those that were involuntary, thus in theory there was no such thing as 'good karma'. For Buddhists, on the other hand, karma was not physical, though it was still a law of the universe. The early Buddhists viewed karma in psychological terms, declaring that it was thirst or craving that led to bondage, and that the fruit of karma depended upon the motivation behind the action. In time these two opposing positions came closer together, as Jains accepted the idea of meritorious action leading to better rebirth, and began to place emphasis on the role of the passions in binding karma. Both the common heritage and the differing understandings of karma and the appropriate religious life are visible in the narratives preserved by each tradition. In particular, stories of multiple lives, which abound in the literature of both Buddhism and Jainism, have much to reveal about attitudes towards the mechanisms of rebirth and the pursuit of religious goals.[3]

Examinations along more traditional lines have been undertaken by traditional Orientalist scholars like Herman Wayne Tull. Tull sets his own work apart from early work, however, by observing that in the "nineteenth and early twentieth century Indologists tended to view... presentations of the karma doctrine in the Upanisads" within what he identifies as a "tendency among these scholars to disparage 'priestcraft', a perspective rooted in the philosophy of the Enlightenment." He claims that "this tendency led scholars to separate the Brahmanas, ritual texts par excellence and the exclusive possession of the Vedic sacerdotalists, from the Upanisads, discursive texts that seek to express the nature of reality".[4] His explanation of karma is thus as a doctrine of ritual action:

> After discussing how the deceased enters into the various planes of the cosmos, a process that replicates the dismemberment of the primordial man, the famed Brahmanic sage Yajñavalkya is asked: "What then becomes of this person?" Yajñavalkya then enunciates the doctrine of action (karman): "Indeed one becomes good by good action, bad by bad [action]." In the context of Vedic ritual thought good and bad apparently refer to a valuation of action based on ritual exactitude; good being equated with the correct performance of the rite, bad with the incorrect performance... This interpretation of the karma doctrine differs from the doctrine's apparent meaning in later texts, which propose that an individual attains a specific state in the afterlife, or is reborn, according to the moral quality of all sorts of actions performed prior to death.[5]

At present, in South Asian as well as all other contexts, karma is commonly used interchangeably with the word "fate" or "fatalism", to represent belief in something other than present human action as responsible for the events that occur during one's life. It is frequently used that way by V.S. Naipaul. For example, in *A Bend in the River* (1979), although distanced from India in time and space by his family's long location in Africa as part of ancient Afro-Asian continental exchanges, the protagonist Salim says:

> I could no longer submit to Fate. My wish was not to be good, in the way of our tradition, but to make good. But how? What did I have to offer? What talent, what skill, apart from the African trading skills of our family? This anxiety began to eat away at me. And that was why, when Nazruddin made his offer, of a shop and business in a far-off country that was still in Africa, I clutched at it.[6]

For Salim, fate and family tradition are one and the same and are set in opposition to the ability to find a place in the world for himself. To choose the former is to choose a sense of being good that can clash with grasping opportunities to "make good", meaning to participate in amassing material acquisitions. He therefore rejects the former for the latter, only to discover that he does so to his own eventual detriment, since diasporic social perceptions make family traditions a lot like fate and as inescapable.

In religious discourse, the concept of "fate" is not to be taken lightly, as it is more than karma and pregnant with meaning. According to David Knipe in his essay "Hindu Eschatology", the Sanskrit term for "fate" is daivam and it is distinct from karma:

> The word [daivam] is derived from deva (god), suggesting a divine source. Often it carries ambiguity in the sense of chance as well as necessity. Melded with the concept karma, daivam therefore implies that karmaphala, the fruits of past human action, are by no means the sole determinative of one's individual status.[7]

Despite Knipe's fairly straightforward definition of fate and karma and his attempt to show how they intertwine, it remains a fairly astronomical task to attach one definitive meaning to the term karma. This difficulty in defining karma is clearly outlined by Wendy Doniger O'Flaherty in the introduction to *Karma and Rebirth in Classical Indian Traditions*. She reminds us for example that:

> Ambivalence in the very earliest texts may account for a number of persistent paradoxes, contradictions, and inconsistencies in the various karma theories – paradoxical statements about whether karma can or cannot be overruled, contradictory statements about the interaction of fate and human effort.[8]

Despite such caveats however, karma is largely understood in terms of a cycle of life everlasting. It involves a process whereby the actions committed in one's past life are seen to influence the kind of life an individual will enjoy in his/her subsequent re-birth. Thus, good actions will bring punya, roughly speaking – merits or rewards, whilst negative actions result in paap which has no adequate translation in English but is rendered in some texts as sin and punishment.[9] For practising Hindus today, explanations such as V. Jayaram's may thus suffice:

> The law of karma is a simple and straightforward concept according to which beings, not just men, are rewarded or punished according to their own actions and intentions. The law of karma makes it abundantly clear that the solution to our liberation lies in our own hands and how we go about it is left to ourselves.[10]

Based on these explanations, in this study karma is distinguished from daivam or fate which represents the idea of predetermined inevitable destiny, the idea that events are out of the realm of human control. These two notions are complex parts of the philosophical context influencing how a Hindu perceives the world.

While it cannot be pursued much further here it is interesting to note that in Samuel Selvon's *A Brighter Sun* the philosophy of daivam is perhaps best summed up in the phrase "what is to is, must is".[11] However Jeremy Poynting in his thesis, "Literature and Cultural Pluralism: East Indians in the Caribbean", talks about the forces against which Tiger rebels and surprisingly identifies what this study considers as a representation of daivam to be "the creole attitude":

> The Indian way is to organise life along a predetermined route; practically, by accepting the given means whereby a modest security can be achieved, illusorily, by attempting to predict the outcome of any action, by consulting the pundit, for instance. Having fixed notions about what ought to happen inevitably sets up disappointments. Tiger, for instance, convinces himself that their first child must be a boy. The creole attitude, frequently summed up by Joe as 'what is to is, must is', becomes too often simply an excuse for passivity and irresponsibility.[12]

Be that as it may, identifying the following as one of the most important ways in which Samaroo's concerns are obvious, this study is particularly interested in the ways in which karma transmutes into fate in V.S. Naipaul's *A House for Mr Biswas* and Shiva Naipaul's *Fireflies*, as much in the sense of daivam as in the Western sense of fatalism.

One of the first occurrences in *A House for Mr Biswas*, located in terms of a post-indenture chronology, is when Mr Biswas's maternal grandfather, Bipti's father, "futile with asthma, propped himself up on his string bed and said, as he always did on unhappy occasions, 'Fate. There is nothing we can do about it'".[13] This sense of fate functions in *A House for Mr. Biswas* as well as in *Fireflies* as a metanarrative as defined by Mark Leffert. According to Leffert, "Narratives exist on two levels – as stories about life events and as stories about how the world works. The latter, subjective personal metanarratives, exert enormous control over the way people experience the world and live their lives."[14] Daivam-fate proves to be such a "subjective personal metanarrative".

Moreover, as J. Vijay Maharaj argues in "A Mala in Obeisance: Hinduism in Select Texts by V.S. Naipaul":

> [V.S. Naipaul's] concern, as critics have observed, is the individual's ensnarement by aspects of Hindu philosophy, particularly the idea of karma. However, contrary to the common critical claims that Naipaul rejects karma, it can be shown that this is not so. He interrogates the concept as "The Hindu killer, the Hindu calm, which tells us that we pay in this life for what we have done in past lives," but he also notes that it is an injunction about "our duty to ourselves [and] our future lives." Karma is a mandate for acceptance of life's events but it is not fatalism. It is also a call to action since it is only through action taken now that one re-pays the debts incurred in the past, ensures a quality life in the present and a better life in the future.[15]

Initially, it is not karma in these terms, but fate-daivam which makes its presence felt in V.S. Naipaul's novel. His concern seems to be that fate-daivam is often used as an excuse, an easy way out, a reason to abdicate any kind of personal responsibility for one's life. Mr Biswas' forefathers are depicted as holding such strong beliefs in fate that it is used to virtually explain every occurrence in their lives, almost to the point of absolving them from any responsibility for anything. This is clearly the case with Mr Biswas' grandfather. Although: "No one paid him any attention" the narrator voices his and the family's acceptance that "Fate had brought him from India to the sugar-estate, aged him quickly and left him to die in a crumbling mud hut in the swamplands; yet he spoke of fate often and affectionately, as though, merely by surviving, he had been particularly favoured".[16]

The tone implies that the act of merely surviving is disdained by all and it provides a context for representations of characters like Salim who will do anything in their power to do more than just survive. Naipaul strongly condemns the kind of mentality exhibited by the grandfather. As Maharaj observes:

> Many aspects of this brief scene negate the principle of action in the term karma that the grandfather would have used. First of all, he is likely to be suffering with asthma because of working on the plantations but he has never taken a stand on this. Secondly, he is on a string bed that cannot add comfort to his breathing. He has abdicated personal responsibility for his own health and Naipaul suggests by the tone of the narrative that financial poverty is not the only problem. There is a greater problem of poverty of mind and spirit.[17]

Mr Biswas' grandfather is one of those individuals who uses fate as a means of explaining away unfavourable things that happen. It is as though he feels people have no control over the pace or direction of their own lives; instead they are wholly controlled by outside forces. Naipaul takes issue with this since it makes people seem like puppets and provides them with an easy way out. They are therefore excused from being accountable for the state of their own lives and the consequences of their actions and behaviour on others.

Bipti, Mr Biswas' mother, is perhaps the character who best personifies the deep sense of fatalism that permeates some of the characters in the novel and it is against that background that Mr Biswas's meagre achievements take on epic proportions, viz:

> Mr. Biswas was forty-six, and had four children. He had no money. His wife Shama had no money. On the house in Sikkim Street Mr. Biswas owed, and had been owing for four years, three thousand dollars. The interest on this, at eight per cent, came to twenty dollars a month; the ground rent was ten dollars. Two children were at school. The two older children, on whom Mr. Biswas might have depended, were both abroad on scholarships. It gave Mr. Biswas some satisfaction that in the circumstances Shama did not run straight off to her mother to beg for help. Ten years before that would have been her first thought. Now she tried to comfort Mr. Biswas, and devised plans on her own.[18]

On the other hand, regardless of what happens in her life: the miserliness of her husband, his death and the eventual dismemberment of her family, Bipti attributes it all to the universal force of fate. In one of his early arguments with Bipti, Mr Biswas vents his anger towards her largely because of her fatalistic thinking. He says things that will strike at her very core, but ends up having little impact on her because she sees even his protests as being part of her fate, because there is nothing she can do about her situation in life, or her relationship with her children. He becomes impatient. "'You have never done a thing for me. You are a pauper.' He had meant to hurt her, but she was not hurt. 'It is my fate. I have no luck with my children. And with you Mohun, I have the least luck of all. Everything Sitaram said about you was true.'"[19]

Naipaul's Mr Biswas is thus depicted as coming from a Hindu-Trinidadian background in which a strong sense of fatalism is evident and this is compounded by a similar ethos in the Creole environment into which he is born. References begin with his birth. He is "six-fingered, and born in the wrong way".[20] To make matters worse, his time of birth is midnight, a time that is often associated with all things inauspicious. From his very entry into the world, Mr. Biswas' existence is fraught with such problems. The midwife, without hesitation, makes the prediction that Mr. Biswas will "eat up his own mother and father" based on his breeched birth.[21]

In fact, throughout the novel the struggle that Mr Biswas wages can be spoken of as one between free will and predetermination. He struggles against the predictions made by the midwife and the pandit at the time of his birth. The pandit, after consultation of his astrological manual, determines that Mr Biswas will have an unlucky sneeze, is doomed to become a spendthrift and a lecher, and needs to be kept away from water in its natural form. Mr Biswas' attempts to escape this unfortunate horoscope are intensified, though it seems, ironically, that the pandit's predictions are coming true when his father dies by drowning in fated water when he dives in mistaken search of his missing son. His only weapon in this fight seems to be his name, "Mohun", a name the milkmaids gave to Lord Krishna, and the only positive feature of his birth. His Krishna-like fight against fate is relentless.

The novel thereby refutes Bipti's assertions. Aside from his role in his father's drowning, Mr Biswas' life does not fulfil his horoscope as given by Pandit Sitaram. At every step, he fights against fate and is determined to be the agent in the events that happen to him during his lifetime. One may posit that his determined pursuit of a house of his own is in fact motivated by his struggle against a seemingly inevitable destiny. Mr Biswas' motto is indeed "paddle your own canoe".[22]

Despite Mr Biswas' motto being the subject of much laughter within the Tulsi household, it nevertheless indicates his assertion of a certain level of independence in an institution designed to promote a hierarchical community and community traditions ahead of individual needs. Even though he achieves independence fitfully and often fleetingly, he still manages to take a stand in order to achieve certain things in life. Thus, as the narrator proudly asserts, he is able, unlike many, to avoid dying as he had been born "unnecessary and unaccommodated".[23]

The numerous efforts made by Mr Biswas throughout the novel to make a home for himself, whether it is at The Chase, Green Vale, Shorthills, Port of Spain and eventually at Sikkim Street, are ways of taking action to defy the fatalistic attitude he has been immersed in since childhood. He is actually doing something, not simply having life pass him by, and the entire novel is reflective of this tension. This view is expressed by John Thieme in "An Introduction to *A House for Mr Biswas*", albeit without a sufficiently nuanced understanding of the complex concepts of fate and action in Hindu philosophy:

> The novel can be read as an allegory which explores a central issue for contemporary Hinduism, the opposition between western-style [sic] action and the quietism encouraged by the doctrine of karma. For Naipaul resignation to karma is the central Hindu failing, an attitude of mind which precludes any form of social action.[24]

In *A House for Mr Biswas,* the Tulsi family represents the kind of Sanatanist Hinduism against which Mr Biswas rebels. His rebellion begins from his very entry into the Tulsi household and can be viewed as the catalyst for his eventual possession of a home of his own. In fact, had he not fought, undermined and rebelled against them at every opportunity, he might not have been given access to the various properties at The Chase, Green Vale, Shorthills and Port of Spain, which prepared him somewhat for the final possession of the house at Sikkim Street.

The Tulsis, like most members of Mr Biswas' own natal family, are resigned to a fatalistic outlook on the world, having adopted it from Pundit Tulsi himself: "What is for you is for you. What is not for you is not for you".[25] This attitude is one Mr Biswas frequently encounters in Shama, who has adopted it from her family. Indeed, nothing enrages Mr Biswas more than when he encounters this fatalistic attitude, as this conversation he has with Shama shows: "'What is for you is for you,' he mocked. 'So that is your philosophy, eh?'"[26] As should be evident, this philosophy of the Tulsi family bears a striking resemblance to "what is to is, must is" in Selvon's *A Brighter Sun.*

Despite the numerous obstacles he encounters, Mr Biswas never really gives up on his desire to own his own home, and this singular drive is represented as his saving grace, the rebellious Krishna-like spark that keeps him going. Eventually, he is able to achieve a certain level of success, "paddling his own canoe". Although his success is brief, as he dies not long after buying his home, it nevertheless provides him with a great sense of accomplishment. In the novel's opening flash-forward:

> He was struck again and again by the wonder of being in his own house, the audacity of it: to walk in through his own front gate, to bar entry to whoever he wished, to close his doors and windows every night, to hear no noises except those of his family, to wander freely from room to room and about his yard. As a boy he had moved from one house of strangers to another; and since his marriage he felt he had lived nowhere but in the houses of the Tulsis, at Hanuman House in Arwacas, in the decaying wooden house at Shorthills, in the clumsy concrete house in Port of Spain. And now at the end he found himself in his own house, on his own half-lot of land, his own portion of the earth. That he should have been responsible for this seemed to him, in these last months, stupendous.[27]

Shiva Naipaul deals with karma in a similar way in *Fireflies*, a novel about the Khojas that can be seen as a sequel to *A House for Mr Biswas* and in a similar relation to their father's short story, "They Named Him Mohun". This novel begins, as Amit Chaudhuri notes in the foreword to the 2012 Penguin edition with "an episode... where the sisters and relations of the clan have gathered at the Khojas' house for a cattha, or an annual religious celebration":

> No Khoja function was ever considered complete without a beating. Any infringement of the rules (they could be invented on the spur of the moment) could be made the occasion for one of these entertainments, and children who were rarely beaten at home would suddenly find themselves liable. The choice of the victim was, in the normal run of things, capricious. At such times the sisters became unpredictable forces and, a beating once administered, its influence percolated through the clan. Several more victims were hastily assembled, although none could surpass the grandeur of that first beating.[28]

In Chaudhuri's reading of the episode, he foregrounds Shiva Naipaul's representation of fate in words that are immensely appropriate for the purposes of this essay. Chaudhuri remarks:

> This mixture of random justice and predestination gives to Naipaul's fiction – in lieu of straightforward linearity – a tantalising, slightly alarming, circular musicality, a kind of pass-the-parcel sequence of shifting the weight from one person, one centre, to another. Naipaul's themes are fate, dissolution, bad luck; but he is also concerned with, beyond the story, the music – that is, a span of time, constituting a narrative or a life, comprising pauses in which the sword falls repeatedly, and in which nothing much is achieved. As a result, the matter of fate and destiny is something he deals with in a way that's unique, and which bears no resemblance to the plotted narratives of others who've had similar concerns...[29]

The point could not have been expressed better. Whereas V.S. Naipaul diegetically explains the functioning of fate-daivam in the characters' lives, Shiva Naipaul expresses its permeation through his characters' consciousness via the very form of his work. Chaudhuri remarks to this effect that "Scene after scene, episode after episode in this terrible pass-the-parcel game, Shiva Naipaul reveals himself to be less an adherent of character and story than a devotee of an exquisite, if deeply odd, formal beauty."[30] This beauty recreates, I think, the beauty Seepersad Naipaul strove for in order to represent Hinduism in his short stories.

Conclusion

It can be concluded that in these novels, in their Hindu-Trinidadian context, the philosophy of karma is action based and exists in tension with the concept of fate which is represented in Sanskrit by a different term, daivam, which is a belief in and fear of predetermination and destiny. In both novels discussed, their authors present the philosophy of karma at work in the lives of their characters. In their presentations of the Hindu-Trinidadian community other perceptions of the term karma emerge. It is noteworthy, however, that the protagonists see karma as being the result of human activity and do not resign themselves as victims of fate. Instead they are determined to take charge of their lives.

Karma, in the Naipaul brothers' work, can thus be seen as capable of performing a similar function to its portrayal in other texts in the South Asian tradition. Theirs may not be stories like those in the Jatak kattha vanyana, which according to Shaw comprises "a multitude of stories preserved by early South Asian traditions that discuss karma and rebirth, giving specific examples of past-life memory".[31] Nonetheless one may borrow Satya P. Mohanty's words, in "Alternative Modernities and Medieval Indian Literature: The Oriya *Lakshmi Purana*", for example, in order to assert that in these works:

> The poetic – in particular, metaphorical – connections among the various actors consolidate the philosophical redefinition of identity in terms of action rather than social ascription, or karma rather than dharma. The individual self is extricated from entanglements of caste and social station as the self of the doer and the devotee. ...[They] may well represent a major stage in the articulation of a subjectivity that is disembedded from caste and class, and available in principle to all human agents, not limited to gods and goddesses.[32]

In fact, in the two novels examined here:

> Karma and inherited social roles (the traditional meaning of dharma) are here wrenched apart; what emerges as an alternative to ascribed identity is the thinking, questioning, critical self – something close to the modern ideal of the individual whose value does not depend on social status but rather on what she or he chooses to do, on intentional action.[33]

The Naipaulian literary production thus performs a great service to the Hindu-Trinidadian community.

Endnotes

1. Brinsley Samaroo, "The India Connection: The Influence of Indian Thought and Ideas on East Indians in the Caribbean", in *India in the Caribbean*, eds. David Dabydeen and Brinsley Samaroo (Hertford: Hansib Publications, 1987), 43-59, p. 56.
2. The understanding of karma that applies to this essay was developed via study of a number of texts, including many not directly referenced such as Naomi Appleton, "Heir to One's Karma: Multi-life Personal Genealogies in Early Buddhist and Jain Narratives", *Religions of South Asia* 5/1.2. (2011): 227-44; Johannes Bronkhorst, *Karma and Teleology: A Problem and its Solutions in Indian Philosophy* (Tokyo: The International Institute for Buddhist Studies of the International College for Advanced Buddhist Studies, 2000) and *Karma* (Honolulu: University of Hawai'i Press, 2011); Balarama Das, "Lakshmi Purana" [An Excerpt]. Trans. Rajendra Prasad Das. *Medieval Indian Literature: An Anthology* (New Delhi: Sahitya Akademi, 1999), 734-738 and *Lakshmi Purana: A Paean to the Goddess of Fortune*. Trans. Lipipuspa Nayak (Bhubaneswar: Grassroots, 2007); Wendy Doniger O'Flaherty, "Karma and Rebirth in the Vedas and Purânas" and *Karma and Rebirth in Classical Indian Traditions*. Ed. Wendy Doniger O'Flaherty. (Berkeley, Los Angeles and London: University of California Press, 1980), 3-37; Saurabh Dube and Ishita Banerjee-Dube, "Introduction: Critical Questions of Colonial Modernities." *Unbecoming Modern: Colonialism, Modernity, Colonial Modernities* (New Delhi: Social Science Press, 2006); Richard F. Gombrich, "Buddhist Karma and Social Control", *Comparative Studies in Society and History* 17/2. (1975): 212-20; Phyllis Granoff, "Karma, Curse, or Divine Illusion: The Destruction of the Buddha's Clan and the Slaughter of the Yâdavas", in *Epic and Argument in Sanskrit Literary History: Essays in Honor of Robert P. Goldman*, ed. Sheldon Pollock (New Delhi: Manohar, 2010), 75-90; Charles F. Keyes and Daniel, E. Valentine. eds. *Karma: An Anthropological Inquiry* (Berkeley, Los Angeles and London: University of California Press, 1992); Yuvraj Krishan, *The Doctrine of Karma: its Origin and Development in Brâhmanical, Buddhist and Jaina Traditions* (Delhi: Motilal Banarsidass, 1997); Bruce R. Reichenbach, *The Law of Karma: A Philosophical Study* (London: Macmillan, 1990) and Robert C. Solomon, "On Fate and Fatalism", *Philosophy East and West* 53/4. (2003): 435-54.
3. *The Jatakas: Birth Stories of the Bodhisatta*, trans. Sarah Shaw, (New Delhi: Penguin, 2006), 4.
4. Herman Wayne Tull, *The Vedic Origins of Karma: Cosmos as Man in Ancient Indian Myth and Ritual* (New York: State University of New York Press, 1989), 2-3.
5. Tull, 2.
6. V.S. Naipaul, *A Bend in the River* (London: Andre Deutsch, 1979), 26
7. David M. Knipe, "Hindu Eschatology", in *The Oxford Handbook of Eschatology*, ed. Jerry L. Walls (Oxford: Oxford University Press, 2007), 185.
8. Wendy Doniger O'Flaherty. "Karma and Rebirth in the Vedas and Puranas",

in *Karma and Rebirth in Classical Indian Traditions*, ed. Wendy Doniger O'Flaherty (Berkeley, Los Angeles and London: University of California Press, 1980), 3-37, 4.
9. See for instance Satya Mohanty's "Alternative Modernities and Medieval Indian Literature: The Oriya *Lakshmi Purana* as Radical Pedagogy", *diacritics* 38.3 (2008): 3–21; "The Epistemic Status of Cultural Identity: On *Beloved* and the Postcolonial Condition", *Cultural Critique* 24 (1993): 41-80 and *Literary Theory and the Claims of History: Postmodernism, Objectivity, Multicultural Politics* (Ithaca: Cornell UP, 1997).
10. V. Jayaram. *Hinduism: Beliefs and Practices*. Web. Accessed November 28, 2014. http://www.hinduwebsite.com
11. Samuel Selvon, *A Brighter Sun* (London: Allan Windgate, 1952), 226.
12. Jeremy Poynting, "Literature and Cultural Pluralism: East Indians in the Caribbean", vol. 2 (doctoral thesis, University of Leeds, 1985), 560, http://etheses.whiterose.ac.uk/821/4/uk_bl_ethos_355497_VOL2.pdf.
13. V.S. Naipaul, *A House for Mr Biswas* (New York: Vintage, 2001), 15.
14. Mark Leffert, *Contemporary Psychoanalytic Foundations; Postmodernism, Complexity, and Neuroscience* (London and New York: Routledge, 2010), 42.
15. J. Vijay Maharaj, "A Mala in Obeisance: Hinduism in Select Texts by V.S. Naipaul", in *Created in the West Indies: Caribbean Perspectives on V.S. Naipaul*, ed. Jennifer Rahim and Barbara Lalla (Kingston: University of the West Indies Press, 2011), 127.
16. V.S. Naipaul, *A House for Mr Biswas*, 15.
17. Maharaj, 127.
18. V.S. Naipaul, *A House for Mr Biswas*, 1.
19. V.S. Naipaul, *A House for Mr Biswas*, 65.
20. V.S. Naipaul, *A House for Mr Biswas*, 15.
21. V.S. Naipaul, *A House for Mr Biswas*, 15.
22. V.S. Naipaul, *A House for Mr Biswas*, 107.
23. V.S. Naipaul, *A House for Mr Biswas*, 14.
24. John Thieme, *The Web of Tradition: Uses of Allusion in V.S. Naipaul's Fiction* (Hertford: Hansib Publications/Dangaroo Press, 1987), 157.
25. V.S. Naipaul, *A House for Mr Biswas*, 165.
26. V.S. Naipaul, *A House for Mr Biswas*, 517.
27. V.S. Naipaul, *A House for Mr Biswas*, 8.
28. Amit Chaudhuri, foreword to *Fireflies* by Shiva Naipaul (London: Penguin Classics, 2012).
29. Amit Chaudhuri, foreword to *Fireflies*.
30. Amit Chaudhuri, foreword to *Fireflies*.
31. Sarah Shaw, (trans.) *The Jâtakas: Birth Stories of the Bodhisatta* (New Delhi: Penguin, 2006) i.
32. Satya P. Mohanty, "Alternative Modernities and Medieval Indian Literature: The Oriya *Lakshmi Purana* as Radical Pedagogy", *Diacritics* 38, no. 3 (2008): 3-21, p. 15.
33. Mohanty, 18

19: SADOMASOCHISM, INCEST AND POWER RELATIONS

MEGHAN CLEGHORN

Studies of sexuality in the Caribbean has been a largely twenty-first century development. The research projects which I have undertaken aim to contribute to the field by exploring problems and issues of sexuality pertinent to the Indo-Caribbean group as these are represented in works of Caribbean fiction. As Linden Lewis states, after all, "the creative writers of the Caribbean have treated the subject of sexuality much more seriously and explored it much more fully than their academic counterparts."[1] These projects are also informed by a gender perspective primarily because in the fiction problems of sexuality are represented as directly related to oppressive, inherited structures of patriarchy which plague the Caribbean.

In addition, Jenny Sharpe and Samantha Pinto, in "The Sweetest Taboo: Studies of Caribbean Sexualities; A Review Essay", argue that: "The complex interplay between sexuality and respectability has historically undergirded scholarship on gender and sexuality in the Caribbean. The topics of women's sexuality and sexual needs were subsumed within studies of kinship and family, while homosexuality was treated as if it simply did not exist".[2] This essay, "Sadomasochism, Incest and Power Relations" examines changing concepts of sexuality and gender, and discusses their relevance to a reading of the Naipauls' works which is informed by the relationship between respectability and sexuality as manifest in the Caribbean and discussed in Caribbean studies. It explores male sexuality in both fictional characters and the real life representation of V.S. Naipaul's sexuality via his biography.

In 1985, at the fourth annual conference on West Indian Literature, in an essay entitled "Psycho-sexual Aspects of the Woman in V.S. Naipaul's Fiction", Elaine Fido compared the work of American writer Norman Mailer and of the Italian Oriana Fallici to that of V.S. Naipaul. She calls the writing of all three authors sadomasochistic, but notes that by comparison, Naipaul's writing is far more sadistic and carries no inherent moral lesson for the reader. She writes for example:

> The case of V.S. Naipaul's treatment of male-female sexuality in three later novels, *Guerillas* (1975), *In a Free State* (1971) and *A Bend in the River* (1979) is more complex and more worrying than the case of Fallici or Mailer, who, whilst possibly serving a desire on the part of the reading public to enjoy vicariously the danger of sadomasochism and anti-social violence, are at least presenting a warning and a moral commentary along with their salacious details.[3]

These 1970s works by V.S. Naipaul have indeed created a wide range of such passionate response. It is for this reason perhaps that Supriya Nair argues for a more complex response to V.S. Naipaul:

> One of his interviewers describes an otherwise dour Naipaul as rather pleased over the impending publication of his disturbing novel *Guerrillas*. When asked what it was about, "'Nasty, wicked people,' he says with relish. For the first time today he smiles," the interviewer observes. In another exchange some years later with Bharati Mukherjee and Robert Boyers, where he admits the novel lost him a substantial readership, Naipaul discusses the comic potential of *Guerrillas* and *A Bend in the River*, both novels that readers could be forgiven for regarding as quite removed from comedy. Sensing the scepticism of his interviewers, he insists, "Do you know *Guerrillas* is full of jokes? If I had read *Guerrillas* aloud you would be roaring with laughter. Really." To which Boyers doubtfully replies, "*This is something I'll have to think about.*"[4]

Nair argues that the interviewers miss an important aspect of the Caribbeanness of work by V.S. Naipaul and other writers:

> The episodic, picaresque fiction of Selvon, Naipaul father and son, and Willi Chen... suggest a national style of humour attuned to local traditions, but also sharing a regional kinship. In some ways the picaroon of colonial society is also a word warrior, but a warrior who enjoys a good joke and is not averse to sharing it.[5]

Nair, published in 2013, is representative of a recent positive turn in Naipaulian criticism and one may add that she could as easily have said sons rather than "son". Previous critical stances are visible in the interviews to which Nair refers as well as to Fido's essay, in which the assumption seems to be that the writer should carry with him/her some sort of moral compass which directs the reader to a "better" reality and should convey a somewhat definitive position on the "rights" and "wrongs" of sexual acts. This kind of assumption was intrinsic to much nationalist literatures and literary criticism across the postcolonial world. Fido also makes a connection between "sadomasochism", "danger" and "anti-social violence" which can be seen as similarly historically positioned.

In this chapter, the types of sexual behaviours, such as sadomasochism, highlighted by Fido, exhibited in the novels of V.S. and Shiva Naipaul, as well as in representations of the life of V.S. Naipaul himself, are analysed with this issue of morality in mind. This is an important undertaking if one considers that often the same society which judges the writers is the very same society that produced them. To place the argument of this essay in context we must first examine changing definitions of sadomasochism. It is necessary to develop a sense of how sadomasochism was conceptualised at the time of Fido's paper, as opposed to how the phenomenon is seen today in a time of common knowledge regarding BDSM as bondage: discipline; domination: submission; sadism: masochism.

Fido's concept of sadomasochism seems to be rooted in the perception that any sadomasochistic act is purely to the disadvantage of and would be detestable to women. In this, she shared common ground with many others then and now, including radical thinkers such as Audre Lorde.[6] Indeed, Lorde vehemently asserts in one interview that:

> Sadomasochism is an institutionalised celebration of dominant/ subordinate relationships. And, it *prepares* us to either accept subordination or dominance. *Even in play*, to affirm that the exertion of power over powerlessness is erotic, is empowering, is to set the emotional and social stage for the continuation of that relationship, politically, socially and economically.[7]

Fido however quotes Brownmiller's similar definition of sadomasochism:

> ...sadomasochism has always been defined by male and female terms. It has been codified by those who see in sadism a twisted understanding of their manhood, and it has been accepted by those who see in masochism the abuse and pain that is synonymous with Woman. For this reason alone sadomasochism shall always remain a reactionary antithesis to women's liberation.[8]

The context of racism in post-slavery America may well underwrite these ideas, of course.

However, such views contrast sharply with current academic discourses about sadomasochism, even in the area of psychology, where the terms have changed dramatically since Sigmund Freud's use of Richard von Krafft-Ebing's treatise on perversion, *Psychopathia Sexualis*, based on the works of Leopold von Sacher-Masoch, which influenced all subsequent work on the issue.[9] Today there are different concepts associated with the term, many of which take Freud's ideas in new directions. Many of the concepts have been proposed by feminist critics including Gayle Rubin, Juliet Mitchell, Elizabeth Grosz and Judith Butler, who have in fact argued that psychoanalysis has many concepts which should be developed. Elena Barrett, in "The Distribution of Power: Sadomasochism and Feminism" studies more recent definitions of sadomasochism which have developed as a result, and concludes that today sadomasochism is "a consensual sexual practice rather than a larger social phenomenon".[10] Refuting a position similar to Savory-Fido's she writes:

> Weinberg, Williams and Moser define the relationship between these two roles as "the rule of one partner over another," wherein one person

dominates the other with given consent. In addition to consent, the necessary elements that define SM are: role play relevant to dominance and submission within a sexual context, as well as mutually agreed upon definitions of SM sex play. Typically, however, SM role-play involves the *illusion* of non-consent, with the submissive pretending to resist the will of the dominant.[11]

By this definition, we see that in the more recent evolution of the terminology, sadomasochism has been taken out of the constraints of gender roles and a reduction of the negative connotations of the term has occurred. This is an aspect of contemporary thought about individuals' power over their choice of sex play and sexual fantasy.

In light of this contrast to earlier notions regarding sadomasochism, it is now possible to interrogate positions like Fido's on the supposedly sadomasochistic writing of V.S. Naipaul. Fido says:

Naipaul is a persuasive purveyor of the psychopathic male-masochistic female relation without providing, by authorial comment or strong counterbalancing characters, a clue to how we are to understand his moral perception of the nature of his cruel men and passive, self-rejecting women.[12]

Fido thus suggests that sadomasochism is scandalous and that the reader needs to mimic the writer and must be told his/her moral position by the writer. Even if one cannot completely answer them, this begs the questions: Does V.S. Naipaul have a moral perspective? If we can gather enough evidence to say that he doesn't, the question is, should he? Moreover, does this supposed morality or lack thereof in any way affect the quality of his artistic representation of society? And finally, do the changing perceptions of issues like sadomasochism suggest that Caribbean works like those by V.S. Naipaul need to be revisited in order to think again about sexuality in the Caribbean?

The role of the author has never been indisputably settled within any particular parameters. If we take a great author's role as comprising at a minimum a believable representation, then a great deal of the Naipauls' success has been predicated on their ability to represent West Indian society as it is, in all its postcolonial trauma and abjection, rather than as a fictional paradise of Caribbean tropes and sun-kissed European morals. We therefore need to ask what critics, such as Fido, are inquiring into in relation to these representations of sexuality in V.S. Naipaul's work.

Most literary work is inspired by that author's life experiences, and therefore their perspectives on these experiences. A large number of biocritical essays on the works of the Naipauls speak of their feelings of abjection, desolation and alienation, as well as struggles with identity, throughout their literary careers and lives. It is not surprising therefore that these melancholy qualities are also manifest in the characters of their novels. Critical comments, such as this by Alpana Mishra's, are common.

Mishra writes, "For his storytelling, [V.S] Naipaul is famous for his searing, unforgiving and controversial portraits of formerly colonised societies struggling towards self-realisation in the postcolonial world".[13] Adjectives such as "searing, unforgiving and controversial" can be extended into the area of sexuality "in the postcolonial world," with its history of colonial rape, its dark areas of incest and its racialised stereotypes.

Since the publication of V.S. Naipaul's authorised biography, it has become possible to draw some parallels between the sexual experiences of Naipaul's characters and the man himself. In order to analyse this concept further, an evaluation of Naipaul's protagonist in *The Mimic Men*, Ralph Singh, is necessary. In Champa Rao Mohan's *Postcolonial Situation in the Novels of V.S. Naipaul*, for example, she quotes Hana Wirth-Nesher on the issue of sexuality in Naipaul's novels, *Guerrillas* and *A Bend in the River*. Wirth-Nesher writes:

> Sexuality in Naipaul's fiction is contrary to that literary tradition in which nakedness implies stripping men and women of their cultural and political roles as well. Indeed, in the post-imperial world political identities become so integral a part of life that intimacy becomes an impossibility. Every sexual relationship forged in the novel is of a perverse nature.[14]

This view of Naipaul's representation of sexuality is evidenced not only in the aforementioned novels, but also in the texts being examined in this essay: V.S. Naipaul's *The Mimic Men*, Shiva Naipaul's *The Chip Chip Gatherers* and Patrick French's *The World is What it is: The Authorized Biography of V.S. Naipaul*, as well as in the novel *Guerillas*, which is examined briefly.

Some of the characterisation in these works can be seen as conforming to the idea of the "masochistic, passive and self-rejecting women" of whom Fido speaks. In Shiva Naipaul's *The Chip-Chip Gatherers,* for instance, the relationship between Rani and Egbert Ramsaran is a pertinent example. Rani, the infinitely melancholy and downtrodden wife of Egbert Ramsaran, dutifully prostrates herself outside his bedroom door every night, bathed, perfumed and ready for the off-chance that he may choose to take her into his bedroom on that night. Instead, he beats her into a different kind of submission, one where she submits to his will to be rid of her, at least for the night. In this case, Egbert's pleasure certainly comes from his power and authority over Rani. In this he is a typifies the machismo portrayed by all the Naipauls in their satirical depictions of those men who feel a sense of power only in destroying others.

Although Shiva Naipaul's representation of Rani is consistent with Fido's definition of sadomasochism, there is none of the role-playing and pleasure associated with more recent concepts of sadomasochism. However, Shiva Naipaul's character, Sushila, is quite the opposite. Sushila is the dominant partner in her relationship. In fact, it is interesting to note the similarities and differences between representations of women in the works of the two brothers. For example, Shiva Naipaul actually subverts Fido's concept of sadomasochism as she perceives it in V.S. Naipaul's work in his depiction of the relationship between Egbert Ramsaran and Sushila the prostitute, in comparison to that between Ramsaran and his wife, who may have died because of his abuse. Egbert Ramsaran, in a sudden alteration of character, submits to a reversal of power roles with the advent of Sushila in his household. This is how Shiva Naipaul depicts it:

> Egbert Ramsaran wilted under her provocations. Indeed, provocation is too weak a description of what was taking place between them. It was more like assault. Sushila pursued him ruthlessly and he seemed to have no defences against her. He did try to avoid too close a contact with her; too prolonged an exposure. But Sushila harried him, forcing a recognition of her presence on him. She would not allow him to forget she was there. Her laughter dogged him, penetrating the locked door of his bedroom and invading his dreams. A voluptuous ease was tempting him, clouding his concentration. It was wearing him down as inexorably as water wears down the toughest stone.[15]

However and notably so, despite his attempts to evade her, when Sushila finally leaves him, Egbert Ramsaran goes into a period of intense grieving in which he refuses his body nourishment, suffers what seems to be a stroke and loses motor functions, inclusive of his ability to speak. He has become so dependent on Sushila for life sustenance that he literally ceases to function without her. It is Sushila who holds the sexual power in their relationship, Sushila who enjoys with sadomasochistic pleasure Egbert's sufferings, according to Fido's definition, and it is Sushila, the prostitute, who ultimately defeats Egbert Ramsaran, the man who conceived of himself in terms of *machismo*, which according to studies in Caribbean masculinity are the terms in which many Caribbean men conceive of their selfhood.[16] Thus, the concepts of sexuality to which Fido, Lorde and others subscribed, in which sadomasochism can only occur with the female in the submissive position, is refuted in Shiva Naipaul's representation of the relationship between Egbert Ramsaran and Sushila.

In V.S. Naipaul's *The Mimic Men*, a similar idea of *machismo* is broached but differently resolved. The young politician, Ralph Singh, struggles with his political role and place in society and most of all with his sexuality. His sexual liaisons become a struggle with power and identity. Kavita Nandan writes in "Exile in *The Mimic Men*":

> Notions of impurity and taint in the novel are linked to women. Ralph sees the English women as a source of escape from the insecurity of his past and through his relationships with them he imagines he can align himself with a secure tradition. His sexual relationships and marriage are viewed by him in terms of their failure to provide the security and connectedness that he yearns for. He reflects: 'How right our Aryan ancestors were to create gods. We seek sex, and are left with two private bodies on a stained bed."[17]

Interestingly, Patrick French's representation of V.S. Naipaul's childhood provides food for thought in this context. French reports in *The World Is What It Is* of a time in young Vidia's life when the Naipaul children lived in close proximity to their cousins, the Capildeos, and were socialised together with them. He writes:

> The cousins – boys and girls of all ages – were not encouraged to associate with people who lived nearby, such as the mulatto family who lived by the road and worked on the estate, or the Indian Muslim family who kept a parlour and had a pretty daughter... One day they put on a play of the trial scene from Shakespeare's *The Merchant of Venice* in the drawing room, and Vido was struck by the beauty of his female cousins. In later years, he 'found it very hard to think of making love to an Indian girl. It had an incestuous sense to it.'[18]

In *The Mimic Men*, Ralph Singh develops strong romantic feelings for his female cousin and he feels as though he could never love another woman. He says of his cousin Sally, "She was the most beautiful person in the world... I was in love with her..."[19] Later in the novel he describes their incestuous relationship as the only pure thing in his life. He narrates:

> Sally had become my partner... bound by that special relationship, we had inevitably drawn closer in the changed house. No word was spoken. We simply came together; and nothing again was to equal that sudden understanding, that shared feeling of self violation, which was for me security and purity. I could not conceive of myself with a girl or woman of another community... Here for me was security, understanding, the relationship based on perfect knowledge, in which body of one flesh joined to body of the same flesh, and all external threat was diminished. Later I would have the reputation of a lecher and whoremaster. But in every relationship I would be aware of taint; I would recognize triumph or humiliation.[20]

Thus, the theme of incest is found in both the author's biography and his fiction. The incest seems to play out with more clarity of introspection within the fiction – the art expressing the reality. For Ralph, incest is not a sordid, disgusting concept as it is commonly perceived. Rather, it is the bond with sameness, sameness of ethnicity, sameness of family, sameness of blood. No moral comment seems to adhere to the point. It is given as a simple observation of one of the narrator's childhood truths. Given the prevalence of the theme of incest in postcolonial writing, one may suggest that the overwhelming desire for sameness, which it may represent, is a postcolonial truth obscured by dark areas of shadowy refusal, an ignorance on which V.S. Naipaul's writings have shed light in many ways.

After conceding that no woman could fill Sally's place after their relationship had ended, in order to participate in sex at all, Ralph seeks out prostitutes of any ethnicity but his own, until he meets a white woman who dotes on him, and reminds him of nothing in his Indian heritage. This is the woman Ralph finds suitable as a wife. Many have noted the autobiographical parallels, because in V.S. Naipaul's actual life he married an English woman, and then he had an affair with a Latin American woman for several years, mirroring Ralph Singh's preference for sexual partners not of his ethnicity. In part this seems way for Naipaul's characters to punish themselves for the incestuous feelings of their childhoods. One can view this scenario as a type of self-directed sadomasochism.

This assertion is based on the recollection of Freud's famous essay of 1919 entitled "A Child Is Being Beaten," and subtitled "A Contribution to the Study and the Origin of the Sexual Perversions". Freud begins by saying, "It is surprising how frequently people who come to be analysed for hysteria or an obsessional neurosis confess to having indulged in the fantasy: 'A child is being beaten'".[21] Freud and later theorists influenced by this observation conceive the fantasy as composed of three distinct phases. In the first, the person imagines, in Freud's words, that, "My father is beating a child". He calls the second phase, however, "the most important and most monumentous" as "My father is beating a child" becomes, "I am being beaten by my father".[22] The third is voyeuristic as in it: "A number of children are being beaten (and I am watching)".[23] Freud and others have been particularly concerned with the guilt and fear that motivates the phases which eventually lead to identification with the powerful one. The superego is formed in the process and self-monitoring occurs. In V.S. Naipaul's case, self-monitoring takes the form of "taint" but still performs the tasks which Freud claims are those of introjected authority figures: "their power, their severity, their tendency to watch over and punish".[24]

Ideas like these are not however taken into account by Fido and others, although Fido does analyse the tendency for V.S. Naipaul's protagonists to become sexually tied to "white women". Referring to Naipaul's most sexually explicit novel, *Guerillas*, she writes:

> The Naipaulian formula... is the non-white male with the white female, thereby exploiting another sexually tense area: white women are supposedly more passive and accommodating, i.e. more classically feminine and masochistic, than the black women, whilst non-white men are supposed to be more aggressive sexually, more potent and more masculine."[25]

Echoing Edward Said, she accuses Naipaul of using his "formula" to exploit the postcolonial condition itself in order to reap financial benefits. Reducing his work to pornography she writes:

> In short, Naipaul, as much as any pornographic writer, may be profiting from the side-effects of conventional sexist social norms, rather than trying (as Fallaci and Mailer do) to comprehend the sickness in men and women which give rise to such behaviours as he portrays.[26]

Fido's opinion that V.S. Naipaul's writing lacks a moral compass can, however, be questioned on the basis of a quote she herself uses. In her analysis of Jimmy's behaviour in *Guerillas,* she quotes Naipaul as saying in another one of his works "The Return of Eva Perón" that:

> The act of straight sex, easily bought, is of no great consequence to the macho. His conquest of a woman is complete only when he has buggered her. This is what the woman has it in her power to deny; this is what the brother game is about, the passionless Latin adventure that begins with talk of *amor. La tuve en el culo,* I've had her in the arse: this is how the macho reports victory to his circle, or dismisses a desertion. Contemporary sexologists give a general dispensation to buggery. But the buggering of women is of special significance in Argentina and other Latin American countries… by imposing on her what prostitutes reject, and what he knows to be a kind of sexual black mass, the Argentine macho, in the main of Spanish or Italian ancestry, consciously dishonours his victim. So diminished men, turning to machismo, diminish themselves further, replacing even sex by parody.[27]

Ironically, this seems to be a clear moral proclamation by the writer allegedly without a so-called moral compass. V.S. Naipaul clearly states that, from his perspective, any man performing the violent and non-consensual, sadomasochistic act of buggering is not only dishonouring his victim but diminishing himself. V.S. Naipaul interprets this as a consequence of male emasculation stemming from a previously colonial society in which masculinity is rigidly defined and conformity demanded because men are without any personal power apart from what they can physically inflict on women. Fido interprets the passage as a denunciation on V.S. Naipaul's part of homosexuality. It is possible to see here, however, that V.S. Naipaul is asserting that by resorting to this type of violence, the macho replaces even sex with parody, a trait many of his main characters display, including Ralph Singh.

Champa Rao Mohan asserts in her book that author and protagonist are one and the same in *The Mimic* Men. However, although it may be enticing to draw similarities between the man and his fictional characters, Mohan's assertion must be questioned. She states:

> While in the preceding novels Naipaul had maintained his separateness from his characters through the use of irony, in [*The*] *Mimic* [*Men*], however, Naipaul makes no attempt to maintain his separate identity. At no point in the novel do we witness Singh becoming the target of Naipaul's irony… The absence of such manipulations in [*The*] *Mimic* [*Men*] leads one to conclude that Singh and Naipaul are in fact one. We are too familiar with Naipaul's artistic expertise to consider it a lapse on his part.[28]

Although the idea that some of Naipaul's main characters bear striking similarities to the man and have similar experiences is certainly supportable, the reasoning behind Mohan's assertion is not easy to follow. It is hard for example, to identify how Mohan arrives at the conclusion that "Naipaul makes no attempt to maintain his separate identity". Moreover there is neither more nor less of a distance between writer and text in this novel than there is in any of his other writing.

However, not all critics are of similar views. Kavita Nandan's point, which she makes by reference to Pamela Mordecai's essay on the character Ralph Singh, is apropos. She notes for example that: "All Ralph's relationships with women according[ly]...never spring from any intent of good towards the woman, all are directed by 'a logic that perceives each woman as a way of grasping the elusive self Singh is after'.[29] A parallel may therefore be drawn to the way V.S. Naipaul's relationship with his mistress is described in the authorised biography by French as sadistic, abusive, perverse and reminiscent of Wirth-Nesher's declaration that "every sexual relationship forged in [Naipaul's novels] is of a perverse nature".[30] In fact, one may agree with Nandan that, "[t]he frequent use of the words 'violation' and 'taint' in the novel suggests that Naipaul subscribes to a discourse of purity which is related to his idea that colonialism resulted in the violation of colonies like Trinidad".[31] Furthermore, the supposed "taint" is perceived as much in the man and in the writer and his works.

Moreover, French writes of other examples of incest between Naipaul and another cousin, this time coupled with trauma rather than simply disgust. French writes:

> ...he [had] his first sexual experience, when he was seduced by his cousin Boysie. The encounter was unwanted. As he put it: 'I was myself subjected to some sexual abuse by an older cousin. I was corrupted, I was assaulted. I was about six or seven. It was done in a sly, terrible way and it gave me a hatred, a detestation of this homosexual thing.[32]

This experience, as Naipaul himself says, led to an entrenched homophobia and was perhaps the source of self-loathing and frustration which inspired his descriptions of sordid sexual abuse and acts in novels such as *Guerillas* and *The Mimic Men*. V.S. Naipaul's instinctive reaction to matters of molestation after this incident in his life is explored by French in the biography. He quotes Naipaul as saying:

> It happened to other cousins. I think it is a part of Indian extended family life, which is an abomination in some ways, a can of worms... After an assault one is very ashamed – and then you realize it happens to almost everybody. All children are abused. All girls are molested at some stage. It is almost like a rite of passage.[33]

How one is to analyse such an acceptance of the molestation of children is a far heavier task than can be dealt with in this essay. However, it is safe to say that in keeping with the theme of his particular representation of postcolonial West Indian society, Naipaul has maintained his "searing, unforgiving and controversial" stance. It is interesting to note that "all children are abused", yet, "all *girls* are molested". This seems to imply that so typical is the molestation of the female Indo-Caribbean subject, that even V.S. Naipaul's post-traumatic reflection must incorporate the fact that this horrendous infringement of personal space happens much more to women than to men.

Undoubtedly, there is a thin line between the biographical assertions and the representations that V.S. Naipaul creates. It is a line that many critics have crossed. Indeed, French's depiction of V.S. Naipaul's life, though authorised by the author, comes with French's own interpretation of certain details, as well as questions even as to V.S. Naipaul's own recollection of his past. For example, just as soon as French quotes Naipaul's own, very sure words of his humiliation over being sexually assaulted, French questions Naipaul's version of his own story. He writes, "Vidia never mentioned it to anyone, at the time or later. He insisted he was never a willing participant, although his denial is not wholly convincing given the similarity in age of the two boys".[34] A similar example of a dispute concerning Naipaul's account of events comes from his sister Kamla, recorded by French in the biography. She recounts the period of World War II in 1941 when Trinidad was used as a naval base for American ships. French writes:

> Vido remembered this period as a time of unhappiness and hunger. He started to get asthma, gasping for missing breath, sucking in air, wheezing his way through the long, hot nights. Often, there would be no proper food available, and he would go to school or to bed on an empty stomach. In Kamla's view, this was the result of wartime food shortages rather than neglect, and she thought Vido's claim of being starved was 'a ridiculous memory, it is a damn stupid memory'.[35]

The difference between Kamla's and V.S. Naipaul's recollection of the same time period demonstrates the quintessential truth about the unreliability of memory and enforces scepticism about representation. As Wesley Crichlow notes, "All representation is constructed and hence partial; it will never be virtual, will never fully reproduce 'reality'".[36] Therefore, it must be remembered that V.S. Naipaul's attempts at factually representing the West Indian society from which he came were just that, *representations*. French's portrait of the author is just that, a *portrait*, designed to represent reality; it can never be exactly that which it represents.

In closing on this note, the words of V.S. Naipaul seem appropriate: "Fiction works best in a confined moral and cultural area, where the rules are generally known; and in that confined area it deals best with things – emotions, impulses, moral anxieties – that would be unseizable or incomplete in other literary forms".[37] As this essay has shown, the Naipaul brothers have immeasurably extended what that "confined moral and cultural area" comprises and how it should be viewed. Looking with Caribbean eyes at a diverse range of societies, they bring to life the relationship between social conditions and sexuality, helping us to understand the deep linkages between individual psychology, community sociology and political structures. They help us to conceive of "the rules" that underwrite them. The writings of the Naipaul brothers and the biography of V.S. Naipaul demonstrate how very complicated human consciousness is, and moreover how the trauma of the collective postcolonial consciousness is manifested and represented sexually within West Indian society.

Endnotes

1. Linden Lewis, ed. *The Culture of Gender and Sexuality in the Caribbean* (Gainesville: University Press of Florida, 2003), 9.
2. Jenny Sharpe and Samantha Pinto, "The Sweetest Taboo: Studies of Caribbean Sexualities: A Review Essay", *The University of Chicago Press Journals* 32, no. 1 (2006): 247-274, p. 248, accessed 3 August 2016, doi: 10.1086/505541.
3. Elaine Fido, "Psycho-sexual Aspects of the Woman in V.S. Naipaul's Fiction", *West Indian Literature and its Social Context: Proceedings of the Fourth Annual Conference on West Indian Literature*, ed. Mark McWatt. (Barbados: University of the West Indies Department of English, 1985), 78-94, p. 83.
4. Supriya M. Nair, *Pathologies of Paradise: Caribbean Detours* (Charlottesville, University of Virginia Press, 2013), 163.
5. Nair, 164.
6. See for example, Audre Lorde and Susan Leigh Star, "Interview with Audre Lorde", in *Against Sadomasochism: A Radical Feminist Analysis*, ed. Robin Ruth Linden, Darlene R. Pagano, Diana E. Russell, and Susan Leigh Star (East Palo Alto, CA: Frog in the Well, 1982).
7. Audre Lorde and Susan Leigh Star, "Interview with Audre Lorde", *Against Sadomasochism: A Radical Feminist Analysis*, 68.
8. Fido, 211.
9. See the collection of essays for example in Margaret Ann Fitzpatrick Hanly, ed. *Essential Papers on Masochism* (New York: New York UP, 1995).
10. Elena Barrett, "The Distribution of Power: Sadomasochism and Feminism", accessed 2 October 2015, http://www.academia.edu/619275/The_Distribution_of_Power_Sadomasochism_and_Feminism, 3.
11. Barrett, 3.
12. Fido, 83.
13. Alpana Mishra, "V.S. Naipaul's *Half a Life*: A Critical Study", in *V.S. Naipaul: Critical Essays Vol. III*, ed. Mohit K. Ray (New Delhi: Atlantic, 2005): 181-225, p. 211.
14. Hana Wirth-Nesher, quoted in Champa Rao Mohan, *Postcolonial Situation in the Novels of V.S. Naipaul* (New Delhi: Atlantic, 2004), 118.
15. Shiva Naipaul, *The Chip-Chip Gatherers* (London: Andre Deutsch, 1973), 157.
16. See for example Patricia Anderson "Measuring Masculinity in an Afro-Caribbean Context", *Social and Economic Studies*. 61.1. (2012): 49-93; Janet

Brown and Barry Chevannes, *Why Man Stay So*. Mona: University of the West Indies Press, 1998; Barry Chevannes and Claudia Mitchell-Kernan, "How we were Grown: Cultural Aspects of High-risk Sexual Behaviour in Jamaica", Kingston: ISER, 1992, Linden Lewis, *The Culture of Gender and Sexuality in the Caribbean* (Gainesville: University of Florida Press, 2003) and the collection of essays in Rhoda Reddock, ed. *Interrogating Caribbean Masculinities: Theoretical and Empirical Analyses* (Kingston: UWI Press, 2004),17; Kavita Nandan, "Exile in *The Mimic Men*", in *V.S. Naipaul: An Anthology of Recent Criticism*, ed. Purabai Panwar (Delhi: Pencraft International, 2003), 138.
18. Patrick French, *The World Is What It Is: The Authorised Biography of V.S. Naipaul* (London: Picador, 2008), 35-36.
19. V.S. Naipaul, *The Mimic Men* (London: Andre Deutsch, 1967), 99.
20. V.S. Naipaul, *The Mimic Men*, 168.
21. Sigmund Freud, "A child is being beaten" [1919], in *Sexuality and the Psychology of Love*, ed. Philip Rieff (New York: Touchstone, 1997), 97-122, 97.
22. Freud, 108,
23. Freud, 104,
24. Freud, 108.
25. Fido, 84.
26. Fido, 84.
27. V.S. Naipaul, *The Return of Eva Perón* (London: Penguin, 1981), 150, quoted in Fido, 86.
28. Mohan, 82.
29. Pamela Mordecai, 641, quoted in Nandan, 136.
30. Hana Wirth-Nesher, quoted in Champa Rao Mohan, 118.
31. Nandan, 138.
32. French, 36.
33. French, 36.
34. French, 36.
35. French, 39.
36. Wesley E.A. Crichlow, "History, (Re)Memory, Testimony and Biomythography: Charting a Buller Man's Trinidadian Past", in *Interrogating Caribbean Masculinities: Theoretical and Empirical Analyses*, ed. Rhoda Reddock (Kingston: University of the West Indies Press, 2004), 185-224, p. 187.
37. V.S. Naipaul, *Reading & Writing: A Personal Account* (New York: New York Review of Books, 2000), 49-50.

20: FINDING SAFE SPACES

V.S. NAIPAUL AND THE REWRITING OF HISTORY: JUXTAPOSING PAST, PRESENT AND FUTURE IN *A WAY IN THE WORLD*

VARISTHA PERSAD

> The one duty we owe to history is to rewrite it.
> — Oscar Wilde

V.S. Naipaul's iconoclastic narrative, *A Way in the World*, like other Caribbean aesthetic works of its type,[1] introduces new ways of interrogating and understanding the conditions in which the postmodern Caribbean subject exercises multiple identities in a globalised world. The character Manuel Sorzano for example is typical in this regard. About him the narrator says:

> My first quick assessment... was that he was an out-and-out Venezuelan, a coastal mestizo, a product of a racial mixture that had started with the Spanish settlement... his curly hair was plaited and tied at the back into a tight little pigtail about an inch long. It gave him a piratical, eighteenth-century appearance.... He was unusual. He could be one thing or the other: it depended on what you thought he was.

A shift away from the traditional ways of reading such narratives is therefore urgently required.[2] Searching for a theoretical stance that encompasses both therapeutic and progressive spatial constructions, this essay seeks to demonstrate that Naipaul's "novel" pushes at the limits and boundaries of Caribbean thought and literary forms; that it fill gaps in traditional concepts of Caribbean history by storying the globalised Caribbean subject into being via the imagination. In so doing, Naipaul demonstrates that the Caribbean has always been a postmodern space due to the fragmentary nature of historical narratives and the insecurities that are often linked to colonial prejudices. Spatial reconstructions in this novel allow the juxtaposition of many different sites of resistance of varying influence in Caribbean history.

One well-known theoretician of this spatial turn is Michel Foucault. His concept of "heterotopia" is particularly useful since it allows for a reading of this novel that yields a complex understanding of the postmodern Caribbean subject in a globalised world. Robert J. Topinka in *Foucault, Borges, Heterotopia: Producing Knowledge in Other Spaces* states:

> By juxtaposing and combining many spaces in one site, heterotopias problematise received knowledge by destabilising the ground on which knowledge is built. Yet heterotopias always remain connected to the dominant order; thus as heterotopias clash with dominant orders, they simultaneously produce new ways of knowing.[3]

V.S. Naipaul, if only instinctively, seems to understand and use this concept to produce alternate ways of understanding the postmodern Caribbean and the postmodern Caribbean subject. The heterotopia of *A Way in the World* problematises history and delivers therapeutic postmodern narratives which offer new insights into existing faulty historical constructs. Each chapter is involved in this tripartite approach: from Prelude: An Inheritance to History: A Smell of Fish Glue through New Clothes: An Unwritten Story and Passenger: A Figure from the Thirties and finally in On the Run.

One may be tempted to think that all Caribbean narratives include this problematising function in dealing with history and reconstructing "identity". As Linda Hutcheon reminds us in *A Poetics of Postmodernism*:

> What the postmodern writing of both history and literature has taught us is that both history and fiction are discourses, that both constitute systems of signification by which we make sense of the past ('exertions of the shaping, ordering imagination'). In other words, the meaning and shape are not *in the events* but *in the systems* which make those past 'events' into present historical 'facts.'[4]

Hutcheon insists that "this is not a 'dishonest refuge from truth' but an acknowledgement of the meaning-making function of human constructs".[5] This has always been seen as an intrinsic task of the literary work in the Caribbean, as Naipaul has long insisted in his well-known contention in *The Middle Passage* that the region needs novelists to help the people to understand who they are. My emphasis in this essay on postmodernism is not in any way an attack on postcolonial studies or other theoretical constructs; it is instead intended to offer a further necessary vantage point for current and future theoretical studies.

Indeed, Caribbean intellectual, Antonio Benitez-Rojo, in his landmark theoretical study *The Repeating Island: The Caribbean and the Postmodern Perspective,* persuasively argues for viewing the Caribbean in relation to the postmodern. Moreover, he shows that when this is done, Caribbean literature usefully complicates inherited "notions of belonging" and as a result carries the future of Caribbean discourse further than other theoretical models. He adds:

> One has to conclude that, with regard to Caribbean culture, the postmodern perspective can also offer interesting angles, since it assumes the impossibility of finding authentic origins and predicable outcomes; that is, it discards the likelihood that the system's components have ever come together or will come together in the foreseeable future inside some kind of revelatory synthesis.[6]

Postmodernism thus challenges existing methods of knowledge production to point out that there are no fixed facts in history for providing a "totalising" narrative.

In the postmodern Caribbean narrative moreover, the fusion of the past, present and future and the incorporation of the reader, author and narrator into the text destabilises traditional narrative structures. Naipaul ensures, moreover, that "identity" in *A Way in the World* is at every juncture analysed as "identities". This moves away from Eurocentric tendencies to privilege one voice over another. Naipaul's novel can thus become the Caribbean subject's guide to recreating notions of identity for belonging anywhere in the globalising world. For instance, Phyllis, a character in his novel can be seen as symbolic of the postmodern human subject, capable of belonging anywhere and everywhere. Michael Peter Smith in *Postmodernism, Urban Ethnography, and the New Social Space of Ethnic Identity* makes an apposite point:

> ...postmodern social analysis problematizes knowledge and meaning. Ironically, despite the fact that the postmodern intellectual current eschews totalizing grand narratives, postmodernism as method offers a totalizing critique of realist and materialist theories of representation. It problematized both the text and context. Epistemologically, at the level of textual representation it questions not only what is *known*, the 'out there' of historical reality, but also the *knower* or *story-teller and* the *reader* or *receiver* of knowledge. Ontologically, at the level of contextual interpretation, it problematizes the *subject* as a bounded social actor inexorably situated in a context that is itself historically contingent, and socially constructed. This immensely complicates the question of human agency.[7]

Smith adds that this method of narrative construction is similar to what Stephen Tyler labels "cooperative story making." Smith explains:

> ... 'cooperative story making' [refers to]... a story produced by mutual dialogue rather than imposed by an authorial script. This approach is intended to produce a 'cooperative evolved text'... Because social reality is historically constituted, because there are no master narratives except those constituted by us, the central task of postmodern ethnography becomes the re-examination of the subject's past, by engagement in listening and conversation in order to explore new meanings and intentions. These meanings are not viewed as pre-given 'data' to be uncovered by the researcher; rather, they are socially constituted and hence contestable representations of history produced by intersubjective dialogue. In this mode of interrogation, one purpose of dialogue is to enable the subject to become an active producer of meaning rather than an object of the projected meanings of the researcher.[8]

Such "cooperative dialogue" and "cooperative story making" can be seen to comprise the narrative strategies of Naipaul's *A Way in the World*, and can also be seen in some of his previous works. They have been part of his evolution into maturity as a writer. The reader becomes enveloped in the process of story-making in his/her engagement with what the author writes. But when the novel ends on the last page, the story continues for the reader and does not end with that last word the author pens. In this way, the text transcends its physical restrictions to come into the real world. The meaning of the text is best grasped, therefore, when the reader appreciates this privileged position that the postmodern author creates for him/her.

To start with, Naipaul presents a text that shifts the usual boundaries of genre. The form of *A Way in the World* may be identified as belonging to many categories of fiction and non-fiction: it has autobiographical elements; makes use of historical facts and "fictionalises" these facts; it has multiple narrators and a shifting, non-linear narrative. This creates for the reader an experience that challenges boundaries and limits in understanding the dynamism of the Caribbean postmodern subject's identity.

Postmodern theorists such as Arjun Appadurai have put forward ideas to explain the nature of the post 9/11 world; Jean Baudrillard has expounded on the impact of technological innovations on the progressive relinquishing of concepts of reality; and David Harvey has made connections between late capitalism, human geography and postmodern discourse, but as this discussion attempts to show, their work only goes so far in helping us to understand and theorise the Caribbean postmodern subject in relation to space. V.S. Naipaul's *A Way in the World* helps us to overcome this problem because its unique narrative structure reflects the complexity of the postmodern Caribbean subject. Its structure shakes the foundations of the art of novel writing.

The 1960s are seen as the main temporal point from which postmodern fiction emerged to bring into being innovative methodologies to challenge those practised by "modernist" writers. However, in the Caribbean this development came much later. A look at the social and economic grounds of this emergence in Europe and North America, in comparison to the Caribbean, goes some way to explain the belated adoption of postmodernism as a critical tool in the Caribbean and why postmodernist fiction has until very recently been a non-Caribbean artefact. In locating the postmodern in Britain and Ireland, Paul Crosthwaithe explains:

> Given the challenges to austerity, authority, and convention that marked Britain and Ireland in the 1960s – the explosion of mass consumerism, the rise of youth culture, the counterculture and anti-Vietnam War movements, the Irish-Civil rights struggle, the emergence of second wave feminism and the "sexual revolution" – it was inevitable that as

the decade unfolded the restored pre-eminence of realistic fiction would come to appear increasingly reactionary and anachronistic.[9]

By contrast, the 1960s, and the immediate decades after in the Caribbean, was a period of nationalist self-definition when the realist, modernist voice in Caribbean fiction remained strong. Thus for a Caribbean writer like Naipaul, writing at the turn of the twenty-first century, the conventional is to be found in the realist work of other Caribbean writers such as C.L.R. James, who is fictionalised as Lebrun in the novel. Naipaul appears to read him as someone who sought to reproduce Eurocentric analyses and interpretive techniques that make his work non-inclusive of the widest range of Caribbean critical thought. The Caribbean, specifically Naipaul's country of birth, Trinidad and Tobago, saw its own revolutionary movements, such as the Black Power movement in the circa 1970 period. It has experienced numerous problems of equality and equity in the post-Independence period; it witnessed Muslim insurgency in 1990 and the creation of groups and pockets of extremists as a result of reactionary politics and inequalities prevalent in the later post-independence period. Tracing these events through history becomes Naipaul's postmodern project. As Crosthwaithe's account suggests, this has taken a different form from the European postmodern project:

> A model for a form of fiction that might adequately channel the disruptive energies of the period came from France in the form of *nouveau roman* or "new novel." Associated with the likes of Michel Butor, Nathalie Sarraute, Claude Simon and, most notably, Alain Robbe Grillet, the *nouveau roman* replaced the novel's traditional concern with character, plot and theme in favour of a systematic working through of the various permutations of a set of textual units, a strategy that tended to emphasise what Robbe-Grillet called "the movement of the writing itself".[10]

Naipaul's novel *A Way in the World* creates a similar movement away from plot and theme and establishes a flow or movement of narrative that is as chaotic and diverse as the historical accounts being narrated. But it has no obvious previous fictive model upon which it is founded. Its structural "fluidity" reveals the "fluidity" that permeates the identity of the subject. The narrative spans geographies and historical periods, including multiple vantage points and characters, both fictional and "real", who do not necessarily interact or intertwine in each other's "constructed lives". They include Sir Walter Raleigh, Francisco Miranda, Blair and other narrators, at least one of whom resembles Naipaul himself. They are the main protagonists in the novel, but they are separated by centuries, language and geography. The textual units in which their stories are told may seem as if they were placed at random – or the reader may experience them as being carefully juxtaposed to create a coherent construction. As with the narrator's experience of Manuel Sorzano, it depends on how one looks. Either way, this can give rise to utter confusion if the novel is not interpreted through postmodern critical and theoretical understandings. A postmodern reading of this text allow us to understand how these narratives, juxtaposed to each other, define the "postmodern self" and the dis/advantages of the postmodern Caribbean subject.

Naipaul creates a space in which the juxtaposition of all these elements becomes possible. As Michel Foucault reminds us in "Of Other Spaces: Utopias and Heterotopias", this is a necessity because:

> The space in which we live, which draws us out of ourselves, in which the erosion of our lives, our time and our history occurs, the space that claws and gnaws at us, is also, in itself, a heterogeneous space. In other words, we do not live in a kind of void, inside of which we could place individuals and things... We live inside a set of relations that delineates sites which are irreducible to one another and absolutely not superimposable on one another.[11]

Naipaul's narrative constructions allow for a stronger postmodern Caribbean subject capable of juxtaposing several realities in themselves and in the world. Combining the facts and fiction of a traumatic history allows us to move forward in a globalising world. In this way, we fill in the gaps in history to make sense of the forgotten and confront the constructed nature of facts that are presented as self-evident.

Apart from juxtaposing past, present and future narratives of Caribbean history, Naipaul also incorporates the reader, author and narrator in the text. Here he points to the possibilities of a healthy, questioning scepticism for the postmodern Caribbean subject. For instance, Naipaul intrudes into the narrative to comment on the writing and even to explain why he does so. In explaining what happens when he is reading Raleigh's book, for example, he writes:

> You feel you've missed something, so you go back. You've missed nothing. It's just something's gone wrong with the writing. This happens many times. So even if you're a careful reader you lose the drift of the narrative. It's not easy, noticing first of all that the writing has changed and then finding exactly where. But those are precisely the places you have to identify. Because these are the places where the writer decides to add things or to hide things.[12]

Naipaul directly addresses the reader here, and in many other places in the text; this manner of intruding into the narrative is one aspect of the metafictional nature of this novel. The reader who is becoming engrossed in the fictional narrative is quickly be brought back to recognise the complex and constructed nature of reality.

Within the narrative, given the location of characters at different points of historical time, Naipaul points not only to the Caribbean intellectual's obsession with the losses of history but offers a way to understand and envision a way forward for the Caribbean subject. The history of the Caribbean has long been acknowledged as fraught with ambiguities; here Naipaul constructs a postmodern narrative that denounces the Caribbean intellectual's obsession with the ills of Eurocentric writings about our history. He designs his narratives around characters who are normally sidelined, overlooked or mentioned too rarely in the litany of so-called historical facts for us to really appreciate their influence on our past. This leads Naipaul to find characters for his novel from documents in the "untouched shelves" of libraries in which they were otherwise doomed to oblivion as dust, with time eating away at the material pages, blurring and making holes in the text. The lives of such characters are presented in all their own obscurities.

The "storying" of experience that Naipaul points to in *A Way in the World* can be summed up in Anderson's statement regarding Carmel Flaskas's (1997) evocations of the "postmodern self" in *Limits and Possibilities of the Postmodern Narrative Self*:

> [Postmodernism] invites a shift from a modernist logical understanding (verifiable reality) of self to a narrative social understanding (constructed reality) of self... the self becomes a narrated self...[13]

This sense of a "narrated self" can be seen to offer an advantage to the postmodern Caribbean subject; specifically, it provides him/her with the ability to discard faulty experience and to therapeutically recreate some sense of stability. The constructions that he/she employs become part and parcel of understanding the various aspects of the Caribbean person.

The modernist conception of the "self" does not offer this kind of fluid complexity. Flaskas states:

> These ideas will be unfolded in the similar pattern of their usual presentation by saying first what the self is not. The self which emerged within modernist discourse became an essential self, an interior self, capable of being thought about as a separate form. If our ideas become limited to this modernist conception which sees self as a thing to be discovered, then it can very easily become a thing which we can either have too much of or too little of.[14]

Naipaul, in *A Way in the World*, echoes the expression of alternative postmodern ideologies in this excerpt:

> The idea of a recent wiped-out past was too big for a child in an elementary school to grasp. Later it became difficult in another way. As soon as you tried to enter that idea, it ramified. And it ramified more and more as your understanding grew: different people living for centuries where we now trod, with our own overwhelming concerns: different people, with their own calendar and reverences and ideas of human association, different houses or huts, different roads or paths, different crops and

fields and vegetation (and seasons), different views, speeds, reasons for journeys, different ideas of the ages of man, different ideas of the enemy and fellowship and sanctity and what men owed themselves. In this way leaving aside the primary notion of cruelty, the idea of a wiped-out, complete past below one's feet quickly became almost metaphysical. The world appeared to lose some its substance; reality became fluid. It was more natural to let go, to let the mind spring back to an everyday, ground-level vision that took in only what could be seen.[15]

The implication here is that it is never wise to live in the space of an assumed "natural" world, since everything that we suppose to be natural may not necessarily be so. Flaskas makes a point that is *apropos* here:

>...[The] modernist picture of the self as autonomous, fixed, and 'owned' by the individual [which] becomes the oppositional pole to the postmodernist framings of self which have begun to be articulated within systematic therapy. Rather than the self being autonomous, the self becomes a relational self; rather than the self being fixed, the self is a self-in-action, always fluid, always being created and re-created in relationship with other; rather than existing as the internal property of the individual, the self becomes a narrative self "storied" and constructed in language with others... Therapeutic change can align itself with the continual narrative process of the changing meanings we give to our lives and to ourselves in relation to others.[16]

Focusing on spatial constructions and discarding the dominance of the temporal is foregrounded in Naipaul's narrative. What David Harvey tells us in *The Condition of Postmodernity* may help us to make sense of the apparently disjointed structure of Naipaul's fragmented novel:

>I begin with what appears to be the most startling fact about postmodernism: its total acceptance of the ephemerality, fragmentation, discontinuity, and the chaotic that formed one half of Baudelaire's conception of modernity. But postmodernism responds to the fact of that in a very particular way. It does not try to transcend it, counteract it, or even to define the 'eternal and immutable' elements that might lie within it. Postmodernism swims, even wallows, in the fragmentary and the chaotic currents of change as if that is all there is.[17]

Naipaul's "fragmentary and chaotic currents" all suggest a positive, complex, envisioning of the Caribbean self. The "textual units" or "fragments" of narrative become keys to grasping a relational sense of self.

In this novel, the movements across time and geography move even to spaces where the concept of time becomes non-existent in creating heterotopias that challenge Eurocentric visions of assimilating a fixed and unitary identity in the real world. Naipaul deals with such an absolute loss of the temporal in the chapter, "New Clothes: An Unwritten Story", where the narrator is being led through the forest by Lucas and Mateo:

>They stop for a while to rest and eat and drink a little. Lucas and Mateo use their machetes to trim a place for the narrator to sit. As they walk

on again, the narrator surrenders to the idea of the antiquity of the forest and this trail. He begins to wonder about the idea of time that men have in this setting. When men know their world well; when they know every tree and flower; all the foods and poisons; all the animals; when they have perfected all their tools; when everything exists in balance, and there is nothing from the outside to compare, what idea can men have of the passing of time? It is the things we pass that give us an idea of speed. When there is nothing to compare, men must exist only in their light and the light of the people they know – the narrator things of the dim lights in the blackness of the mission clearing, thinks of the play of flashlight and the others' as they pick their way back to their cabins. Beyond that, backwards and forwards, there must be nothing.[18]

Naipaul conflates the past, present and future in this short excerpt and creates a manual for generations of Caribbean subjects to use as their guide to living in the globalised world. It points also to the fact that generations will find it difficult to find one source or origin in which they can construct an "identity" or "identities" to belong to, or exercise successfully, if temporal linearity and hierarchy remain important. The Caribbean has the advantage of being in a position to access a multiplicity of narratives, where the fluid construction of one's identity becomes a point of reference and difference for further postmodern theorising, both globally and amongst other civilisations. The history of man and civilisation is, as shown in this novel, not a linear narrative but one involving a juxtaposition of events in time and space that are the outcome of heterogenous motivations both public and private, and the play of chance.

Endnotes

1. In my thesis I look at Nalo Hopkinson's and Wilson Harris's novels as belonging to this same category.
2. See on this J. Vijay Maharaj, "A Caribbean *Katha*: Re-visioning the 'IndoCaribbean' 'Crisis of Being and Belonging' through the Literary Imagination", (doctorate dissertation, University of the West Indies, St Augustine, 2008).
3. Robert J. Topinka, "Foucault, Borges, Heterotopia: Producing Knowledge in Other Spaces", *Foucault Studies* 9 (2010): 54-70, p. 54.
4. Linda Hutcheon, *A Poetics of Postmodernism: History, Theory, Fiction* (London: Routledge, 1988), 89.
5. Hutcheon, 89.
6. Antonio Benitez-Rojo, *The Repeating Island: The Caribbean and the Postmodern Perspective*, 2nd ed. (London: Duke University Press, 1996), 295.
7. Michael Peter Smith, "Postmodernism, Urban Ethnography, and the New Social Space of Ethnic Identity", in *Theory and Society* 21, no. 4 (1992): 493-531, p. 498.

8. Smith, 507.
9. Paul Crosthwaite, "Postmodern Fiction", in *The Encyclopedia of Twentieth-Century Fiction, Volume II*, ed. Brian W. Shaffer et al. (Malden: Wiley-Blackwell, 2011), 309.
10. Crosthwaite, 309.
11. Michel Foucault, "Of Other Spaces: Utopias and Heterotopias", *Architecture, Mouvement, Continuité* 5 (1984): 46-49, trans. Jay Miskowiec in *Diacritics* 16, no. 1 (1986): 22-27.
12. V.S. Naipaul, *A Way in the World,* 165
13. Harlene Anderson, Conversation, Language, and Possibilities: A Postmodern Approach to Therapy (New York: Basic Books, 1997), 212, quoted by Carmel Flaskas, "Limits and Possibilities of the Postmodern Narrative Self", *Australian and New Zealand Journal of Family Therapy* 20 (1999): 20-27, 2, doi: 10.1111/j.0814-723X.1999.00090.x.
14. Flaskas, 3.
15. V.S. Naipaul, *A Way in the World* (New York: Vintage, 1995), 214-215.
16. Flaskas, 3-4.
17. David Harvey, *The Condition of Postmodernity* (Malden: Blackwell Publishers, 1990), 44.
18. Naipaul, 56-7.

21: FROM TRAMP TO TRAVELLER: MIRRORS OF IMMIGRANT EXPERIENCES IN *IN A FREE STATE*[1]

NIVEDITA MISRA

There is a scene in "One Out of Many" from *In A Free State* where Santosh, a character from the foothills of Himalaya, looks at himself in the mirror and realises that he is an individual. He takes the step of breaking away from his employer to seek his own identity in the big city of Washington DC. What does the mirror stand for in the scene? Is the mirror the site of a radical disturbance and breach in his life, the place where he sees for the first time the colonial subservience, economic servility and caste demarcations that he must transcend to achieve individuality? Or is the mirror the medium to bridge the gaps between tradition and modernity, community and individuality, faith and rationality? Ironically, Lewis Carroll uses the mirror in *Through the Looking Glass* to invert the everyday world and reflect on reality. This essay compares "One Out of Many" to Lewis Carroll's *Through the Looking Glass* in order to read it as one part of Naipaul's practice of mirroring of immigrant experiences by presenting various personas from and in different parts of the world. He thereby reveals that his characters' immigrant experiences differ in specifics, but all of them experience alienation from their environment and their communities. The same is reflected in the narrator's experiences in the Prologue and the Epilogue of *In a Free State*, with the tramp and the traveller both being eternally alienated from their fellow travellers.

V.S. Naipaul's early novels were all based in the Caribbean. He then expanded his oeuvre to write travel narratives about Trinidad and India. *In a Free State* marks a break and a return to Naipaul's earlier fictional form. He returns to fiction with a short story format, akin to *Miguel Street*, except that the stories are no longer bound by a time or a place or a region. The three narratives about immigrant experiences – an Indian in America, a Caribbean in England, and two English people in Africa – are framed by the narrator's own travels across the Mediterranean, from Piraeus to Alexandria, and by a trip to the pyramids in Egypt. So, *In a Free State* also marks a break from the form of the novel because Naipaul insists on bringing together separate pieces as a whole. Naipaul recounts that, in 1971, Diana Athill wanted to publish the African novella "In a Free State" on its own, leaving out the other pieces because it was a complete story in itself.[2] However, Naipaul insisted that there was to be no publication unless all the pieces were published simultaneously as a sequence because he felt that the other pieces defined the novella.

There is an extended passage in *The Enigma of Arrival* about "In a Free State", which that narrator says he was writing at the time of his arrival in Wiltshire.[3] In the passage, the narrator writes that he was reworking the theme of a traveller disembarking and entering a new space and returning to the shore only to find that the ship had already left. He has nowhere to go. Naipaul attempts to capture such colonial anxieties across different nation states, through the different geographical settings of the stories and by providing different lineages and legacies to his characters across the stories of *In a Free State*.

This anxiety, and how to make literary material of it has its roots in Naipaul's own arrival in Britain in the early 1950s. Peter Kalliney, for example, argues for the crucial role that BBC *Caribbean Voices* programme and the Bloomsbury group played in providing Naipaul, Selvon, Brathwaite, and Lamming with a literary atmosphere and access to a reading, writing and publishing audience. This literary exchange allowed "modernist tropes of urban alienation [to be] ... readily adapted to representations of migrants suffering racism, deracination, and poverty."[4] Though such a consideration tends to read all West Indian literature of the time as immigrant literature, it also allows Naipaul's personal anxieties as an immigrant in England to be read into his writing. The sense of dislocation that Naipaul must have felt growing up in a Hindu community in the West Indies would thus have doubled in England.

Each of the five pieces of *In a Free State* explores the human psyche and how migration makes unnatural demands on the person. The themes pertain to being and becoming: who is free or not, and whether a nation state can be a free state or not. Equally, the text explores the theme of colonialism and immigration in England at the end of the Second World War. Gillian Dooley argues that the text shows "Naipaul's quest for the correct form", pointing out that the "themes in this novel include the image of the journey, the many facets of the idea of freedom, and the accommodat[ion] of a variety of subject positions."[5] Timothy Weiss argues that while in the early Naipaul novels, journeys or voyages "signify openness, discovery, growth, potentialities in general, ... *In a Free State* recounts journeys of loss, waste, absurdity, humiliation, brutality."[6] Naipaul recognises that immigration, whether voluntary or involuntary, involves a renegotiation of one's ties to family, race, class and/or nation such as in the case of Santosh and his "new" relationships with Priya and the "hubshi" woman. It also involves renegotiating the relations that he had in the "home" country, just like the narrator with his brother in the second tale. However, the English expatriates in the third tale do not renegotiate within their new environment and this proves tragic. Reading the five pieces together, it seems as though Naipaul is presenting various facets of the immigrant experience in a hall of mirrors in which each image is individual and complete yet displaces all previous images, constantly defining and redefining the self.

This essay uses the image of a mirror, which is first used in "One Out of Many", to read the sequence of narratives as variations upon the theme of immigrant experience. The gap between an object and its image or enantiomorph is similar to the gap between the narrator and his writing. One cannot exist without the other and the writing/mirror hides/shows as much as it absorbs/reflects. One of the classic images of the use of mirror in English literature is Lewis Carroll's *Through the Looking Glass* which details the journey of Alice through an inverted nonsensical world. *Through the Looking Glass* has been read as children's literature and as nonsense literature. The popularity of the nursery rhymes and characters playing chess, hide and seek and cards ensure the recall value of the text. But *Through the Looking Glass* can also be read as a challenge to the novel of social manners with its well-ordered plots and neat endings with non-conforming elements being shipped away or transformed and brought within acceptable social norms, thus ensuring everybody "living happily ever after". Supplanting the child with an immigrant, Naipaul is able to make sense of the immigrant's expectations from a parent and a host country by the device of the mirror and similarly challenging the idea of the well-ordered plot. The purpose of this comparison is not meant to imply, however, that Naipaul uses *Through the Looking Glass* deliberately as a model for his own writing but to examine the variations in the familiar trope in both texts. I use references from Carroll's text as a way of commenting on thematic trajectories in the five sections of *In a Free State*. The purpose of this reading lies in recognising subtle patterns of connection that may enable new meanings to be found in Naipaul's text. (It also enables us to read Lewis Carroll's text as a text about the unsettling nature of the experience of displacement.) By articulating a response to their new environment, Naipaul's protagonists renegotiate and "theorise" about the place that they are from, creating a critical distance between their previous selves and their present state, destabilising the idea of any kind of unified subjectivity both at the point of departure and arrival. My interest is in seeing how Naipaul uses the trope of the mirror to reflect an immigrant's anxieties about "home" which, paradoxically, has either been left behind or is deferred to the future but never realised in the present.

"*So I wasn't dreaming, after all, unless – unless we're all part of the same dream*".[7]

In the above lines, Alice, after crossing over to the other side of the mirror, is ruminating about where she has arrived. *In a Free State* begins with a Prologue by the narrator who is travelling on a ship from Piraeus to Alexandria. The location of the narrative's beginning is important because these are international waters, away from strict societal strictures, and the focus is on a tramp who defies these very structures by his nonconformity. The tramp is not particularly English, but as Naipaul writes him he could be an English romantic, wanderer or writer. While the tramp travels cabin class, like the narrator, he is a misfit in society because he wears motley unwashed dress and eats and behaves in a manner that agitates the others, ranging from Lebanese business travellers to American students. Like one of the eccentric characters in Carroll's tale, the tramp idiosyncratically dines alone and tears up his magazine in a fit of anger to gain attention and then runs away. He is completely at odds with himself and others: "He looked for company but needed solitude; he looked for attention, and at the same time wanted not to be noticed."[8] The Lebanese sellers of wares indulge in a cat and mouse game and bully the tramp into fleeing the dining room and hiding in the toilets, but the tramp triumphs by blocking the Lebanese out of their cabin.

The tramp proclaims, "I think of myself as a citizen of the world".[9] The declaration is significant because a world undivided by barriers of class, race and nations does not exist. It is equally ironic that the tramp should feel threatened by perpetrators of these barriers. Hence, the "citizen of the world", rather than being a free individual, is seen by others as a threat to their definitions of freedom by such noncompliance. He betrays an inability to accommodate or protect. The narrator never makes this clear, but the theme of freedom continues in the next narrative with the social misfit becoming transformed into a colonial misfit.

Humpty-Dumpty: "When I use a word, it means just what I choose it to mean – neither more nor less"[10]

In "One Out of Many", Santosh is a lower class Indian immigrant who achieves his American dream but feels hollow in his success. The narrator speaks of "both here and in India".[11] Santosh has a previous history of migration from the hills to Bombay, leaving his wife and children in search of employment and money. In Bombay, he lives a fairly contented life sharing camaraderie within his own community of footpath dwellers. His physical dislocation from the village to the city is a back-story when we first meet him working for a bureaucrat in Bombay. It is the second more comic and dramatic transition, however, that sets the story in action.

His boss is transferred to Washington DC and Santosh accompanies him. The plane journey is a grand comedy of errors with Santosh travelling with his bundle of clothes and spitting betel juice all over the aeroplane aisle and toilet. The claustrophobic journey in the plane is symptomatic of his life ahead in a cupboard-like space he occupies in his boss's apartment. His claustrophobic world collapses when he struggles through the apartment and the even more claustrophobic elevator to reach the world outside where he sees *hubshi*,[12] "real" Americans and familiar dancers with men wearing saffron robes and girls in saris chanting Sanskrit words in praise of Lord Krishna.[13] Yet still, he feels he has nowhere to go because there is no community or friends awaiting him. He realises that people are in communities while he is alone. Santosh finds America invigorating only because its race inequalities do not touch him. However, the feelings of loneliness become more and more exaggerated. He runs away from the employer, starts life afresh as a cook and begins to earn "real money". However, his fear of the unknown and of the past catching up with him makes him unstable and neurotic. In a world where he is free to move around, he wilfully locks himself in his room. He is unable to talk with his employer on equal terms and soon realises that he has to marry the *hubshi* to gain his green card and legitimately live in America.

The desire to see the world and *not to return* remains a very important aspect of immigration. For the immigrant, a return is mired in loss, regret and failure and is never an option. Naipaul obliquely comments on the many layers to Santosh's American dream. In the first place, Santosh never really had the dream, but is sucked into it unconsciously. The narrator allows the transition to be so smooth that the reader scarcely realises when Santosh begins to be possessed by the dream. However, the realisation that Santosh has about the emotional consequences of his success ("All that my freedom has brought me is the knowledge that I have a face and have a body, that I must feed this body and clothe this body for a certain number of years. Then it will be over"[14] and his loneliness ("In this city I was alone and it didn't matter what I did"[15] exposes the hollowness of the dream. Santosh seeks the company of fellow men such as Priya, but fails to keep up the pretence of equality that is part of the myths of the American dream. He does get his way by engineering a clever pay hike, but money and success do not earn him camaraderie and friendship.

Santosh is slowly sucked into a time capsule where events then seem to move so fast that the reader is made to lose track of whether Santosh's success came in one year or a couple or ten or twenty years. His unnamed employer, the black woman and Priya all seem to understand him better than himself. His confessions to them, exposing his ineptitude at victory in his new world, come too late. What endears Santosh to readers is that he is not a trickster or a social climber. His aspirations are clothed in his inability to negotiate. What stands out is his looking into the mirror and finding an image of himself that he does not recognise but desires so deeply that he sets out to acquire it. The mirror becomes a symbol of Santosh's aspirations for money, status and stability in life. Inversely, it makes him aware of his own vulnerability and inability to survive by himself. The motif of seeing – the unnamed employer sees efficiency, Priya sees potential, and the *hubshi* woman finds him attractive – is offset by what Santosh feels – failure. Yet, paradoxically, Santosh is narrating his own story of "accomplishments". Gaining a green card is an ambitious undertaking for the uneducated, unassuming Santosh. Just as Humpty-Dumpty argues in the quotation above from *Through the Looking Glass*: the word means only what he wants it to mean, neither more nor less. The narrator desires that people read his life for what he wishes it to mean, neither more nor less.

The loss of control not only over words but their meaning is compounded in the next story. While Santosh sees himself and then is unable to un-see himself, the narrator of the next story is unable to recognise the image he sees in his mirror. The narrator plays upon 'real' and 'un-real' as benchmarks of living, unable to figure out if he is dreaming or not. Similarly, Humpty-Dumpty's loss of control over his fate, Naipaul presents a narrator who loses control over his words and his fate.

Jabberwocky: "It seems very pretty but it's rather hard to understand"[16]

In "Tell Me Who to Kill", the unnamed narrator conveys his sense of the unreality of living on the islands compared to the realities of living in London. His sense of the un-real nature of living on the island is highlighted for him by the belief that he never had a dream or an ambition to reach somewhere on the island. His home was isolated from the rest of their community, and in his memory, there are no specifics of place or time attached to it. The predominant theme in the early part of his narrative is the narrator's feeling that he had "no life" whereas he thinks he has thrown away his life in England where life is potentially real.[17] The mirror effect is more dominant here than in the other narratives. The contrasts between what he sees in those two places is conveyed through an almost metaphysical awareness of things. His life in London is by no means easier than on the island. In both places, he toils hard for his money while his brother wastes it, presumably on the failed efforts to educate himself: "The ambition [for his own and his brother's success] is like shame, and the shame is like a secret, and it is always hurting".[18] This is similar to Santosh and his fear of his success. Whereas the narrator feels that if he had been given the opportunity through a proper education he would have succeeded in the "real" world, the younger brother fails by not trying.

The hollowness of the narrator's life, caused by his investment in his brother's future, burns him out. Unlike Santosh, the narrator does not respond to his surroundings. He lives in his own world, even while working at the cigarette factory. When he later opens a food stall in England, his hard-earned money fritters away, leaving him embittered, with no hope of escape: "When you find out who your enemy is, you must kill him before he kill you".[19] He suspects that the whites are his enemies, but cannot see *how*, because it is the same culture that seems to offer him the chance to realise his ambitions. The beginning and climax of the story condenses this ambivalence: his brother whom he loves more than anyone is getting married to a white woman, a lasting betrayal.

His story is a twice-displaced narrative about living in the Caribbean, where he feels that "real" life is elsewhere, either left behind at the point of the original departure from India, or ahead of him at the point of arrival in England. Life on the island carries a feeling of transition, a place of limbo before reaching a final destination. Perhaps one can see the roots of this narrative in an account Naipaul gives in *Reading and Writing*, "For five months I was given shelter in a dark Paddington basement by an older cousin, a respecter of my ambition, himself very poor, studying law and working in a cigarette factory."[20] It is tempting to see his cousin in the consciousness of the unnamed narrator, the elder brother, on whom the younger lives almost parasitically before he marries a white woman.

Naipaul claims that he was unwilling to review his own immigrant status: "Hysteria has been my reaction and a brutality dictated by a new awareness of myself as a whole human being and a determination, touched with fear, to remain what I was".[21] His initial anxiety to become a writer soon transformed itself into hysteria at losing the ground beneath his feet, literally. Hysteria begins to affect him only after success and the achievement of his initial goals of leaving Trinidad at eighteen and becoming a writer. Naipaul, at this time of his career, had been contemplating a move to America or Canada but eventually settled in Wiltshire in England for the next ten years.

The narrative of "Tell Me Who to Kill" works through a lot of poses, alternately confiding in and distancing the reader. While on one level, the unnamed narrator is telling his tale, on another level, he does not possess the ability to critically distance himself from the tale he is telling. It is similar to Alice trying to figure out her own experience and pretending to understand the nonsense poem, "Jabberwocky", written in mirror writing. Unlike Santosh, the unnamed narrator fails to tell his story cohesively, falling into unclear reveries. Nonetheless, the story is interesting, not in questioning the boundaries of freedom, like the first tale, but in questioning the boundaries of expression.

Santosh explicitly closes his mind to new learning: "I have closed my mind and heart to the English language... I do not want to understand or learn any more"[22] and he has the awareness to question the gap between words and feelings, between success and accomplishment, between aspirations and failed goals. While Santosh acquires a comfortable life, he fails to make a transition to a new personality although he knows that he has become the image he saw in the mirror. He knows that his green coat is oversized and hangs over him more as a burden than fit attire. By contrast, in the second narrative, the unnamed narrator fails to make eye contact with his image and is locked in a world where conflicting images appear to overshadow the sequence of events leading to a negative self-image, poor self-esteem and poor rapport with his acquaintances. He fails to make any sense of his new world and how it has undermined him.

The Walrus and the Carpenter: "Well! They were both *very unpleasant characters"*[23]

In the third narrative, much like Alice's suspended moral judgment in *Through the Looking Glass,* Naipaul inverses the roles of the travellers from the colonised to the colonisers. Just as Alice passes through the mirror to the inverted world, Naipaul writes from the other side of the mirror about the coloniser's experience of the colony. A transition is also made from an autobiographical mode to the voice of an omniscient narrator who is always hidden and never scrutinised directly within the narrative.

"In a Free State" concerns the journey of two white expatriates, Bobby and Linda, through a fictitious African country which is in the middle of a virtual civil war between the country's president and its king. According to Naipaul, the journey replicates the journey "from Kampala in Uganda to Nairobi in Kenya".[24] The novella explores several facets of postcolonial experience, including, in Naipaul's view, the imposition of nationhood upon "free" people whose tribal cultures did not self-generate that concept. The conflation of various independent African nation states into a single state suggests Naipaul's design of defining the colonial experience without particulars. However, presenting Africa as a single state with no distinctions, exposes Naipaul to the charge of writing a deeply orientalist fiction.

This is the point Agnes Czajka makes when she outlines the features of the African Orient that renders Africa a category lower than its Asian counterpart, as defined by Edward Said. Czajka mentions striking differences in the representations of Africa and Asia that include:

> the notion that Africa lacks all evolution and culture, while Asia has actually de-evolved from a previous state of cultural greatness (albeit one still inferior to that of the Occident); interest in the related cognitive under-development and childishness of the African; and, the obsession with the 'under-evolved' African body.[25]

In Naipaul's text, we see the presentation of this African Orient in Bobby and Linda's brief interactions with the Africans (after all, there can be no meaningful dialogue with them).

There are three public spaces that are in focus in the text: the Bar in New Shropshire, the Hunting Lodge and the Colonel's Resort. All of them display examples of the mutual corruptions of coloniser and colonised. In the Bar in New Shropshire, the whites appear in "native" shirts woven in Holland in bright colours, while the Africans wear suits. A young Zulu African leads the gay Bobby on and then spits in his face. The pattern is repeated with the Africans spurning Bobby's offers whether it is at the Colonel's resort or when he finally reaches the Collectorate. At the Hunting Lodge, Bobby and Linda meet with the American "free bird" in Africa. It is an interesting meeting because the American can claim not to be part of the colonial regime yet enjoy all its benefits, including proximity to Linda. On their way out, Bobby gives a lift to an African, who then asks another African to board the car and then begins to direct Bobby to a different destination. Bobby loses patience and drops them off in the rain. Who has been the exploiter, who the exploited? At the Colonel's Resort, the Colonel repeatedly tries to humiliate Peter by making him say he is foolish. Meanwhile Peter, on the other hand, is using the Colonel's resources for his own social advancement.

Naipaul has been criticised more for the presentation of the Africans than for the presentation of the expatriates. However, if the typical colonial explorer in Africa was characterised as a white, heterosexual, middle-class man, with women either absent or as accompanying partner, Linda and Bobby are social and sexual nonconformists. Even so, they have neither the confidence nor ability to survive without the accompanying paraphernalia of the colonial mission. They rely upon their whiteness, vocal accents, facial expressions and vanity to survive in the colonies. Despite their self-image as progressives, in each instance of interaction with the Africans, Linda and Bobby fail to make genuine contact or conversation. Gillian Dooley believes that Naipaul's presentation of Bobby is "far more damning than Santosh's Hindu-based racism or Dayo's brother's pathological confusion."[26] Since "the colonial state of mind is one that does not accept responsibility",[27] Naipaul condemns both the colonisers and the colonised. Instead of imbuing Bobby and Linda with the values expounded in "Our Universal Civilization", Naipaul shows the colonisers as inept examples of Europeans obsessed with themselves. It is mentioned that Bobby had a meltdown in England and Africa is helping him to heal. Linda is looking for love while the Africans are trying to find their own voice. In the scene when Linda and Bobby go out walking by the Colonel's Resort, they are menaced by dogs. Much like the ganging up of the Africans against the whites, and the latter beating up Bobby upon his entry into the Collectorate, the dogs seem innocuous when they are separate. However, once they are confident in their numbers, Linda and Bobby literally have to run to save their lives. There is recognition that an immigrant is always more prone to an attack than a native because he/she is seen as an intruder, irrespective of who holds the political reins.

"Which Dreamt it?"[28]

The Epilogue, much like Alice's questioning of her experience in *Through the Looking Glass*, presents another transient travel experience, this time through a tourist town in Egypt. The Prologue and the Epilogue are mirror images presenting a narrator who doesn't act in the first and intervenes in the second, but with no better results. The separation from the Lebanese, English, Germans and Italians that the writer maintained in the Prologue is not so neat here. The overall tone of Epilogue is bewilderment. The narrator meets a Chinese circus troupe in Milan in Italy and then at Luxor in Egypt. The Chinese behave similarly in the two different geographical spaces. However, for the narrator, their gestures carry different meanings in the two places. In Milan, their pleasantries are a sign of their culture, in Egypt the very same pleasantries become insensitive displays in their self-obsessed world. The Chinese are no different to the Greek and Lebanese businessmen reading French and English newspapers of the Prologue, because they fail to see the "distress of Egypt" in little children competing to get sandwiches and apples from tourists. The mindless game between the waiter and the children affects the narrator who stops them. But he soon realises that there are too many people in the frame. The cat and mouse game between the waiter and the poor children is reminiscent of the one played between the Lebanese and the tramp in the Prologue.

The various protagonists in the five pieces display different facets of the immigrant experience. The tramp never overcomes the anxieties of a first time traveller. Santosh is an unwilling immigrant who experiences continuity only in travel. The narrator of "Tell Me Who to Kill" travels because he feels hollow in his own country. Bobby and Linda seek rehabilitation from failed relationships by travelling to Africa. The narrator of the Prologue, unlike Santosh and the unnamed narrator in the second story, holds back from action. The narrator of the Epilogue, like Bobby and Linda who are ineffectual in a fast deteriorating colonial Africa, tries to intervene but to no avail. The narrator feels that perhaps his vision is flawed. "Perhaps that had been the only pure time, at the beginning, when the ancient artist, knowing no other land, had learned to look at his own and had seen it complete".[29] Unlike the artist, the narrator discovers that nothing is pristine, that the immigrant is inevitably a latecomer, who must adjust to the inequities of the "new" society because his ship has already left the shores and he can neither go on nor return.

Endnotes

1. This essay was originally published in *Transnational Literature*, vol 9, no 2, May 2017. The essay has been modified and copyedited to suit the requirements of this collection.
2. V.S. Naipaul, preface to *In a Free State* (London: Picador, 2008), v-vi.
3. Though *The Enigma of Arrival* is titled a novel, critics including Gillian Dooley, John Thieme, Rob Nixon, Vijay Mishra and Timothy Weiss have read it as a semi-autobiographical text.
4. Peter Kalliney, "Metropolitan Modernism and its West Indian Interlocutors: 1950s London and the Emergence of Postcolonial Literature", *PMLA* 122, no. 1 (2007), 89-104.
5. Gillian Dooley, *V.S. Naipaul, Man and Writer* (Columbia: University of South Carolina Press, 2006), 60.
6. Timothy F. Weiss, *On the Margins: The Art of Exile in V.S. Naipaul* (Amherst: University of Massachusetts Press, 1992), 208-9.
7. Lewis Carroll, *Through the Looking Glass: And What Alice Found There* (Project Gutenberg, The Millennium Fulcrum Edition 1.7), chapter VIII, ebook, http://www.gutenberg.org/files/12/12-h/12-h.htm.
8. V.S. Naipaul, *In a Free State* (London: Andre Deutsch, 1971), 13.
9. Naipaul, *In a Free State*, 11.
10. Carroll, chapter VI.
11. Naipaul, *In a Free State*, 25.
12. A reference to Afro-Americans. In Santosh's mind, the *hubshi* (black) and the Americans (whites) are two separate entities, even though later, he marries a hubshi to acquire the green card.
13. Naipaul, *In a Free State*, 34. The latter are probably affiliated to ISKCON, the International Society of Krishna Consciousness, which is a Hindu religious organisation, often seen to propagate their religious ideals on the streets through the use of a van, pamphlets, music and dancing.
14. Naipaul, *In a Free State*, 61.
15. Naipaul, *In a Free State*, 60.
16. Carroll, chapter I.
17. Naipaul, *In a Free State*, 67.
18. Naipaul, *In a Free State*, 71.
19. Naipaul, *In a Free State*, 83.
20. V.S. Naipaul, *Reading and Writing: A Personal Account* (New York: New York Review of Books, 2000), 14.
21. V.S. Naipaul, *An Area of Darkness* (New York: Vintage, 1964), 16.
22. Naipaul, *In a Free State*, 61.
23. Carroll, chapter IV.
24. Naipaul, preface to *In a Free State* (2008), viii.
25. Agnes Czajka, "The African Orient: Edward Said's Orientalism and 'Western' Constructions of Africa", in *The Discourse of Sociological Practice* 7, nos. 1-2 (2005): 117-134, p. 133.
26. Dooley, 65.
27. Dooley, 61.
28. Carroll, chapter XII.
29. Naipaul, *In a Free State*, 255.

CONTRIBUTORS' BIOGRAPHIES

J. Vijay Maharaj has lectured at the University of the West Indies since August 2000 and specialises in cultural identity and cultural citizenship in Caribbean Studies. She has essays published in a number of important collections including: *Fires of Hope: Fifty Years of Independence in Trinidad and Tobago*; *Beyond Calypso: Re-reading Samuel Selvon*; *Contemporary Caribbean Dynamics: Reconfiguring Caribbean Culture*; *Postscripts: Caribbean Perspectives on the British Canon from Shakespeare to Dickens*; *V.S. Naipaul's A House for Mr Biswas: Critical Perspectives*; *Critical Perspectives on Indo-Caribbean Women's Literature* and *Created in the West Indies: Caribbean Perspectives on V.S. Naipaul* as well as in journals such as *Anthurium: A Caribbean Studies Journal*, *Tout Moun: A Journal of Caribbean Cultural Studies*, *Journal of the Department of Behavioural Sciences*, and *The Journal of West Indian Literature*.

Kenneth Ramchand is Professor Emeritus of West Indian Literature at the University of the West Indies, Professor Emeritus of English at Colgate University, and former President of The University of Trinidad and Tobago. He has also been a Senior Fulbright Scholar affiliated to Yale University and the University of Tulsa, Oklahoma; a Visiting Professor at Indiana University, and a Fellow of the Guggenheim Foundation. Ramchand's seminal text, *The West Indian Novel and its Background* (1970), influenced the creation and internationalisation of West Indian Literature as an academic discipline and his work transformed UWI's syllabus in English. In 1996, Ramchand was awarded a Trinidad & Tobago Chaconia Medal Gold for his work in Literature, Education, and Culture. In 2012, Ramchand was honoured with a NALIS Lifetime Literary Achievement Award.

Bhoendradatt Tewarie began lecturing at the University of the West Indies in 1977 in the Department of Language and Linguistics. In 1992 he became the Executive Director of the Institute of Business at UWI. He remained in this position until 2001 when he became the Pro Vice Chancellor and campus Principal of St Augustine. Outside of academia Dr Tewarie has had a varied career. He was a secondary school teacher and cabinet minister. He has served on a number of government policy making committees – on a few occasions chairing these committees. He has also served as director in a number of private and public organisations.

Nicholas Laughlin is editor, poet, biographer and memoirist. He is editor of the well-known *Caribbean Book Review* and the arts and travel magazine *Caribbean Beat* (2003–2006, then 2012–present). He is a co-director of the contemporary arts space and network Alice Yard, and programme director of the Bocas Lit Fest, an annual literary festival. He has also published a number of essays (often on Caribbean art and artists) and reviews in various books and periodicals. His book of poems *The Strange Years of My Life* was published in 2015.

Aaron Eastley is Associate Professor of Literatures in English at Brigham Young University in Utah, USA. He holds a PhD from the University of California at San Diego, and specialises in transnational literatures in English, British Modernism, subaltern studies, and diaspora and globalisation studies. Recent publications have appeared in the *Journal of Caribbean Literatures*, *Twentieth-Century Literature*, *ARIEL*, and *Conradiana*.

Brinsley Samaroo is Professor Emeritus of the University of the West Indies St Augustine and former head of the history department. He has written extensively on the history of Trinidad and Tobago with a focus on working class movements, Indo-Caribbean history and political and institutional development. He is recognised internationally as a scholar of the Indian diaspora and a notable Caribbean historian. His more notable works include *The Price of Conscience: Howard Noel Nankivell and Labour Unrest in the British Caribbean in 1937 and 1938*.

Arnold Rampersad is a noted biographer and professor of English. He is the Sara Hart Kimball Professor Emeritus in the Humanities at Stanford University. Elected to the American Academy of Arts & Sciences and the American Philosophical Society, he holds honorary degrees from, among others, the University of the West Indies and Columbia University. His books include *The Art and Imagination of W.E.B. Du Bois*; *The Life of Langston Hughes* (two volumes); *Days of Grace: A Memoir*, co- written with Arthur Ashe; *Jackie Robinson: A Biography*; and *Ralph Ellison: A Biography*.

Robert Clarke is a photographer as well as producer and reporter at Gayelle Television, a station that is well-known for offering 100% local and Caribbean programming, much of which comprises live talk-shows. Robert Clarke's name is associated with his award winning journalism and writing such as that involved in the production of a number of well-executed documentaries, for example, the *Bush Diary* collection.

Shastri Maharaj has been a practising artist for the past thirty-five years. The versatility, originality and singularity of his art can be experienced at http://smfineart.com/. These qualities also describe the man as person and artist as the views expressed in his *Trinidad Guardian* articles reveal. His work has been exhibited internationally over the years.

CONTRIBUTORS' BIOGRAPHIES

Andre Bagoo is a Trinidadian journalist, poet and writer. His poetry has appeared in journals such as *Almost Island, Boston Review, Caribbean Review of Books, Draconian Switch, St Petersburg Review, The Poetry Review* and elsewhere. His books of poetry include *Trick Vessels* (Shearsman Books, 2012) and *BURN* (Shearsman Books, 2015) which was longlisted for the 2016 OCM Bocas Prize for Caribbean Literature. *Pitch Lake* (Peepal Tree Press, 2017) is his third book. The poem "On Wordsworth's The Daffodils" in this collection has been awarded The Charlotte and Isidor Paiewonsky Prize for first-time publication in *The Caribbean Writer*.

Sharon Millar is the winner of the 2012 Small Axe Literary Competition and the 2013 Commonwealth Short Story Prize. Her debut collection *The Whale House and Other Stories* (Peepal Tree Press 2015) was longlisted for the 2016 OCM Bocas Prize. Her work has been anthologised in *Pepperpot: Best New Stories from the Caribbean* (Peekash Press, 2014) and *Trinidad Noir: The Classics* (Akashic Books, 2017). Her stories have appeared or are forthcoming in *Granta, WomanSpeak, A Journal of Writing and Art by Caribbean Women*, and *Griffith Review* as well as other international and regional publications.

Raymond Ramcharitar is a cultural historian, critic, and creative writer from Trinidad & Tobago. He has degrees in Economics, Literature, and History and has published widely in academic journals and edited collections on topics as varied as tourism, literary history, and alternative histories of Trinidad & Tobago. He has published two books of poetry (*American Fall* (2007), and *Here* (2013), and one of fiction, *The Island Quintet* (2009), which was shortlisted for the Commonwealth Prize for Best First Book (Caribbean & Canada, 2010). His most recent project was the co-writing of the autobiography of Anthony N Sabga, one of the Caribbean's foremost entrepreneurs.

Keith Jardim is from Trinidad & Tobago and Guyana. His stories have appeared in many publications, including *Mississippi Review, Kyk-Over-Al, The Antigonish Review, Trinidad & Tobago Review, Atlanta Review, Short Story, Wasafiri, Denver Quarterly, Journal of Caribbean Literatures, Tell Tales 4: The Global Village* (Peepal Tree Press, UK), and *Trinidad Noir* (Akashic Books, NYC). His first short story collection *Near Open Water* was published by Peepal Tree in 2011. In 2008 he was invited to read at the 10th International Short Story Conference in Cork, Ireland. He has a BFA and MFA in literature and writing from Emerson College in Boston, a PhD from the University of Houston's creative writing and literature program.

Kevin Frank is the Empire Studies Chair and Educational Policy Committee Chair at Baruch College Department of English, City University of New York. He is also Enrollment Management Committee Vice-chair, Faculty Senate, Baruch College. He has essays published in a number of respected journals including *Small Axe: a Caribbean Journal of Criticism*, *Women's Studies Quarterly*, *Journal of Caribbean Studies*, *The Atlantic Literary Review*, *Anthurium: A Caribbean Studies Journal*, *Journal of Caribbean Studies* and *Commonwealth Essays and Studies*.

Jim Hannan is Associate Professor and Chair, Department of English, Le Moyne College, Syracuse, New York. He received his PhD in English Language and Literature from the University of Chicago. He has published on Caribbean literature and globalisation in *New Literary History*, *Contemporary Literature*, and *MaComere*. He is currently writing a book called *Anthroposcenes: Literature after the World as We Know It*.

Hywel Dix is Principal Lecturer in English and Communication, Faculty of Media and Communication, Bournemouth University, Fern Barrow, Poole, Dorset. His publications include *The Late-Career Novelist Career Construction Theory, Authors and Autofiction* (Bloomsbury Publishing, 2017), *Postmodern Fiction and the Break-Up of Britain* (Continuum, 2010), *After Raymond Williams: Cultural Materialism and the Break-Up of Britain.* (University of Wales Press, 2008). He has also contributed chapters to a number of edited collections and published in journals such as *Public Resistance, Key Words, C21 Literature: Journal of 21st-Century Writings, Textes et Contextes, Foundation: The International Review of Science Fiction, Margins: a Journal of Literature and Culture, Textual Practice, Anglistik* and *Word and Text*.

Elizabeth Jackson is lecturer and undergraduate coordinator at the University of the West Indies, St Augustine. Her publications include the monographs *Muslim Indian Women Writing in English: Class Privilege, Gender Disadvantage, Minority Status* (Peter Lang, 2017) and *Feminism and Contemporary Indian Women's Writing* (Palgrave Macmillan, 2010) as well as a number of articles in the following journals: *ARIEL: A Review of International English Literature*, *Journal of Commonwealth Literature* and *Women: A Cultural Review*.

Paula Morgan is a professor at the University of the West Indies, St Augustine. Her inaugural lecture was entitled "Healing the Hurts of My People Slightly: Discourses of Societal Violence and Trauma" and is a summation of the work she has done over a long career in academia. Her recent publications include: *The Terror and the Time: Banal Violence* *and Trauma in Caribbean Discourse* (UWI Press 2014); with Valerie Youssef, *Writing Rage: Unmasking Violence in Caribbean Discourse* (UWI Press, 2008); as well as the edited collections *The Arc Memory in the Aftermath of Trauma* (Interdisciplinary Press); *Reassembling the Fragments: Voice and Identity in Caribbean Discourse,* co-edited with Valerie Youssef (UWI Press); *The Culture of Violence: A Trinidad and Tobago Case Study,* co-edited with Valerie Youssef (*The Caribbean Review of Gender*); *In a Fine Castle: Childhood in Caribbean Imagi/Nations* (2010) an online collection with a focus on the impact of violence on children, published in *Tout Moun Cultural Studies Journal*.

Fariza Mohammed is a teacher at A.S.J.A. Boys' College, San Fernando. Since she started teaching here thirteen years ago, she has taught English A (language), English B (literature) and Communication Studies through all years of the school. She earned her BA, Dip Ed and MA at the University of the West Indies, St Augustine. Her MA thesis on which the present paper is based was entitled "Karma, Sectarianism and Gender Matters in Three Trinidadian Novels".

Meghan Cleghorn is a PhD Candidate at UWI, St Augustine. She works as a Teaching Assistant in the Department of Literary, Cultural and Communication Studies at the university.

Varistha Persad is a PhD Candidate at UWI, St Augustine. He works as a secondary school teacher at SWAHA Hindu College and he is also a director of the television station IETV.

Nivedita Misra completed her BA, MA and M.Phil in English at the University of Delhi. She then worked as Assistant Professor, Satyawati College (E), at this university. She is currently pursuing her doctoral thesis at the University of the West Indies. She has to her credit various publications in anthologies and journals such as *Journeys*.

INDEX

26, Nepaul Street, family home of Naipauls, 91-92
A Bend in the River (VSN), 23, 32, 172, 207, 218, 221
"A Christmas Story" (*A Flag on the Island*), 69
A Flag on the Island (VSN), 69, 110, 200
A Hot Country (Shiva Naipaul), 23, 131
A House for Mr Biswas, 12, 20, 27, 30, 31, 35, 37, 51, 52, 57, 68, 95, 105, 112, 117, 131, 156, 164, 176-177, 178-179, 180, 182, 183-184, 187, **188-190**, 191, 194-195, 201-202, 206, 209, 212-213; reflects the discrimination against rural Indian children and access to education, 64; on concreteness and metaphor in, 179-181
A Million Mutinies Now (VSN), 9
A Way in the World (VSN), 15, 23, 57, 63, 66, 108, 181, **230-239**
A Writer's People (VSN), 29
Abidh, Stella, 65
Aitken, Gillon, 27, 36, 37, 43; as agent and first editor of the letters, 37, 40, 42, 43, 48 n. 25, 49 n. 40
Akal, Savitri Naipaul, *The Naipauls of Nepaul Street*, 46-47
Among the Believers (VSN), 37, 155
An Area of Darkness (VSN), 165-167, 172, 173 n. 28,
An Unfinished Journey (Shiva Naipaul), 23
Appadurai, Arjun, 233
Athill, Diana, 25, 241
Aunt "Gold Teeth", of reality and fiction, 99
Bagoo, Andre, 10-11; **102-111**: "Tell Me Who to Kill", 11, 20; **103-112**; references to classic film noir as metaphors for narrator's state of mind, (*Rebecca*, *Rope*, *Strangers on a Train*) 103-104, 105; central character as villain, femme fatale and innocent hero, 103; references suspend time, 104; a film noir based on a wedding story, 104; unnamed narrator as unsuccessful immigrant, 104; film (*Waterloo Bridge*) as mapping of London landscape, 105-106, references to *Rope* as a way of signifying a possible murder in brother Dayo's past, 106-107; homoerotic or homosocial relationship with Frank, and sexual element in relationship to Dayo, 106-107; Patrick French on VSN's contemporary interest in sexuality of gay men, 108; gay characters in "In A Free State", *Guerrillas*, *A Way in the World* and *The Enigma of Arrival*, 108; on E.M. Forster as "nasty homosexual", 108; VSN on his youthful addiction to popular film, 109; echoes of "Tell Me Who to Kill" in *The Enigma of Arrival*, 109-110; on film emulation of characters in *Miguel Street*, 110
Bahadoorsingh, Jang, 97
Baudrillard, Jean, 233
Bayley, Peter, 28, 42
Beacon, The, 61
Benitez-Rojo, Antonio, *The Repeating Island*, 231-232
Best, Lloyd, 14, 143
Beyond Belief (VSN), 29, 37
Beyond the Dragon's Mouth (Shiva Naipaul), 93, 132, 161
Booth, Wayne, 183
Boyers, Robert (and Bharati Mukerjee), 157
Brownmiller, Susan, on sadomasochism, 219
Butler, Judith, 219
Butler, Uriah (Buzz), 68
Camacho, Fabian, J, 81
Capildeo, Simboonath, 97
Caribbean Voices, VSN's involvement with and other Caribbean writers, 20, 21, 28, 241

Carroll, Lewis, *Through the Looking Glass*, 240, 242, 245, 247, 249
Ceraso, Stephen (and Patricia Connolly), 187, 188
Chakrabarty, Dipesh, 14, 171 n. 10, n. 11
Chaudhuri, Amit, on fate and destiny in *Fireflies*, 213
Cipriani, Captain A.A., 68
Clarke, Robert, 11, **91-102**: 26, Nepaul Street, family home of Naipauls, 91-92; St James (Port of Spain), district of Naipauls' family house, 92; fictionalised by Shiva Naipaul, 92-94; Shiva Naipaul growing up in multicultural St James, 92-95; as pan player, 93; Droapatie Naipaul, home and temple-going in St James, 95-96, as Bhola Mausi, 97; Seepersad Naipaul, life at home, as photographer, 99-100; V.S. Naipaul occasional nostalgia for home, 99
Cleghorn, Meghan, 15; on sadomasochism and incest in V.S. and Shiva Naipaul's fiction and VSN's biography, 217-229; studies of Caribbean sexualities in literature, 217-218; Elaine Fido on sadomasochism in VSN's writing, 217-218; VSN's claims for comedy in *Guerrillas* and *A Bend in the River*, 218; Supriya Nair on picaresque humour in VSN's fiction, 218; issues of morality in fiction, 218-219, 220; on shifting social views on sadomasochism from feminism to consensual BDSM, 219-220; interrogating Fido's position, 220-221; VSN's biography and sexuality in his novels, 221, 223, 226; contrary types of sadomasochism in Shiva Naipaul's *The Chip-Chip Gatherers*, 221-222; purity and incest in VSN's *The Mimic Men*, 222-223; Patrick French on VSN's feelings about Indian girls and incest, 223; Fido on non-white males and white women in *Guerrillas*, 224-225; VSN on buggery of women in "The Return of Eva Peron", 225; Fido and Champa Rao Mohan blur author and character, 225-226; alleged abuse of VSN as a child, and French's doubts, 226-227; crossing the line between biography and fiction, 227; VSN as extending the boundaries of Caribbean fiction in dealing with non-standard forms of sexuality, 227-228
Cola Rienzi, Adrian, 68
Connolly, Patricia (and Stephen Ceraso), 187, 188
Crossthwaite, Paul, on emergence of postmodernism in Europe, 234
Crowley, Daniel J., 160
Cudjoe, Selwyn, 157
De Boissiere, Ralph, 61, 68, 84
Deutch, André, 30
Dickens, Charles, 12, 50, 77; *Sketches by Boz*, 50; echoes in *A House for Mr Biswas*, 180
Discovering the working classes in Trinidad, (See James and Mendes), 86
Dix, Hywel, 10; on *Magic Seeds* as late career fiction, **175-186**; on the theory of late career fiction, 175, 174; on use of the idea of authoring in career-construction theory, 176; *A House for Mr Biswas* as early career comparison, 176-177; charges of repetition and inferiority made against "late" work, 177; dialogue between early and late and a continuum of subject positions, 178; on the retrospective status of *A House for Mr Biswas*, 178-179; concreteness and metaphor in, 179-180; the growth of metafictional self-reflection in VSN's novels, 181; contrary images of the house in *A House for Mr Biswas* and *Magic Seeds*, 181-184; *Magic Seeds* as retrospective authorial dialogue with earlier work,

183; lateness as a relational concept; "retrospective" as a better descriptor than "late", 184; the case for applying different criteria for judging late/retrospective work, 185; on decline as a stereotype (see Peter Laslett), 186, n. 23
Donaldson, Roger, *The Bank Job*, 14
Dooley, Gillian, 241, 248
East Indian Advocate, the, 61
East Indian Weekly, 12, 50, 61
Eastley, Aaron, 12, **50-59**: Seepersad Naipaul writes for *East Indian Weekly*, 50; as Chaguanas correspondent for *The Guardian*, 50-51; as "The Pundit", 51; writing about "characters", **53-55**; and serious-humorous articles on politics and politics of religion, 52, 56-57 influence on VSN's early fiction, 52; contrasts between Seepersad's compassionate humanity and VSN's mockery, 52, 55; writing for a predominantly elite Trinidadian readership, 55; "Bogus Mediums…" 56; Gault MacGowan as enabler and mentor, 58
Ethel Street Hindu temple, 96
Ethnicity and literary expression, 10, 18, 153-163
Evening News (Trinidad), 71
Family: Naipaul family relationships, 20, 24, **27-33**
Farrell, Joseph P., 160
Fido, Elaine, on the sadomasochistic in V.S. Naipaul's writing, 217-218, 220-221, 225-226
Film: in VSN's fiction and non-fiction, 11, 55, **103-111** (see Bagoo, Andre); in Shiva Naipaul's fiction, 196
Fireflies (Shiva Naipaul), 12, 31, 131, 187, 189, 190-194, 195, 196-197, 206, 209, 213-214
Flaskas, Carmel, *Limits and Possibilities of the Postmodern Narrative Self*, 236, 237
Foucault, Michel and "heterotopia", 230, 235

Frank, Kevin, 10; on ethnic relations in the work of V.S. and Shiva Naipaul, **153-163**; on racial politics in Trinidad and Guyana, 154; on Seepersad Naipaul's commitment to becoming "West Indian", 156; difference in father and sons' attitude to creole Trinidad, 156-157; critique of VSN's racial position in *The Middle Passage*, 157-158; critique of Shiva Naipaul's racial misanthropy in *Journey to Nowhere*, and the denial of racist attitudes beyond "clannishness" amongst Indo-Trinidadians, 158-159; racist language in Shiva Naipaul's essays, 160-161; on writing for a metropolitan audience, 162
French, Patrick, *The World is What It Is*, 20, 28, 29-30, 31, 36, 37, 39-40, 43, 44, 45, 108, 221, 223, 226, 227
Freud, Sigmund, on "perversion", 219, 224
Friends of Mr Biswas, 15
Funk, Ray, 83
Gay sexuality in VSN's fiction, **107-109**
Gender roles, 12, **187-198**, **199-205**
Gera, Anjali, on VSN as "nomadic", 172, n. 24
Glissant, Edouard, 153
Global writers, VS and Shiva, 15, 17, 19, 24; 164-165, 167, 168, 169, 173 n. 28, 230, **232-235**, 238
Globalisation, 11, 14, 17, 19, 103, 167, 168, 170
Gomes, Albert, 61, 68, 84
Gooding, Margaret, 29
Grieg, Beatrice, 68
Growling Tiger (Neville Marcano), "Lazy Man", 82-83
Guerrillas (VSN), 14, 108, 131, 218, 221; and postcolonial anxiety, 120-121
Gurudeva and Other Indian Tales (Seepersad Naipaul, 1943), 13, 19, 20, 22, 60, 67, 73, 74, 79, 84, 85, 88

Half a Life (VSN), 173, n. 28

Hannan, Jim, 11, **164-174**; VSN's writing as connecting neither to Commonwealth literature or post-colonialism, 164; "Two Worlds": VSN's intuitive global focus, 164-165; India seen in *An Area of Darkness* as failing to distinguish between the modern and the archaic, 165; as recording an experience where fixed distinctions of time and place are upset, 166-167; *The Enigma of Arrival* as expressive of VSN's sense of unbelonging, 165-166; sense of displacement and simultaneity seen as features of the global postmodern, 167; the significance of VSN's visit to his grandfather's village as linking distinct places, 167-168; Naipaul's writing career as pragmatically global, 168, 173-174, n. 34; the complications of writing for a metropolitan audience and the context of colonialism, 168-169; *Mr Stone and the Knight's Companion* as an attempt to escape from one kind of regionalism but falling into another, 169; travel writing as a further attempt to escape from Caribbean regionalism, 169-170; William Dalrymple's criticism of VSN's approval of the destruction of the Muslim mosque at Ayodha as both a misreading of history and a sectarian failure of judgement, 169-170; as a writer in the global market, 170; critique of VSN's Eurocentrism, 174, n. 37

Hardt, Michael and Antonio Negri, 170

Harvey, David, 233; on postmodernism and the fragmentary, 237

Hemingway, Ernest, 12, 50

Hensby, Alexander, 170

Hernandez, Ric, 76

Hirsch, Marianne, 115

Hogan, Patrick Holm, 117

Home and placelessness, 18, 99, 110, 161, 167, 172 n. 24, 173 n. 28, 199, 200, 204, 242

Hudson-Phillips, Henry, 82

Hutcheon, Linda, *A Poetics of Postmodernism*, 231

In a Free State (VSN), 13, 15, 20, 31; "Tell Me Who to Kill", 11, 20; **103-111**

Indian re-emigrants, 19, **65-66**

Indians in Trinidad, 18, 61, 113

Indo-Caribbean women, 12, 227

Jackson, Elizabeth, **187-198**; on notions of masculinity in relationship to race, ethnicity, class and religion, 187; changing history of Indo-Trinidadian gender ideologies, 187-188; masculinity as power and control and female subordination, 188; analysis of masculinity in *A House for Mr Biswas*, 188-191; challenge to assumption that the Tulsi household is female-headed or that it "emasculates" men, 189; similar situation revealed in Shiva Naipaul's *Fireflies*, 189; reverence for patriarchy in both Tulsi and Khoja households, 189; different male/female perspectives between these novels, 189-180; exclusive narrative focus on Mohun Biswas's perspective and apparent assumption that only male experience is significant, 190; perspective of Vimla Lutchman in *Fireflies* and critical but nuanced portrayal of Indo-Trinidadian masculinity, 190-191; absence of development in characterisation of Mohun Biswas, in comparison to Ram Lutchman, 191-192; comparison between Biswas's weakness as a product of situation, and Lutchman's of character and toxic male ideology, 192; alcohol and masculinity, 192; on the construction of Govind Khoja as family patriarch in *Fireflies*, 193; power struggles between patriarchal males, 194-195; patriarchy portrayed as supported by women in both novels, 194-195; the performative nature of masculine roles, 195-197; sexual ownership of trophy woman as badge of masculinity, 196-197

James, C.L.R., 61, 68, 84; discovering the working class in *Minty Alley*, 86

Jardim, Keith, 14; influence of V.S. and Shiva Naipaul on shaping of his writing career, 131-132; on the importance of fiction in an era of "barbarism" and "insanity", 132; extract from "Beauty Surrounds the Darkness", 133-140

Jayaram, V., 208

Journalism in Trinidad, 12, 13, 155; as a literary form that engaged all three Naipaul writers and fed into and shaped their fiction, 50; see Seepersad Naipaul and Jerome E. Rampersad and essays by Hannan and Samaroo.

Karma and fate, 17, 62, 149, 206-208, 209, 214, 215 n. 2

Karma in the work of V.S. and Shiva Naipaul, **206-216**

Khan, Ismith, *The Jumbie Bird*, 66

Khemraj, Harischandra, *Cosmic Dance*, 153

King, Bruce, 168, 172-173, n. 24, n. 31

Knipe, David, 208

Krafft-Ebing, Richard von, on deviant sexuality, 219

Lacovia, R.M., 157

Lakhan, Ralph, 97

Lalla, Barbara, 12

Lamb, Charles as Elia, 78

Lansard, John, 85

Laslett, Peter, *A Fresh Map of Life: The Emergence of the Third Age*, 186, n. 23

Late career writing, 10; *Magic Seeds*, **175-186**; Edward Said on "lateness", 175-176

Laughlin, Nicholas, 12, 13: on *Letters Between a Father and Son*'s publishing history, **35-49**; the letters themselves as a initially a three-way correspondence between Oxford (VSN), Benares (Kamla) and St James (Seepersad), Trinidad, 35-36; letters also from Dropatie and other sisters, 36; VSN as meticulous archivist of his work and correspondence, 36; accidental destruction of Oxford diaries and unpublished first novel, 36; first edition of the letters in 1999, 37; as revelation of VSN influences, 37; of Seepersad's writing ambitions; as background to *A House for Mr Biswas*, 37; reviews, 38; defectiveness of some of the transcriptions and absence of critical apparatus, 38-39; Patrick French's criticism of the edition, 39-40; Nicholas Laughlin invited to re-edit, add significant number of additional letters, retranscribe and annotate text, 40; decisions about how to represent personal idiosyncrasies of expression, 40-41; addition of textual apparatus, 41-42; revised edition, 2009, which adds mother and other sisters to the dialogue; VSN's decision to withdraw this edition and restore the defective 1999 edition, 42-43; suppositions on VSN's reasons, 43-44; French on VSN's attitudes to truthfulness, 44; on what the completer letters show of wider family involvement with VSN's writing, 44; evidence of Kamla Naipaul's writing ambitions, 45; reflections on the notion of authorship, 45; Savi Naipaul Akal's *The Naipauls of Nepaul Street* as a memoir that restores Droapatie to a position of importance, 46-47

Leffert, Mark, 209

Letters Between a Father and Son (Vidia, Seepersad, Kamla Naipaul et al), 25, 27, 28, 29, **35-49**, 99

Lewis, Linden, 187, 188, 189, 194, 196, 217

Lord Invader (Rupert Grant), "McGee", 82-83
Lorde, Audre, on sadomasochism, 219
Lovelace, Earl, 153; *The Dragon Can't Dance*, 156
MacGowan, Gault, as Seepersad's newspaper editor, 58; advice to, 154
Magic Seeds (VSN), 10, 108, 175, 176, **181-184**
Maharaj, Chanka, 68
Maharaj, J. Vijay, 14, 112-119; on Hinduism in V.S. Naipaul, 209-210
Maharaj, Shastri, 14, **112-119**; parallels between paintings and the world of *A House for Mr Biswas*, 112, 117-118; *Fyzabad* and *Cane*: on the connections between sugar and oil, 112-113; on ethnicity, nationhood and universality, 113; *Neighbours* and *Conversation* on interethnic relationships, 114-115; on the language and iconography of the Hindu gods, 115; on cross-religious images in *Ritual*, 115; turn towards abstraction, 116-117; embedded narratives in the paintings, 117-118
Maraj, Bhadase Sagan, 97
Maree, Kobus, 176
Masculinity, images of in the Naipauls' fiction, 12, 62, 63, **187-197**
Mathura, C.B. (Pat), 75
"McGee", 12, **70-90** (see Rampersad)
McIlveen, Peter, 178
Mendes, Alfred H., 61, 68, 84; discovering the working class, 86
Michener, Charles, "The Dark Visions of V.S. Naipaul", 155
Miguel Street, 21, 51, **52-53**, 55, 93, 110, 111, 131, 204, 240
Millar, Sharon, 14; on writing a response to VSN's *Guerrillas*, 120-121; "Buying Horses", 121-130
Minerva Review, 61
Mishra, Alpana, 220, 221
Misra, Nivedita, 13; on the narratives of *In A Free State* read through Lewis Carroll's *Through the Looking Glass*, **240-250**; the image of the mirror in "One Out of Many", 240, 241, 243-245; displacement as limbo in "Tell Me Who To Kill", 245-246; on the coloniser's experience of the colony in "In a Free State", 247; stereotypes of African underdevelopment, 247-248; the immigrant experience and alienation in all three narratives, 240; reflections on *In A Free State* in *The Enigma of Arrival*, 241; VSN's experience of immigrant dislocation and access to modernist tropes of alienation in London, 241; *In a Free State* as a quest for form to give meaning to the humiliations of migration, 241; *Through the Looking Glass* as narrative of displacement and a challenge to the conventional novel, 242-243; the tramp in the Prologue as an alienated figure, 243; The Epilogue as a further expression of the transience of travel and the instability of communicative meanings, 249
Mittelholzer, Edgar, 153, 154, 173 n. 31
Mohammed, Fariza, 15, on Karma in the work of V.S. and Shiva Naipaul, **206-216**; fate in *A Bend in the River*, 207; distinction between karma and fate, 208; in contemporary Hinduism, 208; as a creole concept in Selvon's *A Brighter Sun*, 208-209; fate in *A House for Mr Biswas*, 209-210; Biswas's assertion of free will, 211-213; karma in Shiva Naipaul's *Fireflies*, 213-214
Mohammed, Patricia, 187
Mohanty, Satya P., on karma in Indian literature, 214
Mootoo, Bas, 42
Morgan, Paula, on mothering and motherlands, **199-205**; the continuum from ineffective to powerful, 199; Naipaulian angst as product of deficiencies in moth-

ering and displacement from motherlands, 199; unhomeliness and loss of nurturance in "Tell Me Who to Kill", 199-200; the "enemy" as both history and the mother, 200; the benefits and terrors of the extended family network, 200-201; wives affirming and emasculating frail masculine egos, 201, 205; male complicity and rebellion against the Tulsi system in *A House for Mr Biswas*, 201-202; collective power and the annihilation of the individual, 202; Biswas's anti-female paranoia in his breakdown, 202-203; foetal and womblike images after Biswas's return to Hanuman House, 203; emergence of the writing of Seepersad and V.S. Naipaul out of revolt against Tulsidom, 204; comparisons with the trickster figure of Hanuman in Biswas's survival strategies and beginnings of V.S. Naipaul's writing career, 204-205

Morris, Mervyn, *Making West Indian Literature*, 13

Morton, Sarah, 63

Mothers and mothering, 11, 12, 20, **199-205**

Mr Stone and the Knight's Companion (VSN), 169

Mukherjee, Bharati (and Robert Boyers), 157

Mustafa, Fawzia, 169

Naipaul Droapatie (nee Capildeo), 36, 41, 42, 43, 92; home and temple-going in St James, 95-96; as Bhola Mausi, 97

Naipaul, Kamla, 20, 27, 28, 30, 35, 36, 38, 39, 41, 42, 43, 46, 49 n. 40, 51, 103, 227; as would-be author, 44-45

Naipaul, Mira, 29, 30

Naipaul, Pat (VSN's first wife), 29

Naipaul, Sati, 20, 27

Naipaul, Seepersad, 10, 12, 13, stories, 18; journalism, 18-19, **50-59**, 73; at home in St James, as photographer, 99-100; the obligation on VSN to publish his book, 20; death, 20, 27; library, as influence on Shiva, 21; thwarted literary ambitions, 21-22, 28; nervous breakdowns, 22; establishes the relationship between journalism and literature for his sons, 22-23; wide range of journalistic subjects, 22-23; champions women's education, 22; generosity of spirit, 23; as Chaguanas correspondent, 50-51; as "The Pundit", 51; writing about "characters", **53-55**; and serious-humorous articles on politics and politics of religion, 52, 56-57; influence on VSN's early fiction, 52; contrasts between Seepersad's compassionate humanity and VSN's mockery, 52, 55, 154; writing for a predominantly elite Trinidadian readership, 55; "Bogus Mediums..." 56; Gault MacGowan as enabler and mentor, 58; as crusading journalist, **60-69**; proud of Indian heritage but a committed West Indian, 61; interest in African survivals, 61; campaigns on domestic abuse and rights of Indian women to education, 62-63; focus on Hindu/Presbyterian culture clash in "The Adventures of Gurudeva", 62; sensitivity to war-time cultural changes across communities, 63; campaigned for education for rural Indian children and recognition of non-Christian schools, 63-64; as a self-educated man, 64; limitations on his tolerance, on women's dress, 65, and on cross racial and religious marriages, 100; on Indian repatriation and disillusionment of returnees, 65-66; campaigned for home for destitute Indians, 66-67; campaigned for right of Hindu cremations, 67; SN himself cremated by Hindu rite, 67; interest in cultures of other groups, Hossay and the Spiritual Baptist "Shouters", 68; as anti-colonialist, 68; influence on VSN's writing: the cannibalisation of Seepersad's writing in *A House for Mr Biswas*, 68; on the theme of Presbyterian conversion and converts, 69.

Published works: *Gurudeva and Other Indian Tales* (1943), 13, 19, 20, 22, 60, 67, 73, 74, 79, 84, 85, 88; *The Adventures of Gurudeva and Other Stories* (1976), 31, 67, 69, 154, 156, 204; edited and introduced by V.S. Naipaul; received as V.S. Naipaul phenomena, 28, 29; on ill-treatment of women, 62; on little India and creoleness, 156

Naipaul, Shiva, 20; on growing up in Trinidad, 93; writing about multi-cultural St James, 92-95; as pan player, 93; relationship with VSN, "My Brother and I", 20, 30; refusal to return to Trinidad, 24; at Oxford, 31; benefits from VSN's reputation, 30-31; establishes himself as a writer in his own right, 31.

Published works: *A Hot Country* as despairing expression of anxieties, 23, 132; "A Man of Mystery", 95; *An Unfinished Journey*, 23; *Beyond the Dragon's Mouth*, 131, 161; *Fireflies*, 12, 31, 131, 187, 189, **190-194**, 195, 196-197, 206, 209, 213-214; on racial resentments in *Journey to Nowhere*, 154, 158-159; *The Chip Chip Gatherers*, 25, 131, 221-222; "The Beauty Contest", 93-94; "The Tenant", 94-95

Naipaul, V.S., 10, 11; occasional nostalgia for home in St James, 99; duty/obligation to publish his father's work, 28; hesitancy to do so, 28; period of self-reflection in writing, 29; seeking information from his sisters, 29; interviews with, 32-33; involvement with *Caribbean Voices* and other Caribbean writers, 21, 241; critical attitude to Shiva, 21; shame over striking Shiva, 30; grief over death, 30; relationship as writers, 31; saw Shiva as a weak imitation, 32; biography and sexuality in his novels, 221, 223, 226

Published works: *A Bend in the River*, 23, 32, 172, 207, 218, 221; *An Area of Darkness*, 165; "A Christmas Story", 69; *A Flag on the Island* (VSN), 69, 110; *A House for Mr Biswas*, 12, 20, 27, 30, 31, 35, 37, 51, 52, 57, 68, 95, 105, 112, 117, 131, 156, 164, 176-177, 178-179, 180, 182, 183-184, 187, **188-190**, 191, 194-195, 201-202, 206, 209, 212-213; reflects discrimination against rural Indian children and access to education, 64, 95; on concreteness and metaphor in, 179-181; *A Million Mutinies Now*, 9; *A Way in the World*, 15, 23, 57, 63, 66, 108, 181, **230-239**; as "heterotopia", 230; *A Writer's People*, 29; *Among the Believers*, 37, 155; *An Area of Darkness*, 165-167, 172, 173 n. 28; *Beyond Belief*, 29, 37; *Guerrillas*, 14, 108, 131, 218, 221, **224-225**; *Half a Life*, 173, n. 28; *In a Free State*, 13, 15, 20, 31; *Magic Seeds*, **175-186**; *Miguel Street*, 21, 51, **52-53**, 55, 93, 110, 111, 131, 204, 240; *Mr Stone and the Knight's Companion*, 169; "One Out of Many", 240, 241, 243-245; "Prologue to an Autobiography" (*Finding the Centre*), acknowledgement of his debt to his father, 29, 37; "Tell Me Who to Kill", 11, 20; **103-111, 199-200**; "The Enemy" (*A Flag on the Island*), 200, 202; *The Enigma of Arrival*, 23, 108, 165-166, 170; *The Loss of Eldorado*, 170; *The Middle Passage*, 155, 157-158; *The Mimic Men*, 31, 181, 221-223, 225-226; *The Mystic Masseur*, 41, 42, 43, 51, 52, 131; satire in, 55, 57; *The Overcrowded Barracoon*,

173 n.4, 201; "The Return of Eva Peron", 225; "The Shadow'd Livery" (unpublished), 36; *The Suffrage of Elvira*, 19, 30, 51, 52, 57, 131; satire in, 55, 56; *The Writer and the World*, 29, 174 n. 34, n. 37

Nair, Supriya, on picaresque humour in VSN's fiction, 218

Nandan, Kavita, on impurity and taint in *The Mimic Men*, 222-223

Negritude, 11

Nobel lecture (VSN), 164, 170

Norris, Kathleen, 85

Nurse, Keith, 188

O'Byrne, Darren, 170

O'Flaherty, Wendy, *Karma and Rebirth in Classical Indian Traditions*, 208

Obeyesekere, Gananath, *Imagining Karma*, 206

Persad, Varistha, on *A Way in the World* as postmodern fiction, **230-239**; on VSN's perception of multiple identities in the globalised world, 230; the Caribbean as a postmodern space, 230-231; the fusing of past, present and future in *A Way in the World*, 232, 236; the idea of "co-operative story making" and parallel narratives, 233; the blurring of genres in, 233; on the belated emergence of postmodernist fiction in the Caribbean, 233-234; C.L.R. James as Lebrun and the critique of realist fiction, 234; fluidity in narration and multiple narrators, 234-235, 237; the novel as incorporating author and reader in metatextual ways, 235-236; *A Way in the World* as offering a way for the Caribbean postmodern self and Eurocentric narratives, 236; as a guide to living in the globalised world, 238

Persaud, Bernadette, on Shastri Maharaj, 116

Pinto, Samantha (and Jenny Sharpe), 217

Poynting, Jeremy, 208-209

Presbyterianism (and Canadian Missions), 19, 23, 62, 63, 64, 69, 74

"Prologue to an Autobiography" (*Finding the Centre*), VSN acknowledges his debt to his father, 29, 37; VSN's boyhood pride in father as well-known journalist and the family ledger of cuttings, 51

Puri, Shalini, 10

Queen's Royal College, 21, 75, 92

Rahim, Jennifer, 203, on V.S. Naipaul as Hanuman, 204

Ramadhin, Sonny, 19, 85-86

Ramchand, Kenneth, 11, **17-26**: on writing and nation, 17-18; on the contribution of the Naipauls to understanding Trinidad as a fusion society, 18; on travel and being away in the writing of VSN, 19; on the complex evolution of Indian lives in Trinidad, 19; on the importance of the Naipaul family connections, 20, 24; on the mysteries of place and person, 25; on Shiva Naipaul and the anxiety of influence, 21; on VSN as once part of a literary community, 21; on the bridge Seepersad built between journalism and fiction, 22; on the anxieties of being that bedevilled Shiva, 23; on writing and self-perceptions of the Naipaul brothers, 24; referenced on Lovelace's *The Dragon Can't Dance*, 156; on *A House for Mr Biswas*, 164-165

Ramcharitar, Raymond, 14; *Here*, 14; introduction to *Here* as an exploration of the split personality of Trinidad between Chaguanas and Port of Spain; an exploration of Hinduism and its gods in a Trinidadian setting; on his preferences for form in poetry; on ethnic biases in reading V.S. Naipaul, 141-143; extract from *Here*, 144-152

Rampersad, Arnold, 12, **70-90**. See below: Rampersad, Jerome Ewart